NUMBER 102

Yale French Studies

Belgian Memories

D1114460

Yale French Studies

Catherine Labio, *Special editor for this issue*

Alyson Waters, *Managing editor*

Editorial board: Edwin Duval (Chair), Joseph Acquisto,
   Ora Avni, R. Howard Bloch, Peter Brooks, Mark
   Burde, Shoshana Felman, Catherine Labio, Elisa
   Mader, Christopher Miller, Susan Weiner

Editorial assistant: Joseph Mai

Editorial office: 82-90 Wall Street, Room 308

Mailing address: P.O. Box 208251, New Haven,
   Connecticut 06520-8251

Sales and subscription office:

Yale University Press, P.O. Box 209040

New Haven, Connecticut 06520-9040

Published twice annually by Yale University Press

Designed by James J. Johnson and set in Trump
   Medieval Roman by The Composing Room of
   Michigan, Inc. Printed in the United States of
   America by the Vail Ballou Press, Binghamton, N.Y.

ISSN 044-0078

ISBN for this issue 0-300-09772-7

BELGIUM

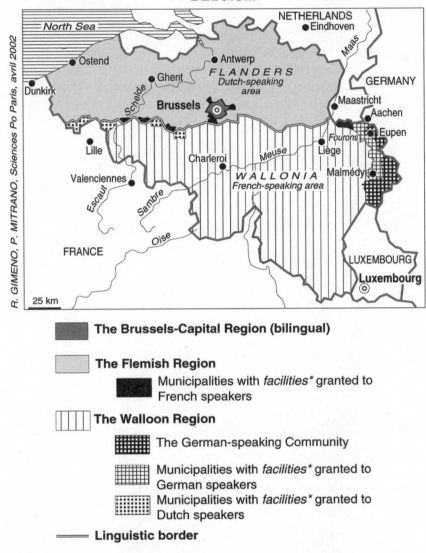

Legend:

- **The Brussels-Capital Region (bilingual)**
- **The Flemish Region**
  - Municipalities with *facilities** granted to French speakers
- **The Walloon Region**
  - The German-speaking Community
  - Municipalities with *facilities** granted to German speakers
  - Municipalities with *facilities** granted to Dutch speakers
- Linguistic border

*The term *facilities* refers to the right to use a particular language for administrative purposes and for primary education in an area where another language is the official language.

Figure 1.

CATHERINE LABIO

Editor's Preface:
The Federalization of Memory

in memoriam,
Daniel Moutafian
Jean-Marie Balleux

Belgian Memories is devoted to an analysis of the nature of the relationship between memory, identity, and culture in a plural and recently federalized nation. Writers, artists, a psychoanalyst, and scholars from a variety of disciplines, including ethnology, linguistics, philosophy, literature, history, film, art history, and geography ask to what extent Belgium's literary and visual environment (from novels to paintings, comic strips to movies, poetry to urban planning) has constituted itself through typically Belgian ways of dealing with the past and culture-specific forms of remembering and forgetting. Such issues have become more pressing since Belgium has reconstituted itself politically and must deal with the prospect that it might itself become a memory.

Belgian society is particularly ill-equipped to deal with its history. Only sporadically patriotic, yet almost constantly on the verge of a linguistic breakdown, it has fewer and fewer unifying myths or frames of reference. Even memories of two world wars have become a source of divisiveness in spite of Belgium's "status" as a victim of aggression. As for the particularly unsavory aspects of its history, these tend, as elsewhere, to be carefully avoided, a phenomenon complicated and magnified by Belgium's internal divisions and the distinctly plural and complex nature of Belgian identity.

Belgium, a country about the size of Maryland with a population of some ten million people, is officially divided into three Communities (*communautés/gemeenschappen*): the Flemish Community, the French Community, and the German-speaking Community; three Regions (*régions/gewesten*): the Flemish Region, the Walloon Region, and the Brussels Region; four linguistic regions, or language areas (*régions*

YFS 102, *Belgian Memories*, ed. Catherine Labio, © 2002 by Yale University.

linguistisques/taalgebieden): the Dutch-language region, the French-language region, the bilingual region of Brussels-Capital, and the German-language region); ten provinces; and five hundred and eighty-nine municipalities (*communes/gemeenten*). Additionally, Belgian society is split along Catholic, socialist, and liberal lines, a phenomenon known as *pillarisation* (*verzuiling*).

Complicated as this picture is, it does not begin to do justice to the complexities of Belgian cultural identities. The dominant Flemish/French binarism, for example—to take up the most obvious fault line—hides important asymmetries.[1] Whereas French culture—from France, that is—provides a strong point of reference for Belgian Francophones, Dutch culture—namely, from the Netherlands—does not play a similar role for the Flemish in spite of the existence of a common language. Whereas Flemish identity can project itself back to the Middle Ages and the Battle of the Golden Spurs of 1302, Walloon cultural identity as it is understood today has even been said, as Jacques Dubois reminds us in this volume, to have found its foundational moment with the deadly strike of 1886.[2] Whereas Flemish speakers of Brussels and Flanders largely belong to the same ethnolinguistic group (hence the Flemish decision to fuse the Flemish Region and the Flemish Community), French speakers of Brussels and Wallonia do not share a comparably strong communal identity even though they both make up what is somewhat confusingly called the "Communauté française de Belgique." For instance, though the imaginary of some French-speaking *Bruxellois* may in some respects be quite Flemish—think of Jacques Brel—the attendant metaphor of bastardy or *métissage* at the core of *Bruxellois* identity does not necessarily sit well with Walloons, many of whom see the existence of the French Community as a threat to their identity.[3] Indeed, one of the paradoxes of Belgium's vexed linguistic

1. This binarism leaves out Belgium's German speakers as well as its large immigrant population. See Hubert Jenniges, "Germans, German Belgians, German-Speaking Belgians" and Anne Morelli and Jean-Phillipe Schreiber, "Are the Immigrants the Last Belgians?" in *Nationalism in Belgium: Shifting Identities, 1780–1995*, ed. Kas Deprez and Louis Vos (Houndmills, Basingstoke, Hampshire and London: Macmillan; New York: St. Martin's Press, 1998), 240–48 and 249–57.

2. "The term *Walloon* as a cultural indicator only began to appear in late-nineteenth-century literary titles, such as the magazines *Wallonia* and *La revue wallonne* (both founded in 1893)" (Philip Mosley, *Split Screen: Belgian Cinema and Cultural Identity* [Albany, NY: State University of New York Press, 2001], 18).

3. Hugues Dumont, "Belgitude et crise de l'État belge. Repères et questions pour introduire un débat," in *Belgitude et crise de l'État belge*, ed. Hugues Dumont, Christian

history is that it also demonstrates the extent to which language is but one element in individual and group identity. This phenomenon partly explains why language issues have not weighed equally heavily in the construction of Flemish and Walloon identities and in Flemish and Walloon demands for greater autonomy. Flemish calls for institutional reforms were prompted primarily by memories of cultural, linguistic, and political victimization by a French-speaking elite, while Walloons' interest in federalization grew out of the devastating sense of loss and abandonment they experienced along with the decline of the coal and steel industries.

Belgian identity is, in short, inescapably plural and sociologically porous. As a result, Belgians' views on Belgium and its constituent parts are often partial and occasionally highly performative. Having said that, I shall now venture a few generalities about the nature of Belgian memories.

In a move unmistakably—and skillfully—designed to have Americans score points with the locals, the section on Belgium of the Department of Defense's *Pocket Guide to the Low Countries* dated August 1953 begins as follows: " 'Brave' has historically been the word used to describe the Belgians. Long ago, although they were overcome by the Roman legions, the Belgians won the praise of Caesar. He wrote, 'Of all the tribes of Gaul, the Belgians were the bravest.' "[4] Every Belgian is indeed familiar with Caesar's tribute.[5] As learned in school, Belgian history is one long laundry list of invasions by (and resistance to) almost every major European power, starting with the Roman invasion of Gaul in 52 B.C.E. and ending with the Second World War. Belgian identity is strongly invested in this history and its image as a small, non-hegemonic nation, a phenomenon reinforced by a history of domestic tensions and discrimination.

The political response to Belgium's internal conflicts has been to in-

---

Franck, François Ost, and Jean-Louis De Brouwer (Brussels: Facultés universitaires Saint-Louis, 1989), 29–30.

4. *A Pocket Guide to the Low Countries* (Department of Defense, Office of Armed Forces Information and Education, PG14, DA PAM 20–185, August 1953), 45. (I am grateful to Alyson Waters for having lent me her copy of this booklet.)

5. Hence, for instance, the playful title of a recent essay by Serge Kribus, "De tous les peuples de la Gaule, les Belges juifs sont les plus braves," in *Belgique toujours grande et belle*, ed. Antoine Pickels and Jacques Sojcher (Brussels: Revue de l'Université de Bruxelles/Éditions Complexe, 1998), 344–48.

troduce a series of four highly convoluted constitutional reforms starting in 1970, a process that culminated in 1993 with the proclamation of a new constitution and the federalization of the country. These reforms have been remarkably successful to the extent that ethnic disputes have never escalated into large-scale violence. Unfortunately, Belgium's relative tranquillity seems to have come at the cost of what one might call a federalization of memory, which I shall define—provisionally—as a tacit agreement that not remembering certain things is best and that leaving misconceptions alone is a small price to pay for peace and prosperity. As a result, though many Belgians can probably rattle off the list of foreign powers that have dominated their country, their pronouncements about, say, their country's linguistic history may on occasion be somewhat more creative.

Belgians' attitudes toward their country's colonial past are even more problematic. First, Belgium has found it difficult to reconcile its self-image as a victim of aggression by larger foreign powers with its colonization of an African country eighty times its size. Second, as noted by Antoine Tshitungu Kongolo later in this volume, the partitioning of Belgium has made it harder for the country to own up to its historical responsibilities toward the Congo and its neighbors. As the national consciousness fades along with the national institutions, so does the national sense of history and responsibility.

Almost paradoxically, however, an alternative memorial culture is also beginning to emerge. In April 2000 Prime Minister Guy Verhofstadt went to Rwanda and publicly apologized for Belgium's role in the genocide. Though he refrained from apologizing for Belgium's colonial past, he did note that his 1996–97 discovery of the Rwandan massacres had forced him "to look inward and confront our own history, as well as our own responsibility" and that "the genocides that have brought shame to the twentieth century are not accidents of History."[6] Such statements would seem to open the door to the breaking up of what Antoon Van den Braembussche rightly identifies as a Belgian taboo.[7]

6. "Discours du Premier Ministre Guy Verhofstadt à l'occasion de la commémoration du 6e anniversaire du début du Génocide rwandais," Kigali, Rwanda, 7 April 2000, <http://premier.fgov.be/topics/speeches/f_speeches12.html> (French version); <http://premier.fgov.be/topics/speeches/n_speech12.html> (Dutch version). Time will tell to what extent the 8 June 2001 conviction by a Belgian jury of four Rwandans charged with having participated in the Rwandan genocide represents an evasion of Belgium's own responsibilities or a growing readiness to face them.
7. The success of *King Leopold's Ghost*, a number one Belgian best-seller in both French and Dutch, is another hopeful sign (see Tamara Straus's interview with Adam

Memory is, of course, not the responsibility of government officials alone. One of the threads that runs through the present volume is that Belgian culture has entered a new phase since the constitutional reforms of 1993. Since the mid-1990s, at about the same time as Belgian commodities suddenly became highly marketable exports, some Belgians have even begun to showcase Belgium's federalization as an exportable political model.[8] Such a view represents a dramatic departure from the disconcerting eagerness with which Belgians have customarily portrayed their country as a scandal-riddled nation.[9] Concurrently, the parceling of the country seems to have made Belgium's past more manageable as well. As noted by a number of the contributors to this volume, Belgian scholars, artists, and writers have recently shown a new-found willingness to do the hard work of memory and to deal, both at the national and regional levels, with a number of sensitive subjects, including wartime collaboration, immigration, and postcolonialism.

Nineteenth-century uses of the past had been subordinated to the nation-building needs of a country created in 1830 and whose elites were, by and large, forward looking. By contrast, the twentieth century was marked by the marginalization of an increasingly contested and fragmented past and by a quasi-apocalyptic vision of Belgium's future. Somewhat unexpectedly, by formalizing, albeit imperfectly, linguistic and regional identities, federalization seems to have made something of a cultural renaissance possible. Belgians must now decide whether the twenty-first century will be known for having excised the past even further or for having entered into a creative and responsible engagement with it. We therefore have to wait and see whether Belgium's "federalization of memory" has signaled a further widening of the amnesia principle or whether it means that a postnationalist emphasis on infranational identities has allowed writers, artists, and scholars to turn being Belgian into a construct open to artistic exploration, and to delve

---

Hochschild in "King Leopold's Ghost Makes a Comeback," 24 September 1999, <http://www.alternet.org/story.html?StoryID=1059>).

    8. On the subject of the "Belgian conquest" of the United States market, see Jerry Shriver, "Belgium: Beer, Trendy Cuisine Are Must-Haves," *USA TODAY*, 19 October 1999, <http://www.usatoday.com/life/travel/leisure/1999/t0625be.htm>. Philip Mosley has noted that Europe has also been experiencing a surge of interest in Belgian food, film, and fashion since the mid-1990s (*Split Screen*, 24).

    9. There is even a three-hundred and eighty-four page long encyclopedia of Belgian scandals: Dirk Barrez, *Het land van de duizend schandalen. Encyclopedie van een kwarteeuw Belgische affaires* [The Land of a Thousand Scandals: Encyclopedia of a Quarter of a Century of Belgian Affairs] (Groot-Bijgaarden, Belgium: Globe, 1997).

into Belgium's contested past as private citizens rather than as people confined or burdened by the now sterile and amnesiac logic of nationalism.

A few words remain to be said on some of the key features of this volume, namely, its interdisciplinary character, its joint focus on literary and visual culture, and its plurilingual and international scope. The interdisciplinary approach at the heart of this issue makes sense inasmuch as separate disciplines have different definitions of memory, not to mention culture and identity. Visual culture is featured prominently, not only because of the long-standing ties between memory and images in European thought, which Paul Ricoeur has recently reminded us of,[10] but because visual culture is particularly crucial to Belgian national identity. It is often through the medium of Belgian art, "the id of the nation," to use Luc Sante's memorable phrase,[11] that silent memories can best be addressed. Literature has had trouble being Belgian; its medium forces it almost immediately to be identified in narrower (Walloon, Flemish) or broader (French/Francophone, Dutch-speaking) terms. Finally, the plurilingual and international aspects of the contributions are intended to underscore that Belgian culture in general and Belgian *francophonies* in particular cannot be thought in isolation from a multilingual context (even in a journal dedicated to French studies) and to provide an opportunity for cross-continental dialogue.

Part 1 focuses on the vexed question of Belgian identity and the plural nature of Belgian memories. In Luc de Heusch's *"Ceci n'est pas la Belgique,"* childhood memories form the basis of a meditation on the sweep of Belgian history and the place of art in a country that has been split by a no-fault divorce. In "What, if Anything, Is a Belgian?" Piet Van de Craen provides a succinct overview of Belgium's new institutions and argues that Belgium's federalization provides a useful political and legal model for the European Union. Reviewing the Belgian taboos that still obtain with respect to the Congolese Holocaust as well as Flemish and Walloon collaboration during the Second World War, Antoon Van den Braembussche argues that the dark zones of Belgian memory and the centrifugal forces of Belgian politics have badly compromised Belgian identity. He then puts forth that these silent zones have recently been challenged by Belgians' response to the collective trauma inflicted by the Dutroux affair, which involved the sexual abuse

10. Paul Ricoeur, *La mémoire, l'histoire, l'oubli* (Paris: Seuil, 2000), esp. 5–66.
11. Lue Sante, *The Factory of Facts* (New York: Pantheon Book, 1998), 175.

and murder of several children and brought out a host of weaknesses in Belgium's sociopolitical system. Rather than focus on the silences of Belgium, Jacques Dubois underscores, "against" Proust as it were, the role voluntary memory should and has begun to play in the recognition of a Walloon identity and of the dignity associated with such a recognition. In particular, he stresses the importance of the role played by artists and writers like poet Jean-Pierre Verheggen, playwright Jean Louvet, and filmmaker Jean-Jacques Andrien in the awakening of an entire community to its own identity.

Part 2 focuses in reverse chronological order on fictional representations of key moments in Belgian history. In the opening pages of Pierre Mertens's latest novel, *Perasma,* the thoughts of the first-person narrator, a librettist, revolve around the notion that buried traumas always seem to resurface in his unnamable country—including the discovery, the previous summer, of the martyred bodies of a pedophile's young victims. In "Colonial Memories in Belgian and Congolese Literature," Antoine Tshitungu Kongolo tells parallel stories of concealment, neglect, and amnesia while also noting the existence of a renewed interest in the colonial past and of the adoption of more genuinely critical stances. In "Death Is Elsewhere," Sophie de Schaepdrijver tracks the different phases of Belgian Great War literature in both French and Dutch, from works in the heroic and the disillusioned mode to the gradual excision of the drama of the Great War from Belgian literature for both international and domestic reasons. In "The Sixteenth Century: A Decisive Myth," Marc Quaghebeur underscores the foundational role played by emperor Charles V and the legend of "black Spain" in the creation of a national identity in Francophone literary and historical works of the nineteenth century and reviews some of the transformations this myth underwent in the twentieth century.

The essays in part 3 deal with images and sites of memory. Serge Tisseron analyzes the means by which Hergé's own family secrets are incorporated in *Les aventures de Tintin,* a body of work that can be studied as the site of personal as well as social memory. Philip Mosley's essay articulates the ways in which Belgian cinema has been dealing with issues of anxiety, place, and memory at the national and subnational levels. Moving from Wallonia to Brussels to Flanders, he focuses on works by the Dardenne brothers, Samy Szlingerbaum, and André Delvaux and wonders whether Belgians' collective amnesia may not be coming to an end. Françoise Aubry traces the paradoxical fate of the works of Art Nouveau architect Victor Horta, whose unique style has garnered worldwide recognition, but whose work has been under-appreciated in Belgium, where some of his most important buildings have been mutilated, destroyed, dispersed, and/or reconfigured beyond recognition. Finally, Alexander Murphy helps us to put the fate of Horta's works in a broader context. In "Landscapes for Whom?" he revisits the vexed question of Belgium's national identity by turning his attention to Brussels's disaggregated landscape and the relative absence of commemorative markers of Belgian history in the nation's capital, which reflects both the establishment's commitment to classical economic liberalism and its desire to create a city that would transcend its political and cultural geography, particularly Belgium's ethnolinguistic fragmentation.

This project would not have taken shape the way it has were it not for the kind and judicious advice I have received from many quarters. At the early stages, I have benefited from a great many suggestions from persons both in Europe and the United States, including Louis Dupré, Thomas Ferenczi, Bart Hendrickx, Nancy Hunt, Françoise Labio, Juliette Loncour, Anne Lybaert, Marianne Mead, Tyrus Miller, Timothy J. Reiss, Henry Rousso, and Noa Steimatsky. Though I have not been able to incorporate every suggestion I have received, I have valued and learned from them nonetheless. I am particularly grateful for the help and advice I have received from Ann Gaylin and Christopher L. Miller, as well as from Richard Boijen, Agnès Bolton, Edward Bolton, Edwin Duval, Françoise Jaouën, David Quint, Susan Weiner, and Jay Winter. I also want to thank Roberto Gimeno for having agreed to create a translated version of his beautifully readable map at the last minute, Barbara Harshav for her wide-ranging translations, Joseph Mai for his thoughtful queries, and Alyson Waters for her keen interest in this project and her careful attention to language. Above all, I want to thank the contributors for their generosity and their willingness to say yes to someone who was, with but one exception, a total stranger.

I. Memory and Identity

LUC DE HEUSCH

Ceci n'est pas la Belgique*

Belgium: sixty kilometers of dunes where the summers were mild and the sea was gray or green, never blue (horrid Mediterranean blue, light without imagination). We didn't travel abroad yet. Only rich children did that. We were children of the north, neither poor nor rich, keen on a North Sea that was welcoming and rowdy, cold and rebellious. We loved the great movement of its tides, with its strong smell of seaweed and mussels. Protected by the breakwaters, it surrendered and recaptured right at our feet vast expanses of dreams.

How do you exile yourself from a happy childhood? Yes, when vacation time arrived, Flanders, with its sixty kilometers of beaches, was sweet for the Belgian children of the interior, who, drunk on salty green horizons, came—if they were children of the bourgeoisie—to build castles doomed to magnificent collapse. My homeland: a federation of fine sand castles, Flemish and Walloon fortresses, side by side, in a make-believe nation, confronting the gray and green sea that laughed at our shouts and our varied accents, covering them with its immense murmur.

This was the time when the great Belgian champions—Romain and Sylvère Maes—were on their way to winning three Tours de France. So, all the Belgian children on vacation at the North Sea became Belgians against the French. I also remember the nails that were (allegedly) thrown somewhere in France under the tires of our champions with the same agitation as I do the Nazi flag I saw hoisted over the Royal Palace of Brussels, where a few moments earlier the black, yellow, and red flag had still waved in the cruel blue sky of the spring of 1940.

To cure chauvinism, that childhood disease, and avert patriotism,

*This article originally appeared in French in Luc de Heusch, *Ceci n'est pas la Belgique* (Brussels: Éditions Complexe, 1992). It has been translated and reprinted by permission of the Éditions Complexe.

YFS 102, *Belgian Memories,* ed. Catherine Labio, © 2002 by Yale University.

11

Figure 1. James Ensor, "Les bains à Ostende," 1899. Etching on China paper. University of Michigan Museum of Art. © 2002 Artists Rights Society (ARS), New York/SABAM, Brussels. Photo courtesy of the University of Michigan Museum of Art.

that adult obsession, requires a very long training period, as well as a partial denial of the Father (*Patrie*) and an initiation. Art—unlike sports—invites us to do that.

But let's not move too fast. I promised my publisher a certain number of pages about Belgium, that country that no longer exists. Flanders and Wallonia are living under the terms of a no-fault divorce.

On that day, in the dazzling spring of 1940, when the war sent Belgium's little ones on vacation before the scheduled date, a few spellbound children followed the German army in the streets of Brussels, deserted by the entire adult male population, as it goose-stepped its way into the city to the fascinating racket of the victory drums. When the black, yellow, and red flag was lowered, I wept with shame. Shame at being a useless thirteen-year-old child abandoned to superb ogres by the adults.

That was the second time since the punctured bicycle tire affair that I felt Belgian. In the enraged throes of a betrayal. In school, we had been taught to be Belgians. Walloon children admired the feats of the Flemish commoners who had wiped out the French knighthood at the walls of Courtrai in the heat of the summer of 1302 [see Figure 2]. The evil king Philip the Fair had wanted to seize the beautiful and flourishing county of Flanders, which he considered an integral part of the future "Hexagon" of France. It's not something often mentioned, but in a sense that was a bilingual battle, since the elegant sons of the Count of Flanders, who led the sturdy battalions of Flemish weavers and fullers into the fray, spoke only French. And during vacation, between two swims, the Walloon children, from their shops of sand, silently, with the language of gestures, sold paper flowers to the distant descendants of those Flemish heroes, prototypes of the indomitable Belgian. Oh, seasons! Oh, castles! Shells were our national currency.

The story of the Count of Flanders (Gui de Dampierre) was indeed touchingly antidialectical. He won back his domain with the help of the wool workers, shaking up the French aristocracy whose help had been enlisted by a local bourgeoisie worried about the revolutionary fervor of the plebeians. Ever since that famous summer day in 1302, the "Flemish question" has been explained in symbolic terms as the legitimate defense of the patriotic lower classes slaughtering the foreign invaders by flailing a weapon called a "hello" (*goedendag*). A few days before the battle, at sunrise on 17 May, the proletarians of Bruges assaulted the soldiers of the French governor who had come to take possession of the county in the name of Philip the Fair. In the confusion of dawn, they dispatched (neatly) all those unable to pronounce correctly the Flemish battle cry: *Schild en Vriend* (Shield and Friend).

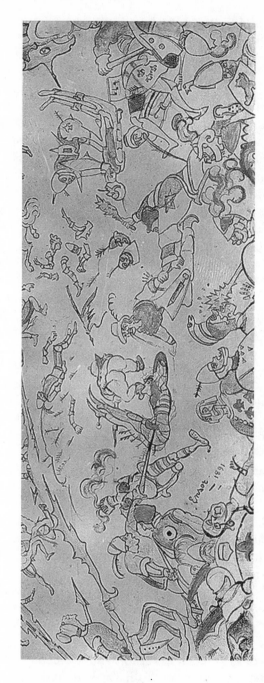

Figure 2. James Ensor, "La bataille des éperons d'or/De guldensporenslag," 1891 (detail). Etching. Royal Museums of Fine Arts, Brussels, Belgium. © 2002 Artists Rights Society (ARS), New York/SABAM, Brussels. Photo courtesy of the Royal Museums of Fine Arts of Belgium.

Yet that good francophone count, whose banner was brandished by the Flemish lower classes, is not part of any nationalist children's library. A few years later, when the weavers of Bruges formed a revolutionary government, another Count of Flanders, Louis de Nevers, would call for help from the King of France. And Flanders would definitely lose its Roman, Gallic half. The "Flemish question," naturally, is also many other things. These feudal muddles were flourishing on the frontiers of France and Germany. The countries between the Escaut (*Schelde*) and the Meuse (*Maas*), which had been the heart of the Carolingian Empire, had been hacked apart by the Treaty of Verdun (843). The Escaut had henceforth formed the boundary between the kingdom of Charles the Bald and the Lotharingia of Lothair, which had had no political future. As a result, while Flanders had become a vassal of the King of France, the Principality of Liège, practically independent, belonged vaguely (and increasingly so) to the Germanic Holy Roman Empire. For patriotic good measure, Flemish schoolchildren—in the days when Belgium existed—pitied the misfortunes of the (Francophone) residents of Liège, who had been massacred by a Duke of Burgundy—the awful Charles the Bold—because they had refused to become Burgundians.

The episode of the Dukes of Burgundy—there's the rub, the core of the Belgian problem, the moment when the Flemish and Walloon cities were brought to heel by history and were forced to finally submit to the good and harsh reasons of state and integrate themselves into a Nation. The mythmakers assigned to write the saga of the Belgian Ancestors would, however, grant the residents of Liège the right to resist the Burgundians. (Charles had not pulled his punches!)

The Liégeois were deemed to have been right, on the whole, for having insisted on their independence. (After all, a prince-bishop is certainly worth a grand duke.)

By contrast, the firm resolution of the Burgundians to rescue the other scattered limbs of the (future) Belgium from a bygone past was to be cause for rejoicing. Schoolchildren accordingly applauded the fierce plan of the Grand Dukes of the West to build a kingdom between France and Germany, to revive the old Lotharingia, and to offer the wonderful possibilities of the modern state to the (future) Belgians. Was not this new political ambition the path to economic progress? Those valiant Flemish commoners who had been right to fight the King of France had had their day. They were now deemed wrong to have impeded the development of capitalism. Let them be demobilized and let the rules of the guild be torn up! The Duke of Burgundy came to be portrayed as a progressive. The painting that blossomed at the time—usually referred to as Flemish—became Burgundian. So did Jan Van Eyck, painter and servant of Philip the Good.

If Philip the Good was not really good, he was not really bad either. After all, he depended on the prosperity of the rich cities of the north to guarantee his power and finance his nascent empire. But that didn't keep him from crushing them with taxes and it didn't keep them from revolting. The reasons of state that forced the Belgian nation into existence humiliated two thousand citizens of Ghent who had come to beg pardon of the good Duke Philip, bareheaded, barefoot, a rope around their neck.

Long live the common Estates General! With the medieval fiefs dispersed, the countries of the Meuse and the Escaut finally became the Burgundian Netherlands, the *pays de par-deçà* (the "countries on this side"): a fine space open to the arts and to trade—not to mention the war against Louis XI, who had his own reasons of state. He overcame Charles the Bold and the political plan of the Grand Dukes failed: Bruges was no longer twinned with Dijon. An abyss was created between the countries "on this side" and those "on that side." The wolves that devoured Charles's frozen face in Nancy also devoured the last traces of Lotharingia.

Strange fate: the (future) Belgium has been the product of an inexorable shrinking. Its lot is fission, segmentation, and disappearance. By contrast, one can recognize (great) nations by the slow and progressive swelling designed by their wise sovereigns. This swelling sometimes looks like a frog's, even though the people concerned like to adopt a more noble coat-of-arms. It is an irrepressible expansion that, rightly or wrongly (depending on whether one is inside or outside), grants from the start to the members of the group (swollen or expanded, depending on one's point of view) a very—too—strong sense of their identity, a feeling one would be ill-advised to challenge for it has now become nationalistic. Nothing like that has been going on in Belgium, where lightning has just hammered out a temporary coat-of-arms, giving the lion back to Flanders and granting Wallonia a rooster. Might the (future) Belgians have dillydallied along the paths of history? They were rich (not all), industrious, creative, whatever you want to call them, but it must be said that their fate rarely seemed to belong to them. Hence their fierce individualism and the notorious absence of a taste for grandeur. René Magritte of Wallonia and Marcel Broodthaers of Brussels have attested to the vitality of that "un-reason," or derision, which Ensor of Flanders made into the cornerstone of Belgian modern art. According to Broodthaers, Belgium is to a starving deserter, only a tricolor bone to gnaw on ("Fémur d'homme belge," 1965). Magritte opens painting to absolute freedom of thought and defies both linguistics and dialectics in the process.

Totally devoid of meaning—that's how the history of the (future) Belgium certainly appears. But is there anywhere else, in the history of others, a significant core, a crux of meaning that is not mythopraxic? Will Europe succeed someday in calmly rewriting the common and unfortunate adventure of the Christians who tore each other apart?

Let's get down to business, to that essence of Belgium the reader may not yet have seen very clearly. After the death of Charles the Bold in 1477, the countries "on this side" remained grouped under the fragile authority of his daughter, poor little Marie. She was quickly married off to a Habsburg prince able to defend the newborn Netherlands against the sly intrigues of Louis XI, who promptly decided to occupy Burgundy, forever depriving the Belgians of the joy of being Burgundians. This is how the future Austrian fate of Belgium began. But not so fast. First (and for a long time), we had to become Spaniards. Here's how: one day, the grandson of Marie of Burgundy and Maximilian of Austria, the so-called "Charles Quint" (Charles V) (1500–1558) became the most powerful man in the world. Born and raised in Flanders, in Ghent, he inherited in succession the Netherlands (which he curiously called, no doubt out of nostalgia, "Circle of Burgundy"), Spain (hence, America), Austria, and part of Italy. Surely that man's heart was on the side of Spain, not on that of his hometown, which he punished harshly when its residents—trailing behind history—refused to pay new taxes to finance imperial enterprises. Charles V imitated his Burgundian great-great grandfather, the wise Philip the Good, and he demanded that 2,000 townspeople, scantily dressed and with ropes around their necks, come grovel before him. No need to add that the privileges of the city were definitely suppressed. That is what is meant by "reasons of state": an unfailing authority in the service of a bright vision of a dark future.

So, the (future) Belgians became Spaniards. They were still united to the (future) Dutch, but that did not last long. The Reformation was the poison distilled by history in the very Catholic veins of the Netherlands. It enjoyed a great success there. Alas for the (future) Belgians, Philip II, the son of Charles V, could not stand the Protestants. He appointed the Duke of Alba to the northern provinces, and there Alba lit the joyous and unifying stakes of the Holy Inquisition. Then, indeed, something that might look like a national sentiment took shape, in the guise of a common revolt against the tyrannical power of Spain. It would, however, signal the end of the political and cultural unity of the Burgundian Netherlands. Holland, which had victoriously stood up to the Spaniards, became a Protestant nation. It devoted itself to conquering the seas, while Flanders (her nose stuck to the ground) remained, along with Wallonia, within the orbit of Spain. So, the (future) Belgians remained Spanish and Catholic. Very Catholic. A strange fact: the arts continued to flourish. Rubens now held the torch of the (future) Belgian art, this time in Antwerp. But Rubens was really a Spaniard, just as Van Eyck had been a Burgundian. And, like Van Eyck, Rubens was busy settling some diplomatic matters for his master.

To complete their European vocation, the (future) Belgians became Austrians in the eighteenth century. The French Revolution—brilliant revenge of Philip the Fair—then made all of them, Walloons and Flemings alike, French. Finally, after Waterloo, eager to build a northern rampart against the ambitions of France, the Holy Alliance took the fate of the (future) Belgians firmly in hand and reconstituted the former Netherlands under the aegis of the king of Holland. Now we were Dutch. Was this the end of the tunnel? Had we reached the conclusion of this fragmented history? Was this the reconstitution of the Circle of Burgundy and of the United Provinces? Yes, of course, but not for long. The French-speaking citizens of the southern Netherlands (Flemings and Walloons) could not bear the authoritarian measures of the Dutch-speaker who was ruling in The Hague. The liberal Revolution of 1830 pitted the Catholic and French-speaking bourgeoisie of the southern Netherlands against the Protestant and Dutch-speaking bourgeoisie of the north in a magnificent Lévi-Straussian structural system. The Holy Alliance was furious, for the European equilibrium was in question once again. The rebellious Belgian bourgeoisie granted itself a liberal constitutional monarchy. In time, it stingily yielded a series of linguistic rights to the Flemish people who occupied half of its territory, and whose representatives, preoccupied only with the business of doing business, did not care very much about those rights. Belgian historians confidently proclaimed that the unity of the country had been realized and, as a result, the little Flemings and Walloons, an undivided people, began studying the marvelous common history of Belgium (each in his own tongue). This history centered on two events of considerable mythic impact.

In the middle of the coast, halfway between France and Holland, at the end of the nineteenth century, while an unknown painter, James

Ensor, was inventing modern art all by himself in his studio, King Leopold II anointed Ostend Queen of the Beaches. The bourgeois—both Flemish and Walloon—cared little for the amorous escapades of that man, who had understood, before Lenin, that there is no great capitalism without imperialism. In Ostend, the king liked to scan, beyond the gray or green horizon, the invisible mouth of the Congo River, where the equatorial forest disgorged fabulous wealth in a stench of rotten wood. Wary at first, the Belgians rejoiced in the royal Testament that granted them as a colony what had long been, under the name of The Independent State of the Congo, the most beautiful private estate of the world. People then undertook to glorify, for the benefit of the Walloon and Flemish schoolchildren, the unpopular king as the empire-builder who had suddenly made Belgium richer and more virtuous. For Belgians had only accepted the tremendous benefits of colonization in order to draw millions of fetishist and polygamous Africans out of savagery by clothing them, converting them, and teaching them to work (see Figure 3).

Soon after came the trial by fire. Albert I, nephew of the colonizing king, faced (with dignity) the first German invasion. In the company of rats, Belgians fulfilled the founding sacrifice of the nation in the horror of the trenches. Their sovereign was dubbed a knight by Europe. In primary schools, Flemish and Walloon children worshipped with the same nationalistic fervor both Sergeant De Bruyne, the hero of the "anti-slavery," that is, colonial campaign, and the lock keeper who flooded the plain of the Yser to stop the German advance.

We had all learned that, once, a very long time ago, six hundred heroes from the commune of Franchimont had been cut to pieces for having tried to seize Charles the Bold, who had been about to sack Liège, the city of the prince-bishop. And we repeated together, with the best possible accent, "Schild en Vriend." The French-speaking children of Brussels, bilingual by fiat, were also invited to savor the superb poetry of Guido Gezelle in a grim anthology of Flemish literature titled "The Gilded Door" (De Gouden Poort); their little Walloon classmates were allowed to ignore it.

But the linguistic issue was gnawing at Belgium like a cancer. In the nineteenth century, a few educators and priests hostile to the French-speaking bourgeoisie of Flanders had reminded the illiterate and exploited masses of the past grandeur of Flanders. For a moment, the social crisis, the rise of socialism, and the great strikes relegated the problem to the back burner. After World War II, intellectuals and politi-

Voyage du prince Albert et de la princesse Elisabeth au Congo

Observons la gravure. — *1. Quels personnages reconnaissez-vous ? — 2. Pourquoi sont-ils habillés de blanc et portent-ils un casque ? — 3. Sont-ils bien accueillis dans notre colonie ? Prouvez-le. — 4. Les petits noirs qui les entourent sont-ils encore des enfants sauvages ? — 5. Pourquoi le prince Albert a-t-il fait ce voyage au Congo ?*

Figure 3. Luc De Decker, "Voyage du prince Albert et de la princesse Elisabeth au Congo." Excerpt from A. Gérard, F. Lermigniaux, and C. Masson, *Histoire de Belgique* (Brussels, 1966).

cians of all persuasions became involved and the linguistic issue became the national question par excellence. The Flemish bourgeoisie suddenly felt close to the lower classes it had ignored thus far. As an indirect consequence, the Walloons became aware of a shared and uncertain cultural identity.

Belgium was done for. Walloons and Flemings everywhere, who had never clashed in the course of a history that was slipping through their fingers, are now looking at each other like cats and dogs, lions and roosters. The two "communities" fight over Brussels, the stammering city where French is spoken as badly as Dutch—Brussels the bastard. I therefore am on the side of the bastards.

The linguistic question, of course, is of interest to the literati. It leaves painters indifferent or perplexed. It is the Cultural Services of Flanders and Wallonia that have imposed a Flemish or Walloon identity on artists. Their chancelleries have done their utmost to oppose a Flemish expressionism to a Walloon surrealism. Yet, art in Belgium has always been interregional, international. The expressionism of Sint-Martens-Latem is not a random by-product of Flemish soil. It is the regional manifestation of an immense European wave. As for Surrealism, do we need to recall that its seat is not La Louvière, but wherever there exists a certain state of mind of which a few artists (from everywhere) first became aware in Paris? In the Dadaist period, Magritte sketched the frontispiece for the work of the Flemish poet Paul van Ostayen, *Het Bordeel van Ika Lock* (The Bordello of Ika Lock).

Rubens spent eight years in Italy before settling in Antwerp. In those distant days, as now, there were Flemings and Walloons, caught up in the same whirlwinds, the same exchanges of goods and ideas. The basins of the Escaut and the Meuse are tiny compared to those of the Volga. Sensual and greedy, the artists of this small land, which has also been a marvelous battlefield, have known how to paint and draw to ward off the seriousness of death. Now that peace has returned, there are more and more falsely serious Flemings and Walloons who roar or crow whenever they are asked an intellectual question. They have not only lost their sense of humor, they have also lost their sense of the absurd. True, we see this elsewhere, in other, bigger countries. The bigger the country, the greater the absurdity.

COBRA. In the middle of the twentieth century, a retiring man of talent had the happy idea of uniting three small countries in order to have more opportunities not to let humor escape. His name was Christian Dotremont and he knew how to reconcile the art of writing and the art of drawing. For a time, he created the intellectual union of three small kingdoms: Denmark, the Netherlands, and Belgium. CO for Copenhagen, BR for Brussels, A for Amsterdam. Alechinsky the Belgian, Jorn the Dane, Appel the Dutchman, mined a new province of the universal art of painting, with all national frontiers abolished.

Art in Belgium is first of all European—neither Japanese nor African—and open to all winds of the mind (even Japanese and African). It is impossible to nationalize or regionalize COBRA. Even if it was basically northern, it had friends and accomplices in Paris and Germany.

It is impossible to nationalize or regionalize Dada, Surrealism, abstract art. Issues of paternity are pointless when an aesthetic extends over vast regions, precisely escaping provincialism. Besides the consecrated Flemish expressionism, there existed in Flanders a neglected abstract art. And Marcel Broodthaers participates in a vast general renewal of the Dadaist spirit. His originality no doubt is that he opens new breaches in the rifts of the *esprit de sérieux*, on the very ground that Magritte had started to shake up. This is undeniably a matter of spiritual parentage and geographic proximity, but one that has nothing to do with a Flemish or Walloon genius.

In that sense, Rubens is no more Flemish because he paints plump women than Delvaux is Walloon because he paints skeletons. It is by accident that *Ceci n'est pas une pipe* is written in French and not in Flemish or Polish. Belgium is a marvelous accident of history. Did James Ensor of Ostend, who wrote in French, paint in Flemish? Surely, Walloon painting is neither Burgundian nor Spanish, contrary to that of Van Eyck or Rubens. It is quite recent. It was born in an obscure town of the Hainaut province, called Lessines, where Magritte came into the world. It is difficult to relate it to the sculptors of Walloon romanesque art of the eleventh century. And Magritte, like Rubens, owes a lot to Italy. But it is not the same Italy. De Chirico is his teacher, his instigator. To save the regional face, shall we say that there are a lot of Italian immigrants in Wallonia today? Hugo Claus, the itinerant Fleming, and Alechinsky, the Walloon from Bougival, friend of the *Gilles de Binche*, continue to communicate with each other.

If you go far back in time, you can spot the name of the Belgians, written in Latin: *Belgae*. That was long before Belgium. That was the time when Julius Caesar had come to impose his law on Gaul. He confronted a turbulent, undisciplined combination of Celtic tribes of that name and gave them very high marks in his campaign journal (*De Bello Gallico*): "*Omnium Gallorum fortissimi sunt Belgae*" (Of all the peoples of Gaul, the Belgians are the bravest). But they are loath to show it. This is what makes them appear fearful (or idiotic), unlike the French and the Spaniards who have (too much?) flair.

The sixty kilometers of dunes that were once hospitable to Belgian children have been devastated by hideous concrete—Flemish or Walloon—poured onto the sand by vile money. Ensor had foreseen it: "Ugliness will soon spread its dull veil over all things."

—Translated from the French by Barbara Harshav

Figure 4. "In the company of rats..." From the World War I papers of Lt. Gen. Adrien Labio. © 2002 Catherine Labio. Handwritten legend of the back of the photograph reads: "Une chasse à l'ennemi du cantonnement: Le Rat" (Yser front, ca. Spring 1915).

PIET VAN DE CRAEN

What, If Anything, Is a Belgian?

"I was born in Belgium" says the Dutch-speaking poet Leonard Nolens, "but Belgium was never born in me."[1] "Look at the gardens in front of the houses in Flanders and Wallonia," affirms the bilingual dancer Thierry Smits, "there are as many garden gnomes in Flanders as in Wallonia."[2] "Maybe the country itself is a work of art," another artist wonders,[3] while others proudly proclaim—though rarely in writing—that "Belgians are bastards."

It is not difficult to find contradictory statements about Belgium and the Belgians. The book from which the quotations above have been taken, *Belgique toujours grande et belle,* edited by Antoine Pickels and Jacques Sojcher and published in 1998, is a wonderful collection of contradictory statements made by Belgians on their country and its inhabitants. Reading the nearly 600-page volume makes one realize that Belgium and the Belgians consist of a nearly infinite number of characteristics clustered around the unsolvable question *"what and who am I?"* And yet the book is inspiring and not at all gloomy. The reason for this is simple: Belgians do not take themselves too seriously when writing about themselves. Have you ever met French, German, or Dutch people who insist they are bastards? Their fellow countrymen would put them away. Belgians, on the other hand, have elevated bastardy to a way of life while also downplaying some of the rather unpleasant aspects associated with nationalism.

1. Quoted by Kristien Hemmerechts, "Belgique-België," in *Belgique toujours grande et belle,* ed. Antoine Pickels and Jacques Sojcher (Brussels: Éditions Complexe, 1998), 119 (my translation).

2. Thierry Smits, "Il y a autant de nains de jardin en Flandre qu'en Wallonie," in Pickels and Sojcher, 114.

3. Jan Fabre, "Peut-être que la Belgique est une oeuvre d'art," in Pickels and Sojcher, 403.

YFS 102, *Belgian Memories,* ed. Catherine Labio, © 2002 by Yale University.

In Belgium, matters of identity did not emerge until the beginning of the twentieth century. In a famous letter to the King, the Walloon politician Jules Destrée wrote in 1912: "Let me tell you the truth, the grand and horrifying truth . . . there are no Belgians. . . . No, Majesty, there is not such a thing as a Belgian soul."[4] In the sixties, Pierre Wigny, who had been Minister of Foreign Affairs from 1958 to 1961, said: "As was once said by a stand-up comedian, Belgium is the only country in the world where various oppressed majorities coexist, three groups that each have a certain supremacy and that feed an inferiority complex."[5]

Outsiders have sometimes taken part in the debate, as, for instance, in the case of British writer Bill Bryson: "As countries go, Belgium is a curiosity. It's not one nation at all, but two, northern Dutch-speaking Flanders and southern French-speaking Wallonia. The southern half possesses the most outstanding scenery, the prettiest villages, the best gastronomy and, withal, a Gallic knack for living well, while the north has the finest cities, the most outstanding museums and churches, the ports, the coastal resorts, the bulk of the population, and most of the money. The Flemings can't stand the Walloons and the Walloons can't stand the Flemings, but when you talk to them a little you realize that what holds them together is an even deeper disdain for the French and the Dutch."[6] This is an overgeneralization of popular street talk but it reflects more or less what outsiders think Belgium is and what the Belgians are and/or stand for. Remarkably, Bryson makes no mention of Brussels and the *Bruxellois* (the inhabitants of Brussels), i.e., the people who make up Wigny's third group.

In this contribution I would like to present Belgium and the Belgians in a slightly unusual manner. It has been said over and over again that the country will fall apart, that there is no reason for it to exist, and so on. While all this may be true to a certain extent, it may not be true of Belgium alone. Europe's post World War II economic and political evolution has been behind the creation of the European Union. While the Union is still a vague and unfamiliar concept to some, it is clear that the role of the nineteenth-century nation-state is diminishing rapidly. At the same time, the role of regions is on the rise. In this paper, I hope

4. Quoted and translated by Kenneth D. McRae in *Conflict and Compromise in Multilingual Societies: Belgium* (Waterloo, Ontario: Wilfried Laurier University Press, 1986), 10.

5. Also quoted and translated by McRae, 10.

6. Bill Bryson, *Neither Here Nor There: Travels in Europe* (London: Black Swan, 1998), 70.

to show that Belgium and the Belgians have an important role to play in this new context, and that whether or not their country is falling apart may well be totally irrelevant. More specifically, I argue that the Belgian system can be held up as a model for its ability to reach compromises and for its legal organization and that this makes Belgium important for future developments in the European Union. It is in this sense that Belgium can be said to be a kind of miniature Europe and that Belgians may be looked upon as Europeans *par excellence.*

THE BELGIAN ISSUES

Belgium has been plagued by a number of political issues since the foundation of the state.[7] The first major problem, the language issue, arose in the nineteenth century shortly after the country gained independence in 1830. The 30,000 km^2 country is divided by a linguistic border that probably came about between the fourth and seventh centuries.[8] The northern part is Dutch-speaking and the southern part is French-speaking. While the constitution guaranteed freedom of language, in practice French became the only official language of the Belgian state. In Dutch-speaking Flanders, where the middle and upper classes spoke French, a social and political struggle emerged, led by the Flemish Movement. This struggle was enhanced by the fact that in the nineteenth century the linguistic border also became a social border, opposing the industrialized south to the agrarian north. While this battle officially ended with the linguistic laws voted in 1962–63, the language issue still plays a role in Belgian politics, albeit a much less prominent one. Generally speaking, however, it would be fair to say that the language issue is directly responsible for the creation of the near-federal state that is Belgium at the beginning of the twenty-first century.

The second issue that opposed Wallonia and Flanders came up after World War II when King Leopold III was forced to abdicate in favor of his eldest son, Baudouin/Boudewijn I. The "Royal Question," as it became known, divided the more politically left and less Catholic Wallonia, and the more politically right and Catholic Flanders. The former were, generally speaking, against Leopold's return to the throne, while the latter favored it.

7. See also Denise Van Dam, *Flandre, Wallonie. Le rêve brisé* (Ottignies: Quorum, 1997).
8. Danny Lamarcq and Marc Rogge, *De taalgrens. Van de oude tot de nieuwe Belgen* (Leuven: Davidsfonds, 1996).

A third source of political tension concerns significant differences in points of view on the language question. Though Flanders has adopted a territorial approach and made Dutch the official language on Flemish soil, Wallonia finds this both unjust and imperialistic because it means that French-speaking citizens living in a Dutch-speaking territory do not get any official service in their language. Today, apart from the Brussels area, territorial unilingualism is the rule. However, in six *communes* bordering Brussels French speakers have what is known as "language facilities," which means that they can use French for administrative purposes. Likewise Dutch speakers have "language facilities" in a number of other *communes* along the linguistic border.[9]

A fourth source of conflicts between the Walloons and the Flemish concerns social benefits, which are dealt with at the national rather than the regional level. The Flemish have been insisting for a number of years that the richer Flanders "has paid enough for Wallonia" and some Flemish politicians are accordingly demanding that social security become a regional matter.

Finally, a fifth factor that divides Flemish and Walloon politics is Brussels, which consists of nineteen *communes* and is an officially bilingual area. Brussels is situated to the north of the linguistic border and is also the capital of Flanders despite the fact that only 15–20 per cent of its inhabitants are Dutch speakers. The exact figure is unknown because language censuses were declared unlawful in 1947 for fear that the Francophone group might take over power in the city. Nevertheless, some figures can be used to illustrate the sociolinguistic situation in more detail. Some six million people live in Flanders, while Wallonia has about three million inhabitants. About one million people live in Brussels, of which a quarter are foreigners. Let us assume that, out of the remaining 750,000 Belgians, 20 per cent are Dutch speakers and 80 per cent are French speakers. This means that only 2.5 per cent of the total Dutch-speaking population lives in Brussels in contrast to more than 33 per cent of the total French-speaking population. This makes Brussels the largest Francophone city in the country. Nevertheless, the Dutch-speaking minority is protected by language laws and is guaranteed administrative, medical, and educational services in its language. The status of Dutch-speakers in Brussels has been in the forefront of Belgian politics for the past fifty years.[10]

9. See also Alexander B. Murphy, *The Regional Dynamics of Language Differentiation in Belgium* (Chicago: University of Chicago, Geography Research Paper 227, 1988).

10. See Els Witte and Hugo Baetens Beardsmore, *The Interdisciplinary Study of Ur-*

While these critical issues have been responsible for many political crises over the years, it is certainly not true that Walloons, Bruxellois, and Flemish "can't stand" one another, contrary to what Bryson affirms. Because of their historical ties and shared cultural background, a kind of intercultural togetherness does exist despite political frictions.[11]

In the 1990s Belgium became a near-federal state. It is not entirely federal because the status of the Brussels region remains unclear;[12] unlike Flanders and Wallonia, Brussels is not a wholly independent region. Figure 1 illustrates the distribution of power in the newly federalized country. At the national or federal level, power is shared among the federal government, the two chambers of parliament, and the Crown, although the latter has very little power. Belgium is divided into distinct geographical areas, Flanders, Wallonia, and Brussels to which correspond three officially recognized *Regions*, each with their own executives and legislative bodies. Additionally, the country is concurrently divided into three officially recognized *Communities*. In the case of Flanders, Community and Region coincide. Such is not the case for the Walloon Region and the French Community, however: the French Community includes French speakers who reside in Brussels, but the Walloon Region does not. And there is also a German-speaking Community (although there are only some 60,000 German speakers in Belgium, they are responsible for the fact that the country is officially trilingual).

To complicate matters further, Brussels also has an independent executive for the Brussels community as a whole as well as another executive layer made up of two "Colleges": The College of the French Community (COCOF) and the College of the Flemish Community (VGC). These language-specific executives are devoted exclusively to looking after the interests of French and Dutch-speaking citizens in so-called "personalizable" matters. These include education, medical care, and other administrative matters that are of such immediate concern to citizens as individuals that they require special and separate treatment in the mixed-language region of Brussels.[13]

---

ban Bilingualism in Brussels (Clevedon, Avon, England, Philadelphia: Multilingual Matters, 1987) and Els Witte, André Alen, Hugues Dumont, and Rusen Ergec, eds., *Het statuut van Brussel/Bruxelles et son statut* (Brussels: De Boeck & Larcier, 1999).

11. See Van Dam, 163 ff.

12. See Witte et al., *Statuut van Brussel.*

13. See Jan Gijssels, "De toepassing van de taalwetgeving in het Brusselse en de persoonsgebonden aangelegenheden" [The Enforcement of Language Legislation in Brussels

Level	Institutions			
	Belgium	*Wallonia*	*Brussels*	*Flanders*
National	The federal government, the two houses of Parliament, the Crown			
Community		The government of the German-speaking Community / The government of the French Community	The College of the United Community (The College of the French Community (COCOF) / The College of the Flemish Community (VGC))	The government of the Flemish Community
Region		The government of the Walloon Region	The Council of the Region of Brussels-Capital & the Brussels government	
Language area		German 60.000 / French 3.000.000	Brussels-Capital bilingual area 1.000.000	Dutch 6.000.000

Figure 1: The organization of the Belgian near-federal state in 2000

This rather complicated situation is the result of numerous compromises and has led to many a heated debate in parliament. Yet, to say that the system outlined in Figure 1 is *but* a compromise is to ignore the fact that none of the Belgian issues mentioned here has led to any killings, with the notorious exception of the murder of communist leader Julien Lahaut. At the abdication ceremony of Leopold III on 16 July 1951, Lahaut shouted "Long live the Republic." He was shot one week later and the murderer(s) were never found. No other conflict area in Europe can claim such a record. It suffices to compare the Belgian compromise to the history of Northern Ireland, the Basque country, and the former Yugoslavia.

BELGIUM AND THE EUROPEAN UNION

Belgium has successfully managed to neutralize conflicts springing from socioeconomic and linguistic issues. In their study of the Canadian and Belgian situations, Peter H. Nelde *et al.* point out that four general strategies have been used in these areas: (1) the limited application of the territoriality principle (limited, that is, to key areas such as administration and education); (2) institutional multilingualism allowing for unilingual networks, i.e., for the fact that individuals within multilingual institutions need not be plurilingual themselves, and granting equal opportunity to majority and minority speakers; (3) measures of linguistic planning that are not exclusively based on linguistic censuses (specific contextual characteristics are taken into account); (4) linguistic groups are not judged merely quantitatively (more rights and possibilities of development are given to minority groups than their numbers alone would warrant).[14]

One of the challenges facing the European Union is the creation of linguistic and cultural policies that take into account members' linguistic and cultural diversity, while uniting them in a common social and civil project. How to achieve this is the center of an on-going debate among both individuals and organizations.[15] How can we relate the points above to possible paths for policy development in the Union?

---

and the Problem of 'Personalizable Matters'], *Language and Social Integration* 3 (1981): 61–86.

14. Peter H. Nelde, Normand Labrie, and Colin H. Williams, "The Principles of Territoriality and Personality in the Solution of Linguistic Conflicts," *Journal of Multilingual and Multicultural Development* 13/5 (1992): 387–406.

15. See for instance European Cultural Foundation, *Which Languages for Europe?*, Conference Report (Oegstgeest, The Netherlands, 1998) and European Language Coun-

Limited introduction of the territoriality principle. The Union, of course, does not challenge any territorial claims in any European country, that is, it recognizes each country as an entity. It is clear that the strict application of the territoriality principle would be disastrous in those areas where mixed populations reside. In such cases, the minority groups ought to be given rights that allow them to deploy their culture, language, and traditions within the common system. In other words, in some areas some form of language and/or cultural "facilitation" is needed.

Institutional multilingualism. While institutional multilingualism leading to unilingual networks is a good thing in itself, language policy should strive toward individual plurilingualism by promoting plurilingual education. This will enhance citizenship, tolerance, and communication. Although this was a stated goal for European policy according to the 1995 White Paper,[16] plurilingual education is still far from being a widespread phenomenon in Belgium and/or Europe despite increasing interest.

Linguistic planning not based on census and the relative importance of figures. As I have pointed out, linguistic censuses have been forbidden in Belgium since 1947. As a result, measures protecting the Dutch-speaking minority group in Brussels were implemented regardless of the number of Dutch speakers. If we consider the fact that Brussels is a melting-pot, albeit small, with a bilingual (Dutch-French) population of 33 per cent, disregarding figures has proved to be the right way of maneuvering. If the language policy had been based on census figures, we would have had a French-only policy since French is clearly the dominant language and the city's *lingua franca*. This would undoubtedly have been a source of resentment and unrest.

The above reasoning also has implications with respect to another debate in Europe, namely that of the role of English. As of 2001, for instance, the European Union had eleven official languages plus a number of working languages, such as Catalan. With new members waiting in the wings, such as Hungary and Poland, the language issue is not likely to disappear from the agenda in the coming years. For some,

---

cil, *Higher Education and European Language Policy,* Workshop (Berlin: Freie Universität Berlin, 2000 [see *http://www.fu-berlin.de/elc*]).

16. White Paper, *Teaching and Learning: Towards a Cognitive Society* (Brussels: European Commission, 1995).

adopting English as the sole *lingua franca* is the solution to the Union's language problems. Others think that a more diverse policy has to be pursued. Here again the Belgian solution to linguistic diversity may be considered as an example for Europe, where the territoriality principle has been adopted in nearly all cases and the official language of an area is therefore also the primary language of education. As a result, the first foreign language learned in Belgium is either Dutch (in the case of Francophones) or French (in the case of Dutch speakers). Today, there is an increasing trend in primary schools in Belgium to use this other language in a more sophisticated way by implementing some form of immersion or bilingual education. In this way, individual plurilingualism is enhanced and learners benefit from the positive cognitive effects that accompany this form of education,[17] with English becoming the third or, in some cases, fourth language after German. While there is some evidence that bilingualism has in and of itself little impact on social or ethnolinguistic identity,[18] the fact that it facilitates interaction (especially between groups with a similar cultural background), enhances learning, and enriches one's life are more than enough reasons to encourage and expand the Belgian example within the Union.

WHAT, IF ANYTHING, IS A BELGIAN?

Belgium has been at the center of a heated debate since its creation. The relatively young country has had little time to develop any nationalistic feelings in comparison to, for instance, the Netherlands or France. The fact that the country is divided by a linguistic border has condemned it to cope with multilingual and plurilingual issues since its very beginning as a nation-state in 1831. Part of its history is evidence of a struggle for equality of language and power between the French-speaking south and the Dutch-speaking north. This has resulted in the establishment of complicated political structures in order to find a balance between the demands of the parties involved. Today, it is a near-federal state dominated by two large regions.

The evolution of the European Union opens up new opportunities for Belgium, which has become an example of good practice for future

17. See Piet Van de Craen, "Reinforced and Bilingual Language Education in Dutch-speaking Schools in Brussels," in *The Construction of Knowledge, Learner Autonomy and Related Issues in Foreign Language Learning*, ed. Bettina Missler and Uwe Multhaup (Tübingen: Stauffenberg, 1999).

18. Paul Lamy, "Language and Ethnolinguistic Identity: The Bilingualism Question," *International Journal of the Sociology of Language* 20 (1979): 23–36.

European development as it strives toward compromise while maintaining its social and linguistic equilibrium. As a result, a Belgian citizen is a kind of European citizen who had European ideas *avant la lettre*. The country's political history may therefore be seen as a model for political compromise in a multilingual yet monocultural area. One multifaceted European culture together with societal multilingualism and individual plurilingualism might well be the slogan for Europe in the next decade. The Belgians can lead the way.

Figure 1. Everlyn Nicodemus, "Confrontiers. La België," 1997. Wooden case, chalk, glass, reproduction, tourist souvenirs, 34 × 28.5 × 10 cm. Photo: Felix Tirry. Reproduced by permission of the artist.

Artist's commentary: "La België does not exist. The Flemish who write in Dutch call the country 'België' and the Walloons who speak French say 'La Belgique.' A common joke argues that there exist only two "Belgians": the King and Manneken Pis, the tourist icon in Brussels. If one were to clone the latter (easy, as every tobacco shop is full of these souvenirs), the two of him would speak Dutch and French, turn their backs to each other, and even refuse to pee together.

The year I made 'Confrontiers. La België,' I represented Belgium in an exhibition of Flemish art in Spain, and I wrote in the catalogue about my perplexity before the seemingly irreconcilable war between the languages: 'If you come from a country with around one hundred and twenty languages and cultures (Tanzania), where part of the ties that bind the multiplicity together is a complex system of negotiations through jokes, mutual ragging and bickering, and tacitly specified responsibilities between groups, then you are puzzled by the dead seriousness of the wrestle that goes on in a state of bilingual conflict.'

I chose the extreme ambiguity of the Hieronymous Bosch reproduction as a backdrop to comment upon the ambiguity of Belgian identity. Three hundred and fifty years before Belgium was constructed as a nation-state in 1830, at the time Bosch was painting, a big part of what is now Belgium and of what is now the Netherlands belonged together in one set of provinces within an emerging urban Europe."

ANTOON VAN DEN BRAEMBUSSCHE

The Silence of Belgium: Taboo and Trauma in Belgian Memory

BELGIUM AND AMBIGUITY

"I am born in Belgium, I am a Belgian./ But Belgium was not born in me," writes the Flemish poet Leonard Nolens.[1]

There is surely some kind of uneasiness in being Belgian. And if Belgium simply did not exist? It would still be a memory. Or perhaps one should say a loss of memory, a loss of identity, an absence, a silence. A slip of the tongue?

The uneasiness that comes with being Belgian stems from two long-standing problems. The first proceeds from the perception that Belgium is an *artificial* construction, a nation made up of at least two different peoples and always on the edge of breaking up into its linguistic communities. The linguistic conflict between the Dutch-speaking Flemish and the French-speaking Walloon communities has indeed divided the country ever since its creation in 1830. This conflict has always been and continues to be a destabilizing factor in Belgian politics. The other endemic problem, not unrelated to the previous one, is related to Belgium's image as a corrupt country with a precarious policy-making tradition and an obscure and arbitrary administration, in which crude party politics and vested interests predominate as a rule. When the "Dutroux affair" became widely known, the international press characterized Belgium as one of the most corrupt countries in Europe. The resignation of Willy Claes as Secretary-General of NATO because of the "Agusta scandal" and the recent revelations of massive fraud in the well-known Lernhout & Hauspie company have only reinforced that perception.

1. See "Plaats en datum" [Place and date], in Leonard Nolens, *Hart tegen hart. Gedichten 1975–1990* [Heart Against Heart: Poems 1975–1990] (Amsterdam: Querido, 1991), 308. Translations are mine, unless otherwise noted.

YFS 102, *Belgian Memories,* ed. Catherine Labio, © 2002 by Yale University.

But Belgium is also an ambiguous country. The uneasiness is matched by a certain pride, which cuts across the linguistic division and even transcends the corrupt image to a large extent. In French, the word *belgitude* refers not only to the fact of being Belgian, but to the fact of feeling at home in Belgium. *Belgitude* stands for a unique lifestyle, a Burgundian way of life, in which the enjoyment of food and drink makes life a real pleasure. And, in a much larger sense still, *belgitude* stands for a kind of conviviality and coziness that is quite unique and unquestionably makes Belgium an attractive country, not only for tourists but for political refugees as well. And, its endemic mismanagement notwithstanding, one should not forget that Belgium is a true welfare state, with public health legislation that no doubt ranks among the best in the world. So, in spite of the linguistic conflict, in spite— and maybe to a certain extent because—of the corrupt administration, life is comparatively easy and rewarding in Belgium.

Yet there is more that can be said about Belgian pride in relation to the question of Belgian identity. On a cultural level there undeniably exists a Belgian imaginary, characterized by a unique blend of realism and magic. This characteristic can be found not only in Flemish painting, as in the work of Peter Breughel the Elder (or even Hieronymus Bosch, a Dutch painter influenced by the Flemish primitives), but also in the symbolist writings of Emile Verhaeren, Maurice Maeterlinck, Georges Rodenbach, and J.-K. Huysmans. (In France it is frequently forgotten that these symbolist writers, though they wrote in French, in fact came from a Flemish background.) One sees this same unique blend of realism and magic at work in Belgian comic strips and surrealist painting, especially in the works of Hergé and René Magritte, two world-famous Belgian icons. Additionally, one of the most telling currents to emerge in Flemish literature after World War II was the so-called "magical realism," represented most fully by the novels of Johan Daisne and Hubert Lampo. In this magical realism one also meets a dark side of Belgian identity, a kind of metaphysical and sublime depth, an abyss that seems to underlie the daily devotion to conviviality and sociability.

One can find a striking representation of the inner tensions of Belgian identity in "Confrontiers: La Belgïe" (1997), a glass-fronted wooden box with mixed media by the Tanzanian artist Everlyn Nicodemus, who has been living in Belgium for a number of years (see Figure 1). Here, the above-mentioned Burgundian delight and metaphysical abyss are embodied in fragments of Hieronymus Bosch's well-known

Garden of Delight. Additionally, the dark side of Belgian politics, confronted, as it were, with the steady possibility of linguistic division and with an apocalyptic vision of the central state—and *a fortiori* of the monarchy—is here represented in two identical statues of *Manneken Pis* that are standing with their backs to each other and peeing in opposite directions. Here the lighthearted cultural and tourist symbol of Brussels is used satirically to underscore the centrifugal forces of the nation. The use of glass and of the box—and particularly the grid-like structure that is so typical of Nicodemus's work[2]—ties together in one conceptual vision both the fragmentary and ambiguous as well as the alleged, almost imprisoned unity of the Belgian nation. The possible abyss is not far away, but is counterbalanced by the marvelous pictorial synthesis of the work.

In any event, this potential abyss has always threatened the unifying myth behind Belgium's official motto—"L'union fait la force/Eendracht maakt macht" (Unity creates strength)—and which has been most effective in times of war. Indeed, it has been above all in times of war, when the very existence of the Belgian nation was at stake, that the Flemish and Walloon communities were able to mobilize and thus become united against a common enemy. The unifying myth was then most appealing, but at the same time most fragile. A case in point is the so-called "Royal Question," which took place shortly after World War II and was without a doubt the most severe crisis ever faced by the Belgian monarchy. Anti-unitarian forces, especially on the Walloon side, rejected King Leopold III because of his alleged collaboration with the German Nazis. The whole nation was in a state of upheaval. Leopold III, who had already been replaced by Prince Charles as regent as early as 1944, was soon replaced by young Baudouin, the "sad king," who managed to restore the popularity of the royal house.

The challenge of unifying the centrifugal forces of a divided nation and of reconciling thoroughly contradictory interests tells us something important about Belgian political identity. The centrifugal forces are indeed multiple: Flemish versus Walloon interests, federal (and even separatist) against unitarian tendencies, capitalist against socialist pressure groups, Catholic against "humanist" convictions, indigenous against immigrant claims, and so on. Because of these centrifugal forces Belgium has always been and still is a nation in search of itself.

2. See Jean Fischer, "Everlyn Nicodemus: Between Silence and Laughter," *Third Text* 40 (Autumn 1997): 41–54. On the use of glasses and grid-like materials, see 49–50.

Its political identity has always been and still is "in the making," in constant adaptation and adjustment to the necessities of the moment. In this respect Belgian politics has shown a remarkable flexibility, exemplifying an unusual ability to balance conflicting and even incompatible interests, which as a rule leads to ingenious compromises. Prime ministers such as Wilfried Martens and Jean-Luc Dehaene proved to be masters in compromise and would not have been able to rule the country otherwise.

The Belgian notion of compromise is quite famous. Though it has the negative flavor of clumsy texts that are difficult to disentangle and that are open to the most diverse, even conflicting (!) interpretations, it has also been considered a prolific model for the ongoing European process of unification. In particular, the whole Belgian process of federalization, in which the autonomy of three linguistic communities—French-, Dutch- and German-speaking—and the special status of the Brussels region had to be reconciled with the autonomy of the central state apparatus, is widely considered as a kind of exemplary test case for the challenges facing Europe. This symbolic role model of Belgian politics is strengthened by the central location of Brussels, which is frequently called the "capital of Europe."

THE SILENCE OF BELGIUM

But let us now concentrate on the dark zones of Belgian memory, the silence of Belgium. The many centrifugal forces within the Belgian nation have undeniably prevented Belgium from coming to terms with a sometimes difficult, compromising, and unbearable past. They have frequently prevented or postponed a much-needed national debate on Belgium's historical responsibilities, and even on its traumatic experiences. It is as if Belgian historical consciousness is blocked by the many divisions from within, perhaps first and foremost by the indelible, unrelenting opposition between a *unitarian* versus a *separatist* politics of memory. This has undoubtedly activated a fragmentary and extremely biased—almost kaleidoscopic—strategy of remembrance. From this perspective one surely has to speak of Belgian memory in the plural: Belgian memories. As a result, it is extremely difficult to disentangle the historical truth or shed light on the historical responsibility and even the unique suffering of Belgium as a national entity.

There is indeed, to name but one example, albeit a crucial one, a world of difference between the unitarian and separatist memory of

Belgian history. The unitarian strand always sees the past in terms of a strong central state apparatus, which has (and will) overcome all possible attempts at destruction, be it from without or within. Its ideology is purely nationalist: it is devoted to nationalist symbols and commemorations; it tries to strengthen national unity and collective identity. And it is—as a matter of course—strongly committed to the monarchy. The separatist memory is likewise nationalist, but here Flemish and Walloon forms of nationalism are at stake. In this instance, the driving force is not the Belgian state, but the emancipation and autonomy of the linguistic communities themselves. In its ideal-typical manifestation it is thoroughly anti-unitarian, anti-royalist, and pro-federalist; its collective memory speaks the idiosyncratic language of blood and soil, a nostalgic longing for the final emancipation of unique Flemish and Walloon identities that have been repressed ever since the Belgian nation was created. Belgium symbolizes here an artificial yoke, a historical conspiracy against the deep aspirations of the Flemish and Walloon communities and their respective self-images, authentic cultures, and unique folk-spirits.

There is, in spite of these internal divisions, a silence that affects Belgium as a national entity and cuts through its centrifugal forces. This silence is in a way *shared* by the linguistic communities and by the many interest groups that normally divide the country in its daily politics. It reveals, albeit in a negative way, something of Belgium's peculiar identity and ambiguity, which I tried to sketch in my introduction. Maybe, after all, it is not entirely unjustified to speak of a "Belgian soul" (*âme belge*), which according to the famous Belgian historian Henri Pirenne (1862–1935) had its roots in Roman times and established itself during the Middle Ages. The organic development of a Belgian soul was all the more remarkable because "Belgium" had been split horizontally by a linguistic boundary since Roman times. In the North the "Flemish" embodied the *Germanic* element, whereas in the South the "Walloons" represented the *Roman* element. However, as Pirenne emphasized time and again, apart from the linguistic division, the Flemish and Walloon people were united for centuries in an identical political, economic, and partly cultural alliance, which in his view finally led to the creation of a Belgian nation as a historical necessity, a historical self-evidence.[3]

3. See Henri Pirenne, *Histoire de la Belgique des origines à nos jours* (Brussels: La Renaissance du Livre, 1952 [orig. publ. in 1900–1932]). See for a useful recent overview of

THE SILENCED PAST:
A CONCEPTUAL INTERMEZZO

The silence of Belgium is indeed firmly rooted in the "historical necessity" of the entire nation, in the destiny, and maybe in the *construction* of a common soul. This silence forces us to confront the absence of the past, the collective amnesia, and the politics of forgetting that cut through the centrifugal forces of the Belgian state. In order to highlight the shades of this Belgian silence, its differing roots and coping strategies, a word has to be said about the concepts *historical taboo* and *historical trauma,* which are contrasted here as two *archetypical or ideal-typical forms* of silencing the past.

As I have argued elsewhere in greater detail, there is, at least from an analytical point of view, a crucial distinction between historical taboos and historical traumas.[4] Whenever historical taboos are at stake, the silence is rooted in the *present demands of collective identity:* they are, as a rule, closely linked with the prevailing *historical consciousness.* In the case of historical traumas, on the contrary, the silence is rooted in an *overwhelming and mostly catastrophic or utterly painful experience:* they are, as such, embedded within *past experience itself.* But let us make things more explicit.

Though historical taboos may acquire traumatic overtones, they always pertain to the ideological challenge past events create for the present. Those past events, which are considered to be detrimental to the maintenance and enforcement of present collective identity, are simply silenced or re-adjusted in order to become less harmful. Sometimes those past events are even transformed into sheer myths in order to satisfy present demands. In any case, historical taboos always involve some kind of "sacred" prohibition, which makes certain elements of the past, if not unmentionable, at least untouchable. Any attempt to break the silence is severely condemned. As a result historians and citizens frequently, if not always, exercise self-censorship in order to escape the risk of being excluded, stigmatized, or punished. As we shall see, a good example of this kind of self-censorship is the way Belgian

---

Belgian history: Else Witte, Jan Craeybeckx, and Alain Meynen, *Political History of Belgium: From 1830 onwards* (Antwerp: Standaard; Brussels: VUB University Press, 2000).

4. "The Silenced Past: On the Nature of Historical Taboos," in W. Wrzoska, ed., *Swiat historii. Festschrift Topolski* (Poznan: Historical Institute, 1998), 97–112. See also my entry on "History: Historical Taboos" in Derek Jones, ed., *Censorship: A World Encyclopedia* (London: Fitzroy Dearborn Publishers, 2001), vol. 2: 1060–62.

historians long avoided writing about the taboo of Flemish and Walloon collaboration during World War II.

The most straightforward way in which communities try to cope with historical taboos is pure censorship. For example, those German historians who in the 1930s tried to explain the rise of Nazism in terms of continuities with the German past, were either thwarted in their professional career or sent into exile.[5] Similarly, Aleksandr Solzhenitsyn was forced into exile because he broke a taboo by mentioning Stalin's extermination camps in *The Gulag Archipelago*.[6] Sometimes crucial evidence is either neglected or even destroyed, while threatening past events are put into a mythical framework that not only makes them acceptable, but even celebrates the collective identity, as we shall see in the case of the Congo Holocaust.

Historical traumas, on the contrary, emerge from historical experience itself. The silence is here part and parcel of the past event itself: it is only in and through its inherent forgetting that the event is experienced at all.[7] In contrast with historical taboos, historical experience is not suppressed later on, but is *dissociated* from consciousness the moment it occurs. There is a kind of *numbness* that goes along with the experience and wipes it out at the very moment it is happening. The denial is therefore not a conscious, but an unconscious process. It is neither a conscious manipulation nor a downright falsification of the past event. The coping mechanism does not consist in a deliberate silencing of the past event, but in an unconscious rejection, a fateful but involuntary form of collective amnesia. The silence is here rooted not in ideological but in psychological reasons: the past event is simply too painful and even too inconceivable to be experienced fully and henceforth to be remembered at all. This is the reason why it is wiped out, cut off, suppressed, and for the time being "forgotten."

In their most telling and pure form, historical traumas tend to banish the past event from memory for a long time. The traumatic event is still experienced long after the fact as a constant threat to the psychic

5. See Georg G. Iggers, "Die deutschen Historiker in der Emigration," in Bernd Faulenbach, ed., *Geschichtswissenschaft in Deutschland* (Munich: Verlag C. H. Beck, 1974), 97–111. See also Georg G. Iggers, *New Directions in European Historiography* (Middletown, Conn.: Wesleyan University Press, 1975), 87.

6. See Aleksandr Solzhenitsyn, *The Gulag Archipelago*, 3 vols. (Boulder, Colorado, Westview Press, 1997).

7. Cathy Caruth "Unclaimed Experience: Trauma and the Possibility of History," in *Unclaimed Experience: Trauma, Narrative, and History* (Baltimore: The Johns Hopkins University Press, 1996), 10–24, esp. page 11.

equilibrium or the self-image of the collective identity. Just as at the moment the event occurred, all sorts of defense mechanisms continue to serve as an automatic pilot in order to remove systematically from consciousness the threatening vestiges of the past event. The past event is, or rather, *seems* completely neutralized and actually forgotten. In fact, it still remains operative, in spite of—or precisely because of—the initial dissociation, on an unconscious level: it is simply displaced toward the collective unconscious.

A case in point is the experience of the Holocaust. Survivors of the Holocaust remained silent for a long time, as though the experience was wiped out from memory, as though it had not happened at all. But the experience remained operative in the collective unconscious, to the point of reappearing in disguised forms such as nightmares and long-lasting anxiety. The Holocaust experience confronted and still confronts survivors with the limits of representation.[8] The integration of the experience within historical consciousness is mostly a drawn out process of "acting out" and "working through" that is always accompanied by the possibility that one might fall apart or regress into the numbness that had initially silenced the event the moment it had occurred.

Historical taboos are not likely to become historical traumas. By contrast, historical traumas may become exploited by historical consciousness and acquire many of the characteristics of historical taboos. A well-known and much debated example is precisely the way Israeli policy sometimes tends to exploit the Holocaust to justify or at least extenuate some of its own debatable actions, such as, for instance, the settlements in the West Bank.[9] However, historical traumas may also trigger a collective resistance to the overt ideological use (and misuse) of past experience. They may challenge the comfortable and reinforcing image of a past that has been ideologically constructed and serves the vested interests of a collective identity. Even though—and to a certain extent *because*—historical traumas are unspeakable as such, they nonetheless challenge the way the past is silenced by historical consciousness, as we shall see in the case of the "White March." Here the

8. See, on representation and the Holocaust, Saul Friedlander, ed., *Probing the Limits of Representation: Nazism and the "Final Solution"* (Cambridge, Mass.: Cambridge University Press, 1992); Dominick LaCapra, *Representing the Holocaust: History, Theory, Trauma* (Ithaca and London: Cornell University Press, 1994).

9. See, for instance, the controversial but thought-provoking book by Norman G. Finkelstein, *The Holocaust Industry: Reflections on the Exploitation of Jewish Suffering* (London and New York: Verso, 2000).

Dutroux trauma was released into a unique mass mobilization directed against a long-standing corruption, manipulation, and apathy within the Belgian administration, thereby breaking a historical taboo that had been silenced since time immemorial by a comforting but at the same time misleading historical consciousness!

The historical consciousness of Belgium is indeed a good starting point to engage in the problematic of its collective memory. I will focus on the silence of Belgium, the various ways in which Belgium tried to cope with an unmasterable past, a past that more than once has challenged its alleged unity and put definite limits on its ability to compromise with that past. I shall now discuss some of Belgium's long-enduring historical taboos and traumas, to which I have already referred in passing. I shall look at them not only as illustrations of basic mechanisms but also as means to identify the typically Belgian ways of dealing with the past, more particularly the culture-specific ways of silencing an otherwise unbearable past.

THE CONGOLESE HOLOCAUST:
A HISTORICAL TABOO

The historical consciousness of Belgium as a national entity typically pertains to a specific *ideology:* it is normally embodied in an overt and explicit discourse, which serves vested or reclaimed interests of the Belgian state. The emphasis is on the construction of a past and of an identity wrapped in a historical consciousness that serves as its ideological justification. It is here that the different versions tend to be transcended by a common destiny, sometimes even a command blind spot, which normally leads to a politics of memory, or maybe better, a *politics of forgetting,* in which past events are silenced because they pose a real threat to the feeling of mutual trust and to national identity. Historical experience is silenced because it cannot be reconciled with—or made useful for—present concerns.

A good example of a historical taboo is offered by the mass killings that occurred before and during Belgium's colonial rule. That King Leopold's colonial adventure—his systematic exploitation of the Congo—relied on slave labor on a massive scale, which even provoked at the time a worldwide protest movement, is still unknown to the average Belgian citizen. More telling and surprising still is the complete silence about the atrocities. Millions of lives were taken, which probably makes the Congolese Holocaust one of the most forgotten mass killings of modern times. This dark episode of Belgian history has been wiped out of collective memory. It is surrounded by silence and a politics of forgetting. The Congolese Holocaust is now largely forgotten, a footnote in the margins of history, with which only those specializing in African Studies are somewhat familiar.

It is only very recently that the American writer Adam Hochschild revealed in his *King Leopold's Ghost: A Story of Greed, Terror, and Heroism in Colonial Africa,* how all of Europe—and the USA—contributed to King Leopold's Holocaust of the Congolese people.[10] The book is indeed a revelation of the horror hidden in the Congo's colonial past, a horror that reminds one of Joseph Conrad's well-known *Heart of Darkness.* It is likewise only very recently that the Flemish sociologist Ludo De Witte has shown in detail the responsibility of Belgian leaders and officers in the murder of Lumumba, which had been completely denied, a denial that had been reinforced by the publication of Jacques Brassine's so-called historical research in the early 1990s.[11] De Witte's book eventually led—more than forty years after the facts—to the establishment of a parliamentary Commission of Inquiry, which has tried to seek out the Belgian responsibility in the murder of Lumumba.[12]

10. Adam Hochschild, *King Leopold's Ghost: A Story of Greed, Terror, and Heroism in Colonial Africa* (New York: Houghton Mifflin, 1998). On the CIA's involvement, see George Lardner, Jr.: "Did Ike Authorize a Murder? Memo Says Eisenhower Wanted Congolese Premier Dead," *Washington Post,* 8 August 2000, A23: "The official note taker at that meeting, Robert H. Johnson, vividly recalled Eisenhower turning to CIA Director Allen Dulles 'in the full hearing of all those in attendance and saying something to the effect that Lumumba should be eliminated.' After that, 'according to Mr. Johnson, there was a stunned silence for about 15 seconds and the meeting continued.'"

11. Ludo de Witte, *De Moord op Lumumba* (Leuven: Van Halewyck, 1999). See, for the English translation, *The Assassination of Lumumba,* trans. Ann Wright and Renée Fenby (London and New York: Verso, 2001). This book presents a thorough criticism of Jacques Brassine, *Enquête sur la mort de Patrice Lumumba* [Inquiry into the murder of Lumumba], unpublished Ph.D. thesis from the Université Libre de Bruxelles (Brussels: ULB, 1990) and Jacques Brassine and Jean Kestergat, *Qui a tué Patrice Lumumba?* [Who murdered Patrice Lumumba?] (Paris, Louvain-la-Neuve: Duculot, 1991). In these books Brassine "proved" that the Belgian government and the Belgian military's top leaders had nothing to do with Lumumba's murder, and that the Congolese themselves, more particularly soldiers of the ANC, had been responsible for the murder. In his book, Ludo de Witte debunks Brassine's thesis and shows convincingly, by relying on overwhelming documentary evidence, that both the CIA and the Belgian establishment played a crucial role in the murder of Lumumba.

12. The public hearings of the Lumumba Commission, which were to start on Monday, 29 January 2001, were initially postponed because of the murder of President Laurent-Désiré Kabila, which had aroused anti-Western and anti-Belgian feelings in some quarters. In the meantime the Commission has started and completed its investigation.

In retrospect, Leopold's colonial reign looks like a "crime against humanity," but it has not yet entered the historical consciousness of the nation and it may never do so. In that sense it is still a full-fledged historical taboo. The evidence about the mass killings and the murder of Lumumba does bring into question the legitimacy of the monarchy, the role of the Belgian authorities, and the responsibility of the Belgian state. It reveals the hidden logic of colonial and neocolonial exploitation (Hochschild, 294). The silencing of the past is a deliberate one. It is a conscious forgetting, an attempt at erasing the past, including its manifold traces. This is exactly what Leopold and the Belgian colonial officials tried to do. It is why in August 1908, shortly before the colony was officially turned over to Belgium, the Congo state records burned for eight days in a furnace of the Royal Palace. They were turned into the ashes and smoke of forgetting, which darkened the luminous sky over Brussels: "'I will give them my Congo,' Leopold told Stinglhamber [his young military aide], 'but they have no right to know what I did there'" (Hochschild, 294).

At the same time, the Palace ordered the destruction of the state records that were in the Congo. Colonel Maximilien Strauch, who was Leopold's adviser on Congolese matters, stated very meaningfully: "'The voices which, in default of the destroyed archives, might speak in their stead have systematically been condemned to silence, for considerations of a higher order'" (Hochschild, 294)! This inspired Hochschild to conclude: "Seldom has a totalitarian regime gone to such lengths to destroy so thoroughly the records of its work. In their later quests for a higher order, Hitler and Stalin in some ways left a far larger paper trail behind them" (Hochschild, 294–5).

Nevertheless, some crucial evidence escaped from the furnace of 1908. Among this evidence were the transcripts—never published—of the testimonies given by African witnesses before a Commission of Inquiry that was convened in 1904–1905. Unfortunately, this evidence was neatly kept under censorship. When Jules Marchal, an ex-ambassador in West Africa, who also lived and worked in the Congo (and in Zaïre) for nineteen years, learned that these records were piled up in the archives of the Belgian Foreign Ministry, he went to ask for them. His request was denied: "The testimony papers were stamped *Ne pas à* [sic] *communiquer aux chercheurs*—no access for researchers. Marchal

---

The Commission found that the Belgian government and the Crown appear to have been involved in one way or another at the time, though no proof was found of a direct command to 'physically' eliminate Lumumba.

protested that it was seventy years after the commission had delivered its report, and that he was of ambassadorial rank. It made no difference. He was not allowed to see the files."[13]

One encounters a conscious forgetting, a pure denial or even a kind of self-censorship, in the Royal Museum of Central Africa in Tervuren, Brussels, which contains one of the world's largest collections of Africana. In none of the twenty large exhibition galleries is there any explicit reference to the Congolese mass killings. In fact, the Tervuren Museum offers us another type of coping strategy, which has proved very effective, namely the *mythical type of repression*. In order to silence the Congolese Holocaust another past has been invented, or at least amplified into an emotionally appealing myth. In this myth the civilizing and Christianizing role of Belgium in the Congo is time and again celebrated, not only in Belgian education and in Belgian textbooks, but also in the textbooks that circulated in the Congo and were written by the colonizers themselves. In this mythical transformation, the Catholic mission and the Belgian monarchy symbolize a redemptive liberation from savagery, barbarism, and primitivism, also in the eyes of the Congo's official memory. So not only does the myth mitigate and overrule colonial tyranny, it also obscures the traumatic experience of the Congolese people. This traumatic experience, which is preserved in local legends about *"la guerre du Blanc"* (the white man's war), or, as it is called in the Mongo language, *lokeli,* "the overwhelming" (Hochschild, 300), still challenges the silence of Belgium. It is a historical trauma, which likewise challenges, in and through its inherent forgetting, in and through its fragmentation and suppression, the official and canonized memory of the Congolese regime itself!

13. Hochschild, 297. See also the interesting interview with Jules Marchal on the website devoted to the "Histoire de la colonisation belge du Congo," where Marchal confirms that the Belgians do not know about the crimes committed during the colonial past in Congo. He also complains that his *magnum opus* on the history of Congo has systematically been silenced by the national press. See *http://www.cobelco.org/ Interviews/interviewjm.htm,* 3. I am grateful to Catherine Labio for having given me the address of the interview. For the first volume of Marchal's lifetime work, see Jules Marchal, *Travail forcé pour le cuivre et pour l'or. L'histoire du Congo 1910–1945,* vol. 1 (Borgloon: Ed. Paula Bellings, 1999). Marchal, not always considered to be reliable by professional historians, was not the only one who wrote about the Congolese disaster. Some books by Jean Stengers, for instance, already published in the fifties and sixties, contain a lot of the material described by Hochschild. Stengers even edited, together with Roger Louis, *E. D. Morel's History of the Congo Reform Movement* (Oxford: Clarendon, 1968). For a recent historical account, see Daniel Vangroenweghe, *Rood rubber. Leopold II en zijn Kongo* [Red rubber: Leopold II and his Congo] (Brussels: Elsevier, 1985), translated into French as *Du sang sur les lianes* (Brussels: Didier Hatier, 1986).

SILENCE AND WORLD WAR II:
ON COLLABORATION AND THE "NEW ORDER"

The Congolese Holocaust could have been an ideal instrument in the hands of the separatist forces that were trying to undermine the claims of the unitarian Belgian state and its monarchy. The separatist forces were not at all interested in giving a voice to the Congolese traumatic suffering, however. They remained, on both sides of the linguistic boundary, largely insensitive to the excrescences of the colonial past. Is it because both the Flemish and the Walloons shared in the economic wealth stemming from the Congo exploitation? Is it because they did not want to criticize openly military authorities, the Catholic church, and its missionaries? Or were they simply too concerned with their own emancipation movement, in which a right-wing ideology was too far removed from any leftist critique of colonialism and neocolonialism?

The fact is that the separatist forces missed a historical opportunity to question thoroughly the legitimacy of the Belgian state. They only saw such an opportunity when the Second World War offered them a chance to embrace the "New Order" that announced itself with the Nazi regime. It is significant that the "New Order" appealed to both Flemish and Walloon nationalists. In the case of Flemish nationalism, there was already a fertile breeding ground for collaboration with the Germans. The long repression of Flemish language and culture within the Belgian state made Flemish nationalism extremely sensitive—and vulnerable—to an almost utopian integration within a Third Reich that would fully acknowledge and even celebrate the allegedly Germanic spring of Flemish culture.

That the "New Order" also awakened a totalitarian seduction on the Walloon side reveals to what extent the separatist forces were unified in their antidemocratic, antiliberal, and right-wing ideology. Even Léon Degrelle and his Rexist movement, which was initially fueled by a Great-Belgian, and thus "unitary," ambition, were forced during the occupation to put their collaborative ideology into a Walloon straitjacket in order to be both appealing and successful. Nevertheless, notwithstanding the many traumatic overtones, which indubitably affected the Belgian people under German occupation, especially the members of the widespread and often heroic Resistance movement, one is struck by the historical continuity at work during this strange period. In a recent symposium on the impact of the Second World War on Belgian culture, historical continuity was indeed emphasized time and again.[14] On the cultural level, so Paul Aron testifies, the occupation must be considered as a *non-event*, a cultural intermezzo, a parenthesis, an insignificant interlude. In this vision, the German occupation led to a widespread political and cultural modus vivendi among the Belgians. This apparently smooth integration into the Nazi worldview could only have happened because an extensive breeding ground had already been in place before the war, namely, Flemish and Walloon nationalism, in which authoritarian, conservative, and restorative tendencies were strengthened by a fascination with timeless myths. This breeding ground explains why cultural collaboration was so extensive. Very often, however, there was not even a cultural collaboration, but a strange coexistence with the German occupation, which was largely due to the somewhat obscure administrative structure of Belgium—so that even leftist writers could publish their novels without being censored by the German occupying authorities.

In spite of the fact that the war period did not represent a radical rupture, or perhaps because it left the Belgian apparatus largely intact, collective memory became frozen, blocked, and difficult to set in motion after the war. Again the silence of Belgium revealed its profound ambiguities: the ambiguity of both Flemish and Walloon nationalism, and even the ambiguity of the Royal circles, which had all showed an unusual readiness to collaborate with the Nazi regime. The silence of Belgium was—and still is—extremely ambiguous, because it was and still is to some extent a historical taboo both for the separatist and the unitarian forces. It lays bare the deep and unconscious layers of a rightwing dream, a conservative utopia, which not only proved to be a fatal illusion, but provoked as well the unspeakable suffering of so many innocent people. It was the Flemish writer Louis Paul Boon, who tried to capture the devastating effect of the war on the people in his masterly little novel *Mijn kleine oorlog* [My Little War].[15]

14. The large symposium on *Maatschappij, cultuur en mentaliteiten. De impact van de Tweede Wereldoorlog in België* [Society, Culture, and Mentalities: The Impact of the Second World War on Belgium] took place from 23 to 27 October 1995 in Brussels. See, for the sessions on literature, Dirk de Geest, Paul Aron, and Dirk Martin, eds., *Hun kleine oorlog. De invloed van de tweede Wereldoorlog op het literaire leven in België* (Leuven: Peeters, 1998). For the French equivalent, see Paul Aron, Dirk de Geest, Pierre Halen and Antoon Van den Braembussche, eds., *Leurs occupations. L'impact de la seconde guerre mondiale sur la littérature en Belgique* (Brussels: Textyles-CREHSGM [Centre de recherches et d'études historiques de la deuxième guerre mondiale], 1997).

15. Louis-Paul Boon, *Mijn kleine oorlog* [My Little War] (Groningen: Wolters-Noordhoff, 1994 [orig. publ. in 1947]). For the most important novel, which deals with

It is only recently that the Walloon and Flemish collaboration has been reconstructed in its proper dimensions by professional historians.[16] This reveals just how long self-censorship among historians prevailed. It was in fact not a historian, but a journalist who first confronted Belgium with its continuing silence about World War II. Impassioned journalist Maurice De Wilde literally awakened collective memory with his early-eighties television series on the "New Order." It still managed to outrage, after forty years of silence, a substantial segment of public opinion. This proved that wartime collaboration was still a full-blown taboo, which had hardly been neutralized or overcome by the silence originating from the above-mentioned Flemish and Walloon ambiguities. De Wilde showed in great detail that the New Order that was to be established by the Nazis was welcomed by both Flemish and Walloon nationalists as a unique opportunity to realize the totalitarian dreams they had begun to cherish long before World War II. In that sense he revealed the intimate connection between collaboration and nationalism, which had simply been silenced or otherwise accommodated in terms of an unwilling and "forced" acceptance of German occupation.

TRAUMA AND BELGIAN POLITICS: THE "WHITE MARCH"

Belgian historical consciousness, with its endemic taboos, its on-going silence about national responsibilities, and above all its politics of forgetting, which has time and again been embraced and perpetuated by cover-up politics, has recently been acutely challenged by a major traumatic experience. Indeed, when the facts about the "Dutroux affair" became widely known, something of a national trauma was inflicted upon the Belgian people as a whole. The Dutroux murders initially kept the country spellbound: the very atrocity of the crimes led to a paranoid and unspeakable numbness, a kind of disbelief and unconscious rejection of the very possibility of ultimate terror within one's own society.

the theme of collaboration, see Hugo Claus, *Het verdriet van België* (Amsterdam: Bezige Bij, 1983). English translation: *The Sorrow of Belgium*, trans. Arnold J. Pomerans (London: Viking, 1990).

16. See, on the Walloon collaboration, Martin Conway, *Collaboration in Belgium: Léon Degrelle and the Rexist Movement* (New Haven, Conn.: Yale University Press, 1993). On the Flemish collaboration, see Bruno De Wever, *Greep naar de macht. Vlaams-nationalisme en de Nieuwe Orde* [Grabbing for Power: Flemish Nationalism and the New Order] (Gent: Perspectief; Tielt: Lannoo, 1994).

Let us recapitulate the facts.[17] On 15 August 1996 the missing girls
Sabine and Laetitia were liberated alive from the cellars of Marc
Dutroux, thanks to a small team of investigators working with magistrate Jean-Marc Connerotte in the provincial town of Neufchâteau.
Two days later the mortal remains of Julie and Mélissa were found
buried in the backyard of the home of Michèle Martin, Dutroux's "former" girlfriend. Three weeks later the remains of An and Eefje were
then dug up from one of his gardens. The whole Belgian nation was
shocked. It soon became clear that the police and the judicial apparatus had utterly failed. Not only had Dutroux, who had been condemned
for pedophilia, been paroled early, but a number of clues that had
pointed in his and his gang's direction had also been systematically ignored. The whole investigation seemed fatally flawed.

The public indignation finally led to the so-called "White March":
a silent and spontaneous mass manifestation of at least three hundred
thousand Belgian citizens. The immediate cause of this march was the
removal of the popular magistrate Jean-Marc Connerotte from the judicial inquiry into the Dutroux murders on the grounds that he had attended a party organized by the parents of Laetitia and Sabine to celebrate the girls' liberation and had on this occasion eaten a plate of
spaghetti. The *Court of Cassation*, the highest court in the land, found
that Connerotte had broken the law of impartiality and should not be
allowed to continue as a member of the research team. Connerotte's so-
called "spaghetti arrest" was perceived as a maneuver to block the inquiry and to sweep the responsibilities under the carpet once again.

Though the White March has been studied until now mainly from
a sociological point of view,[18] the "Dutroux affair" undoubtedly has
many characteristics of a historical trauma, though it lacks the long period of silence and "working through" that is so typical of classic examples. First, the affected society was initially completely paralyzed or

17. For a detailed reconstruction of the facts, see Fred Vandenbussche, *Meisjes verd-
wijnen niet zomaar. De zaak-Dutroux. Het falen van de Belgische justitie en politie*
[Girls Do Not Just Disappear: The Dutroux Affair and the Failure of Belgian Justice and
Police] (Utrecht/Antwerp: Kosmos-Z&K Uitgevers, 1996); Hans Knoop, *De zaak Marc
Dutroux* [The Marc Dutroux Affair] ('s Gravenhage: BZZTÔH, 1998); Anne De Graaf,
Witte stippen. De zaak-Dutroux: een reconstructie [White dots: The Dutroux Affair, a
Reconstruction] (Groot-Bijgaarden: Scoop; Houten: Van Reemst; Antwerp: Icarus, 1988).

18. See *Wit van het volk. De zaak-Dutroux en de protestgolf in België in de herfst
van 1996* [White with People: The Dutroux Affair and the Protest Gulf in Belgium in the
Fall of 1996], special issue of the *Sociologische gids* 5 (1998): 282–375. The editor of this
issue was Staf Hellemans.

numbed and did not fully perceive the "Dutroux murders" as they occurred or became widely known. The dissociation from consciousness expressed itself initially through professions of disbelief: this could not have happened in Belgium. Second, the dissociation then led to a delayed response, a period of latency, during which the suppressed "Dutroux murders" lingered on in the collective unconscious and left behind deep imprints on the collective soul. In spite—better yet, *because*—of general disbelief and unconscious rejection, the suppressed "murders" lived on vehemently and most typically re-emerged in the form of nightmares, flashbacks, hallucinations, and so on. This certainly explains the generalized paranoia. This paranoia was in a way a collective "acting out" of the traumatic event and manifested itself in the feeling that every child was in danger, that there were networks of pedophilia everywhere in the country, and so on. Pedophilia suddenly became a hot issue. It led, among other things, to the fictitious accusation that the homosexual vice-president di Rupo had abused young boys. Third, the traumatic experience of the murders was reintegrated into collective memory thanks to a collective mourning. Finally, this collective mourning acquired in the case of the "White March" a much-needed social ritual, which not only facilitated the public process of mourning, but at the same time the process of "working through."

For Freud and many others mourning is indeed considered as a crucial precondition of "working through" a traumatic experience, of slowly integrating it into normal consciousness.[19] The "White March" clearly embodied a collective mourning, which led to a collective catharsis of the "Dutroux murders." But it also shows how a collective trauma may finally burst into collective anger, into a spontaneous protest movement, a mass mobilization against long-standing historical taboos. In that specific sense the "White March" presents us with a unique example of mass mobilization[20] and of *expressive politics*, to

19. See Freud's two important studies: "Remembering, Repeating and Working-Through" from 1914, *The Standard Edition of the Complete Psychological Works of Sigmund Freud* 12 (London: Hogarth), 145–56 and "Mourning and Melancholia" from 1917, in *ibid.*, 14, 237–60. See also Dominick LaCapra, "Conclusion: Acting-Out and Working-Through" in his *Representing the Holocaust*, 205–23. See also Peter Homans, *The Ability to Mourn: Disillusionment and the Social Origins of Psychoanalysis* (Chicago: University of Chicago Press, 1989).

20. In their contribution to the special issue of the *Sociologische gids*, Walgrave and Rihoux argue that the White March movement is unique and distinct from other social movements. The reasons are threefold: (1) there was no homogeneous but heterogeneous

use Gusfield's terminology, in which the Dutroux affair finally became the efficient catalyst through which deeper discontents could be enacted and expressed.[21]

This takes us a back to the introduction and earlier sections of the present essay. Indeed, in the "White March" the silence of Belgium cuts once again through the centrifugal forces, linguistic or otherwise. In all its mourning, it also manifested a deep discontent with Belgian politics as usual: it embodied, beyond party lines, a rejection and deep distrust of the judicial apparatus, the police forces, and the ongoing political machinations and manipulations. It was as such a collective resistance to the crisis of the Belgian state and the host of historical taboos that have so badly compromised the very identity of Belgium. Whether the "White March" has actually been able to debunk the "old politics" is still an open question, however. It remains to be proven that a new generation of politicians, who have been inspired by the "White March" to take a stance for a "new politics," have really left the "old politics" behind.

---

backing, (2) the driving force was not a well-defined political goal but an emotional appeal, (3) the mass mobilization was not supported by available organizations or institutional networks, but evolved spontaneously. See Stefaan Walgrave and Benoît Rihoux, "De Belgische witte golf. Voorbij de sociologische bewegingstheorie?" [The Belgian White Gulf: Beyond Sociological Movement Theory?], in Staf Hellemans, ed., *Wit van het volk*, 310–39.

21. See Marc Hooghe, "De 'witte mobilisatie' in België als *moral crusade*. De vervlechting van emotie en politiek" [The "White Mobilization" in Belgium as Moral Crusade: The Intertwinement of Emotion and Politics], in Staf Hellemans (ed.), *Wit van het volk*, 289–309. This contribution is inspired by Joseph R. Gusfield, *Symbolic Crusade: Status Politics and the American Temperance Movement* (Urbana: University of Illinois Press, 1963). Hooghe is especially using Gusfield's thesis that emotionally or symbolically loaded themes, which may have small intrinsic interest, can lead to long-lasting political mobilization. In Hooghe's view, the White March was triggered by an intertwinement of emotional and political meaning. One must not forget the enormous influence of the mass media in the Dutroux Affair, something that was absent, for instance, in the early days of the Congolese Holocaust. The Congolese Holocaust was for a long time only a matter of concern for Belgium's elites, not for the Belgian people as a whole. See, on the growing influence of mass media on politics and public opinion, Els Witte (with Anja Detant and Bart Distelmans), *Media en Politiek* [Media and Politics] (Brussels: VUB University Press, 2002).

JACQUES DUBOIS

Wallonia: The Will to Remember

To Jeannine Paque

14 December 1960. Place Saint-Lambert in Liège, seventy-five thousand people, led by metal workers, demonstrate against austerity and
social recession measures concocted by a conservative government.
The socialist Fédération Générale du Travail of Belgium—a majority
in Wallonia, a minority in Flanders—has launched the movement to
oppose the "single law" (*la loi unique*) but, against the advice of the
Walloon branches, it does not want that movement to go too far. On
the Place Saint-Lambert, in the heart of a city that, along with its sub-
urbs, is one of the bastions of the old industry, a violent feeling of revolt has seized everyone: the real target, far beyond the current governmental measures, is clearly the Belgian state in its unified form or
else that monarchy already opposed by the Walloon working class ten
years earlier, an opposition it had paid for with its own blood. That was
in 1950, during the "Royal Question" that forced King Leopold III to
abdicate in favor of his son Baudouin, under the pressure of leftist opinion. André Renard, a charismatic leader of the metal workers of Liège
and a respected orator, is galvanizing the crowd this day, but he also
tempers it. For the shout of "Let's March on Brussels" has risen from
the masses. The marriage of the young king is to take place in the capital the next day. A republican wind is blowing through the gathering.

A few days later, as the union leadership shilly-shallied, the strike
erupted spontaneously, first in the public and then in the private sector: workers wanted it to be general and unlimited. It initially reached
a large part of the country, drawing some Flemish cities and Brussels in
its wake, but eventually became essentially Walloon. It hardened and
paralyzed a whole region for a good month. At times, it even took on
an insurrectional character, accompanied by violence and threats to de-

YFS 102, *Belgian Memories*, ed. Catherine Labio, © 2002 by Yale University.

stroy the industrial infrastructure. For a few weeks during that harsh winter, all the European media concentrated on Walloon Belgium. Yet, the longer the strike continued, the more it was tinged with despair, a despair that found its only outlet in violence. Soon reduced to a few centers of resistance, the strike eventually laid down its arms. Shortly afterwards, the Belgian population would be called upon to elect a new Parliament. A center-left government would emerge from these elections, which can be said to have broken up the "single law" only to better implement it piece by piece.

The movement was coming to a sudden halt after having gone very far. At any rate, it could not have played out its revolutionary momentum. Neither domestic nor foreign powers would have allowed a radical socialist regime to take hold in the heart of Western Europe—like a little Walloon Cuba—while, in the world, the tension between the power blocs was at its height. Nevertheless, in the medium term, the events had important political consequences for Belgium. For if the strike was primarily an act of opposition, it would gradually be transformed into a movement of proposition. As such, it undoubtedly generated the profound transformations that affected Belgium in its centralized form in subsequent decades. Quite soon, in fact, André Renard, the conscience of the movement, issued a rousing slogan, calling for federalism and structural economic reforms for Wallonia.[1] Immediately after the strike, he established a "Walloon Popular Movement," dedicated to the fulfillment of these two demands. He understood that, contrary to appearances, Wallonia had as many reasons as Flanders, which had long adopted an autonomist discourse, to demand at least partial independence within a federal framework. As many reasons, certainly, but not the same ones. Triumphant Flanders intended to enjoy its new prosperity, and to increase it even. Declining Wallonia had to give up on its former sources of wealth (collieries, and the steel, glass, and even textile industries) in order to embark on a vast and painful economic conversion, relying only on itself.

Twenty years later, after complicated negotiations and various reforms of the Constitution, Belgium was indeed transformed into a federal state. It preserved a central government, but granted the regions entire portions of its powers and budgets. Thus, a Flemish Region, a Walloon Region, and a Brussels Region appeared, each complete with

---

1. Notably, it was proposed that the public sector make up for the failures of the private industrial sector.

parliaments and governments and each responsible for a variety of economic and social matters. A number of other social questions, especially cultural issues, were entrusted to "Communities" that did not coincide strictly with the Regions. Thus, a French Community appeared, which merged Walloons and the French-speaking inhabitants of Brussels into a single whole and became responsible for the implementation of cultural and educational policies.[2]

The collective self-awareness that accompanied these transformations was nonetheless not a pure epiphany. First of all, the Walloons—from political leaders to simple citizens—needed time to admit that their economy was in decline and that the industrial revolution that had put them at the head of European expansion in the nineteenth century had come to an end. They also needed time to understand that the earlier dynamic economy had not created the conditions that would be needed, when the time came, for a thorough conversion. Thus, an economist like Michel Quévit revealed to Walloons that their former prosperity had in a way been something of an illusion.[3] It was not the Walloons themselves who had been the primary beneficiaries of their economic expansion, but those who had managed their industries from the outside, from the Société Générale—the most powerful holding bank in the country—to the central government, and who were now abandoning Walloons to their sad fate. Thus, a region and a people that had produced time and again such remarkable elites of skilled workers and technicians had barely had the opportunity to acquire the managerial class indispensable for any control and recovery. This was one more reason in fact for the Walloons to learn to take responsibility for their own situation, albeit with the knowledge that the road ahead would be long. Such was the climate in which the state was federalized, allowing regional policies to be undertaken in the last quarter of the century.

It would take an especially long time before political awareness would be accompanied by its natural extension and its best support, that is, an ethical consciousness. A founding event, the strike of 1960 had also postulated that the Walloon collectivity would affirm itself as a people and fight for its recognition as such. Yet, despite the warnings issued by a few minority groups, this did not occur. No doubt it is heart-

2. It is estimated that 80 per cent of the people living in the Brussels Region are French-speaking.
3. See Michel Quévit, *La Wallonie. L'indispensable autonomie* (Paris: Éditions Entente, 1982).

ening that the Walloons never yielded to a rigid nationalism, which would in any case have been alien to their traditions of openness and tolerance. But it is also to be regretted that on that occasion they lacked a basic concern for their identity. Was this the result of an ancient modesty? Perhaps. Ready to think of themselves as inferior, the Walloons have never shown a strong preoccupation with their culture, their history, or their heritage, except for some regional variations of traditional or folk inspiration.

From this perspective, the uniting of *Bruxellois* and Walloons in a "French community of Belgium" did not help anything. No doubt this political arrangement had aimed, and is still aiming, at presenting a united front based on a shared language and the values it conveys in the face of what Francophones perceived as a certain Flemish *esprit de conquête*. Nevertheless this union obliterates Wallonia's own reality and curbs its construction of an assertive self-image, as a variety of groups and individuals have underscored and bemoaned.[4] Although it is highly significant, this point will not be treated here as such. It does, however, bring immediately into relief the problematic aspect of the "struggle for recognition," in which Walloon society was engaged at a specific point in its history.

A FUNEREAL CELEBRATION

The strike of 1960 carried within itself this affirmation of a "national" identity. However, for obvious reasons, it could only bring it forth in terms of failure and nostalgia for better days. This is because, as we have suggested, the strike could only work itself out in the observance of a double mourning: mourning for an industrial power that had once been glorious and mourning for the aggressive proletariat to which that power had given birth. Certainly, the laborers who had stopped work in 1960, and who were not all proletarians in the classic sense, did not know that they were waging the final battle in a long series. They did not know they were experiencing the slow disappearance of that Walloon working world that had been at the vanguard of the proletariat in winning social rights.[5] They nevertheless still fought to create a new

4. See particularly the "Manifeste pour la culture wallonne," a tract issued on this subject by a hundred artists and intellectuals in 1983. It was reissued in *La revue nouvelle* 1 (January 1984): 62–64.

5. This disappearance is obviously quite relative. There is still a Walloon proletariat today, but it no longer has the strength previously provided by heavy industry on the one hand, and by an aggressive union organization on the other.

world out of the old, declining forms, a world that would be completely different from the world of oppression into which they had been born. This was an exemplary case of the dialectic of the past and the future, and of a past that sacrifices itself giving birth to a future.

Thus, as though in spite of itself, the strike of 1960, that great eruptive and savage event, took on the role of commemorative theater. It reenacted previous social movements with their dramatic charge. It was reminiscent, for example, of the deadly strike of 1886 which, begun in Liège, had spread like wildfire to the Hainaut province, and has even been described as having given birth to a new Walloon identity.[6] Moreover, the movement of 1960 abounded in gestures that resonated beyond their strategic *raisons d'être* and acquired a theatrical and symbolic dimension. This was true of all the acts aimed at the time at the transportation networks and the media: the fires that were set to buses, the use of dynamite at different points of the railroad network, the attacks on the railroad station of Liège or on the offices of the populist daily paper, *La Meuse,* which the next day could then carry the cynical headline: "Nos lecteurs mécontents" ("Our readers miffed"). It was not simply about striking the vital centers of power, but also showing, with spectacular gestures, that history was being staged and that, as a result, the present was reconnecting with an entire past.

Hence we see that even in its most desperate and cataclysmic aspects, the "great strike" was far from having a negative impact. It initiated a necessary work of mourning. It set off a process of remembering that called on the community to take hold of itself once again. With the strike, a past that had been extraordinarily obscured until then tended to resurface, a past that had to tell itself, but could not find the words to do so. True, from the perspective of those in power, it was in no one's interest to have this new voice come forth too quickly and call too fast on the identity of a people. From the start, the political right alarmed public opinion by stigmatizing the "strike culture" of the Walloon and socialist worker. On the other hand, the leaders of the movement, who had set themselves the immediate goal of transforming political structures, were afraid their plan would be tainted by a superfluous sentimentalism and associated with the specter of anarchy. This worked so well that what should have been seen was not seen, and became the object of a peculiar denial.

6. Marinette Bruwier, Nicole Caulier-Mathy, Claude Desama, Paul Gérin, *1886. La Wallonie née de la grève?* (Brussels: Labor, "Archives du futur," "Histoire," 1990). Acts of a colloquium held in 1986.

Failed opportunity? The work of identity would somehow be post-poned. It demanded an effort of memory, the carefully thought out decision to take on history. And not only the history of labor, but also of a much vaster and never recovered past. For, until then, the official History of Belgium had, in all its "manufactured" aspects, excelled at obscuring the much more real histories of the Flemish and Walloon peoples. As a result, the culture of the Walloons in particular was long confined to dialectal and folk forms of expression. It has been true, historically, that these same Walloons have never formed a politically united entity, but have instead lived on through the centuries in the relative isolation of their various provinces. Nevertheless, this has not prevented them from sharing common and sometimes very ancient lifestyles that have eventually formed a genuine and identifiable culture. In short, the Walloons first of all share a language, that Walloon dialect that gives them a name.[7] Moreover, they occupy a specific geographical position, that *"marche romane"* at the northern border of *francophonie* that is caught between Germany, Holland, and Flanders. Finally, they share a great tradition of exploitation of natural resources, which has for centuries made them into glassmakers, coal miners, and metal workers. The great historian Jules Michelet has already evoked this high tradition in his *Histoire de France.*[8]

A whole lost memory thus haunted the movement of 1960, but it had no structured means of expression. Now, it would have been desirable for this memory to support the current political project in order to give it meaning and provide the newly-won autonomy with a frame of reference. In modern societies, there is no genuine access to identity—of an individual, a group, a people—except under these two conditions: the securing of rights that allow for freedom of action and the recognition of a number of common values.[9] As a result, for Wallonia to manage its complete autonomy, it would not only have had to be accepted as a self-reliant political entity, but it would also have needed to acquire that particular kind of dignity that comes from having a dis-

7. This dialect can be broken down into numerous varieties, which reflects the fact that Wallonia has been extremely fragmented in the course of history. Moreover, a fraction of the population speaks a Picard dialect while another speaks a Lorrain dialect. Each live at the ends of Wallonia.

8. See Jules Michelet, *Histoire de France,* Volume VI, *Louis XI et Charles le Téméraire* (Paris: Hachette, 1844), book XV, 133–288.

9. On this subject, see the remarkable work of the philosopher Axel Honneth, *Kampf um Anerkennung* (Frankfurt: Suhrkamp Verlag, 1992); *The Struggle for Recognition,* trans. Joel Anderson (Cambridge: Polity Press, 1995).

cernible identity. It is here, of course, in the spirit of a heritage that would have reflected people's life experiences over long periods of time and presented itself as rich in promise, that the identification of a common past would have garnered its full value.

Yet, can it be said that nothing happened? True, no strong cultural assertiveness accompanied the political changes. As already mentioned, however, this assertiveness can only occur gradually and in conjunction with a collective work of self-construction. Historians, artists, and writers have since committed to this work, which has always seemed to involve confronting the forgotten continent of a cultural memory. We would now like to mention the road taken by some of them.

THE WORK OF MEMORY

A significant part of this work would be done by writers and filmmakers, and would owe a great deal to a climate favorable to the problematics of identity found throughout Europe in the 1970s and 1980s. As noted, once great ideologies crumbled and ceased to provide frames of reference, communities were gripped by a powerful need to affirm their identity and found their moorings in the local, the regional, or the national.[10] In this general movement, the Walloons had not only to reconnect with their past; they also had to bring it to light in order to construct it. This was a difficult undertaking that clashed both with the institutional sluggishness we have described and with the great general amnesia.

This work involved conferring on places, practices, and figures a dignity that would take Walloons from repression to a clear and active awareness of their true past. The social struggles conducted over a century by the Walloon workers are the best example here. They constitute a great heritage even for those who do not feel strongly connected to them. Yet, they are barely beginning to be objects of knowledge and recognition. They continue to be defined as violations of order, including the order of the Kingdom of Belgium. Schoolchildren therefore do not learn about them. True, a nineteenth-century writer like Camille Lemonnier was able to portray the Walloon world of miners and metal workers, but Lemonnier is not taught in school. A whole past is still being humiliated and is not granted representation because people have

10. See, among others, Claude Dubar, *La crise des identités. L'interprétation d'une mutation* (Paris: PUF, "Le lien social," 2000).

always conspired to keep it down. We are dealing here with a collective inferiority complex that many people have learned to live with.

Creating one's memory in this case involves breaking with diffidence and shame. It also involves making it clear that returning to the past is not an end in itself, but means getting a hold on the future. Thus the work of memory has motivating properties: it gives meaning, feeds pride, and stimulates creation. A number of artists began working in this spirit in the late 1970s and early 1980s, without entertaining exaggerated illusions about the immediate impact of their action. Themselves products of an obliterated culture, operating often within unknown networks, they knew they would not be heard. They also knew that they were performing a political act. Breaking with powerful taboos, they knew they would create a scandal and would not be well received. They took the risk anyway, clearing the hurdles. Here we will limit our discussion to the work of three creative artists whose exemplary contributions will lead us from poetry to cinema, through the theater.

POETRY: JEAN-PIERRE VERHEGGEN

Representative of an avant-garde that intended to wed textual revolution and political revolution, Jean-Pierre Verheggen (born in 1942) first burst on the scene in 1978 with a caustic poetic text, *Le degré zorro de l'écriture*. The writer's entire effort is here concentrated on the provocative manipulation of the language, and in particular, right from the title, an unbridled use of puns to both burlesque and creative ends. As for subjects, Verheggen gladly draws on childhood memory. Always allusive, his recollection of past companions and pleasures is a pretext for a critical questioning of the most immediate present. Most importantly, the past flows back into the present through the use of language, that is, through the irruption into current French of the language spoken or heard in childhood, the Walloon dialect (occasionally written "oualon" as a challenge to the French pronunciation "valon"). As Verheggen joyously writes: "The apparently contradictory use I very often make of popular *"bas oulaon"* and the *"amerloque"* [American language] of cartoons, stems from the fact I am, perhaps, ignorant through and through—a Walloon from Wisconsin?"[11] Or: "What pleases me above all doesn't have a name, is somehow anonymous. It is a language,

11. Jean-Pierre Verheggen, *Le degré zorro de l'écriture* (Paris, Bourgois, "TXT," 1978), 74.

my groundswell language: Walloon. The vernacular *bas wallon*, the spoken Walloon, strongly tinged with that lower-class accent" (73). Thus, frustrating expectations, Verheggen re-establishes the old dialect—which continues to be spoken by large working-class groups— in a throbbing language of ironic and obscene demand, and defolklorizes it in the same breath. If this speech is scandalous—and it is—it is primarily because it involves a whole sexually marked affective base.

But in addition, behind the words, an entire culture, trivial and intense, is limned, as are people, ways, works, suffering. Allusively, but highly effectively, a whole universe looms up in the reader's mind. It is, needless to say, a scorned, humiliated, and dispossessed universe. Verheggen's stroke of genius is to make it reappear not in the plaintive or even demanding mode, but in a petulant and provocative form that disarms conventions and good manners (including literary ones). In this respect, some have spoken of a verbal carnival, with everything that notion evokes in terms of a spirit of revenge of the low on the high, the vulgar on the noble. In his subsequent work, Verheggen does not deviate from that carnivalesque spirit even if the resumption of Walloon speech has been more episodic in his later texts.

THE THEATER: JEAN LOUVET

Jean Louvet (born in 1934) came to the theater right after the "great strike" and echoed that event in *Le train du bon dieu*,[12] a work written directly following the events and produced some time later. However, the real struggle against oblivion would not take shape until 1977, with a play titled *Conversation en Wallonie*. From then on, several of his plays would address that recovery of a past. Aside from *Conversation en Wallonie*, we will discuss three plays which, in their very diversity, conjure up the path taken by the playwright.

Gateway to a history, *Conversation en Wallonie* is intimist in subject and tone.[13] Autobiographical in nature, it portrays a young adult who confronts the image of a dead father. The pair forms a stark social contrast: the father has led a miner's terrible life and has left his spirit

12. Jean Louvet, *Le train du bon dieu* (Louvain: Cahiers théâtre, "Documents dramaturgiques 2," 1976). Note that the title of that play seems to echo that of the great classic of the literature in Walloon dialect, *Li pan dè bon Diu* (*Le pain du bon Dieu*) by Henri Simon (1909). Dialectal literature itself has no heirs.

13. Louvet, *Conversation en Wallonie*, followed by *Un Faust* (Brussels: Labor, "Espace Nord," 1997). The first edition of *Conversation en Wallonie* was published in Brussels by J. Antoine (1978).

in the pit; the son has gone to university and become a high school teacher; as the play begins, he is supporting a labor strike. *Embourgeoisement* of the son of a proletarian in a climate of social struggle: here is definitely a problematic of heritage, and Louvet excels at depicting the double cultural dispossession, of both the proletarian and his son.

With *L'homme qui avait le soleil dans sa poche*,[14] the playwright portrays a unique personality in the history of Belgium, that of Julien Lahaut, chairman of the Communist Party. Shortly after shouting "Long live the Republic!" with his group as the young King Baudouin was swearing his oath of office before both houses of Parliament, Lahaut was assassinated in his house in a Liège suburb. The perpetrators were never discovered. The Lahaut affair was the dark face of the Royal Question, that great national trauma mentioned earlier. Let us note that, despite the historic and heroic framework, the play's characters are, with the exception of Lahaut and his wife, ordinary individuals who belong to a recent period and to different social classes and are confronted with the return of a figure who had once shone forth, but whose "golden voice" they no longer hear.

Simenon,[15] the third play, was produced in 1994. It, too, is dominated by an exceptional character, in this case the world-famous writer Georges Simenon, who was of Walloon origin. He is the object of an intimist approach: the play speaks of the man more than of the writer, and of an ultimately banal man at that, who finds the cure for personal, family, and social torments in writing.

The past Louvet revives through the three plays is a painful one, synonymous with suffering and disappointment. Memory can only retrieve it with difficulty. Thus, the three major figures—Simenon, Lahaut, and the miner father—come back only as ghosts. Not only do they return from the kingdom of the dead, but revived, they prove to be strangers to the world as it is. Emanating from a bankrupt history, the generous Lahaut ("he had the sun in his pocket") is no longer heard by those—selfish or brotherly—who struggle with their current problems. As for

---

14. Louvet, *L'homme qui avait le soleil dans sa poche* (Brussels: Ensemble Théâtral Mobile, "Textes pour Didascalies 2," 1982), translated as *The Man Who Had the Sun in His Pocket*, in *An Anthology of Contemporary Belgian Plays 1970–1982*, edited and with introductions by David Willinger, trans. David Willinger and Luc Deneulin (New York: The Whitston Publishing Company, 1984), 533–74, 577–656.

15. Louvet, *Simenon*, "Théâtre à vif" (Carnières-Morlanwelz: Lansman, 1994), translated as *Simenon* by Kirsten Johnson for the Foundation Beaumarchais, S.A.C.D. (unpublished but available from the Éditions Lansman in Carnières, Belgium).

Simenon, he actually is only able to guarantee his presence through the myth he has concocted for himself, with Maigret's help. As one scrutinizes the recesses of his personal legend, one discovers that his private life was far from glorious and that writing was never anything for him but a way of escaping the worst. The relationship between Jonathan and his father Grégoire progresses more encouragingly in *Conversation en Wallonie*. A dialogue is established, but it is based on a misunderstanding: a proletarian's son, Jonathan has merely realized the *petits-bourgeois* dreams of his father. Thus, the past is filled with melancholy and, each time, it crushes the present instead of revitalizing it.

It is the very beautiful and expansive Scene 12 of *Conversation en Wallonie* that draws the lesson from the experience of memory. It shows us the working class as a dispossessed rather than an oppressed class. To be the son of a worker, as Jonathan realizes, amounts to being the son of no one, with no culture of one's own, or only the culture of indignity:

> GRÉGOIRE: Don't be silly. Everybody knows what we are. They know our flowered carpets, our porcelain birds, our bad paintings, our henhouses. Everybody talks about them. They pity us, they hate us. You know very well. [85]

And yet, dispossession is never total. Louvet excels at uncovering that "culture of the poor" where the individual succeeds against all odds in preserving some margins of creativity, despite an overwhelming determinism. The memory of little is a memory nonetheless. In Louvet's work, the history of the Walloon proletariat certainly appears as the story of a long frustration, but it is still the history of everyone. And it deserves to be preserved, especially since it is the history of loss and failure. It is certainly from this failure that the hybrid figures of Lahaut, the popular orator, and Simenon, the *petit-bourgeois* writer, are constituted. Neither of them has found a place in the memory of a people. Lahaut's ostracism from memory has been intensified as it were by the absence of a solution to the crime. But Simenon himself did not find anything in his fame that enabled him to pose as a monument of a history, becoming embodied with great difficulty in the fetishized character of Maigret. Moreover, the great plans of both Lahaut and Simenon survive only in blurred and disappointing images. Lahaut's ideal, in particular, fed by utopia and hope, did not escape the shipwreck that swept all of Communism away. And so, the new generation, facing the previous generation, demands in a way the right to forget:

ÉMILIE: We learned about it right away, on the radio. Julien Lahaut was assassinated by two strangers. Terrible night. They lowered the blinds in Seraing. Seraing the Red was in mourning. Julien, the golden mouth, had been killed in a wave of blood.

. . . . .

VINCIANE: Walloon who laughs, Fleming who cries. Walloon who cries, Fleming who laughs. I don't give a damn about your stories, your Walloon tricks, little Flemish priests, affected French-speaking Belgians of Ghent, from the nineteenth, twentieth, and twenty-first centuries. Night spider, great hope. All is lost except honor. A king abdicates, a man dies. I play on the steps of your temples, on the altars of your churches. In the parks of your most illustrious figures. A pigeon shits on the stone heads of Godefroid de Bouillon and of Julien Lahaut. [32]

Nevertheless, it is precisely when the emblematic figure of Lahaut forces them to mourn for ancient hopes that the characters of the play come to raise the disturbing question of their identity, and they do so in relation to him. And despite the denials of the rebellious young bourgeois woman, Vinciane, this identity cannot be built on a void, that is, on disdain for a past, confused as it may be.

FILM: JEAN-JACQUES ANDRIEN

The work of memory in Louvet clearly did not take place without critical labor. This same labor is found in the career of Jean-Jacques Andrien, but adapted to the demands of cinema. Thus, his films make a broader place for narrative construction and also represent more concretely and immediately the worlds to which they refer. Here we shall examine two films, *Le grand paysage d'Alexis Droeven* (1981) and *Australia* (1989), which are based on the same scenario. Both films portray run-down regions: an agricultural area in the first, the city of Verviers and its wool industry in the second.[16] Two young heirs, the first a farmer, the second the head of a firm, are in financial difficulties and threaten to give up. A member of the family intrudes from the outside and encourages them to break away, holding out the prospect of a more modern lifestyle and its advantages. Gripped by doubts, the two char-

---

16. Luc Sante, a New York novelist originally from Verviers, has evoked that city and its decline in a beautiful narrative of a search for origins titled *The Factory of Facts* (New York: Pantheon Books, Random House, Inc., 1998). It has been translated into French by Christine Leboeuf as *L'effet des faits* (Arles: Actes Sud, "Un endroit où aller," 1999).

acters nevertheless end up sticking it out and trying to salvage what is essential. In this way they own their heritage.

In each of the films, memory is initially filtered through the melancholy that suffuses the landscapes. Each time, the sustained quality of the gaze and the photography enable Andrien to pay homage to rural or urban settings, which become the most tangible witnesses of a past and a lost grandeur. It is as though films had to direct all the resources of their art toward salvaging the memory of a culture that had long permeated the sites of human labor. Andrien does not, however, indulge in nostalgia for its own sake. Thus, in *Australia,* as the two backgrounds alternate, the modest Walloon landscapes are placed in a difficult rivalry with the sumptuous views of the Australian natural environment. But, laden with history and poetic for that very reason, they bravely take that contrast on.

If the two films have similar themes, the second develops them more powerfully and more brilliantly. It is also true that *Australia* is a more expensive production than *Le grand paysage,* and stars Fanny Ardant and Jeremy Irons. In retrospect, this makes *Le grand paysage* look like a draft of *Australia,* but one that is remarkably able to evoke the difficulty that lies in self-expression and the concomitant labor that goes into reconquering one's speech.

The central character of *Australia* is Edouard Pierson, the son of a wool manufacturer from Verviers, who goes to Australia for professional training before World War II. The war catches him by surprise and keeps him there: he establishes a family there (even though his wife soon dies) and a small wool trade. Thus in this phase he breaks with his origins. We then witness his return to his homeland after the war. He has been summoned by his brother Julien, who has carried on the family business and finds himself threatened with bankruptcy. Edouard shows his brother that the local industry is functioning according to obsolete principles, and that, in any case, wool washing and subsequent operations will henceforth be taking place on another continent. Edouard then leaves, but not without obtaining a financial respite for his brother.

Thus the film is constructed on a strong contrast between the old world and the new. Andrien's innovation consists in having the character from the new world who is critical of the old world also be heir to this declining world. A subtle form of distancing takes place: the external perception is internalized as the action develops, according to a dialectic that Irons handles very well. What is being questioned is not so much obsolete economic management as the lack of awareness vis-à-vis this obsolescence, which is expressed in the way the bourgeoisie portrayed here calmly indulges in its pleasures: a violin contest for the ladies and gliding for the gentlemen. Moreover, Edouard, who began by disowning the world from which he came, reestablishes a relationship of desire with it, through the sudden passion stirred in him by Jeanne, the wife of a solicitor, who draws a strange authenticity from her peasant origins and her personal intensity. Julien, the brother, engulfed in old habits, is himself extremely passionate, even in his desire for death (see the beautiful sequence of his gliding in the night sky). In this very gentle film, a violence smolders, a hope takes effect: they are those of a world that has preserved, no matter how severe its decline, more than just the memory of the dynamism and conquering spirit of its founders. Is this why, at the end, a thin ray of hope remains, even if the facts do not justify it?

As in Louvet's work, the experience of memory is also problematic in Andrien's. First in its form: while the former reconstitutes a past as bravely as its fragmented anamnesis allows, the latter manages the appropriation of memory in a more linear, but also more slowly progressive fashion. Then in its content: the film does not bring us glorious episodes, but tales of dilapidation stained with impotence and failure. The choice to show the truth was made without needless pathos, because the two works are based on a materialist conception of history, whose embrace enables one to take note calmly of what was while detailing how things happened, without being afraid to point out errors and contradictions. It is best not to sugarcoat the pill when one is addressing a forgetful society.

Verheggen, Louvet, Andrien, and others—poetry, theater, cinema. Seen up close, these represent so many scattered attempts, not a concerted movement. But these attempts have not been without effect. To give only one example, if the young Walloon government has recently stood out for its unprecedented heritage policy, classifying and restoring monuments and sites, this "cultural good will," limited though it may be, can be seen as a continuation of the momentum begun by filmmakers and writers. Above all, however, these artists have set in motion a new relationship to memory. They have awakened a whole community to the significance of identity. They have taught it to consider the productions of the past as the fundamental elements of a social personality. They have made it understand that every people has a right to its image and that this image depends on acts, works, and persons that will likely determine how others will come to see it. In short, they have provided the impetus for a will to remember that is unprecedented among Walloons.

—Translated from the French by Barbara Harshav

II. The Work of Fiction

PIERRE MERTENS

Perasma*

Summer has finally returned. . . . We might want to begin with the
coming, at long last, of a new summer. The first wasp had entered the
parlor at dawn. In the courtyard, the daughter of the Portuguese con-
cierge was smoothing the coat of a resigned Labrador with an iron
comb. On the balcony of the building next to mine, on the top floor, a
young woman was coming and going, euphoric or furious, orating with
grand gestures into her cell phone. I told myself that, in other times,
she would have been considered mad, as would have the old maid on
the seventh floor who feeds all the stray cats of the neighborhood, but
finds "that animals sometimes lack gratitude." For now, she was trying to tame a hedgehog half dead with fear in the nascent heat wave.

I turned on the radio, tuned into a cultural program. The theme music of a broadcast aimed at lovers of the humanities—a harmonious
blend of a piano and the trills of a nightingale—brought tears to my
eyes: the same thing had been heard at this season for several years, and
so it reminded me of so many summers past, with women whose love
I had lost, too, as I went along.

The news bulletin that followed informed us that in the federal Parliament, a deputy had proposed a law to limit the activities of pigeon
fanciers throughout the national territory. In my heart, I was pleased
about that, although the disappearance of the pigeons seemed to correspond, metaphorically, with that of love. Love in general.

Two days ago, on my balcony, I discovered two new-born pigeons,
whose still crumpled feathers looked like raw silk. I cast one of them
into space, hoping that, at the last moment, it would open like a para-

*From Pierre Mertens, *Perasma* (Paris: Éditions du Seuil, 2001). Translated and
reprinted with permission of the author.

chute. But it crashed on the lawn, where a tomcat soon took care of it. I remembered a great Spanish poet's words about "murderers of doves." I no longer know to whom he referred, perhaps to Franco's soldiers, who put Iberia to fire and sword sixty years ago. I blushed with shame. I really feel that, from now on, I'm going to take care of the remaining pigeon, devote myself to its survival: feed it, give it something to drink— or, impotent, numb with remorse, witness its slow dying from day to day, while its mother walks around us, sometimes releasing droppings as milky as spurts of sperm on the parapet . . .

I wonder why I am developing such an aversion to those feathered creatures: aren't they always in couples? Don't they embody affection and fidelity? (Unless that is precisely why, in the current state of my sentimental life, I find them so unpleasant? They are so *bound*, so professionally conjugal.)

Now, by saving one of the two winged infants—out of cowardice or moved by repentance—I know that I am going to attach its parents to me, and they will want to nest on my terrace at any cost. To get rid of them, I will have to wage total war on them. But no doubt, in vain: the spirit of family triumphs over everything. . . . Yet that's me all over, doing everything to save one baby, after arbitrarily sacrificing another.

On the airwaves, a Debussy prelude is flowing now, like a delicious poison, drop by drop, like a meditative imitation of the passage of time.

So, let's go to lunch at the Armada. The Andalusian waitress, Ophelia, tells me she won't be there on Thursday. She's getting married that day. Yes, yes, she'll be back on Friday. (She can't know that, in fact, she'll also be away on Friday, for on her wedding night, the husband— badly in need of immigration papers—will tell her he is a homosexual and HIV positive. Poor Ophelia: you will experience a very contemporary tragedy. Will we ever see you again at the Armada?)

I unfurl the newspaper rolled up on the wooden frame at the entrance to the restaurant. I read that a world heavyweight champion was disqualified for biting his opponent's ear at a casino in Las Vegas. I learn that Marlon Brando presented to a gathering of Athenian journalists his list of grievances about global warming, the erosion of the ozone layer, the spread of tobacco addiction in the world, and the preservation of the caste system in India. An Associated Press dispatch states that the actor, who now weighs about 300 pounds, seemed to be a bit tired at the end of his performance.

Here and there, they're still going on and on about the crushing de-

feat of the world chess champion, Garry Kasparov, in the sixth game—
in one hour and nineteen moves—by the super-computer "Deep
Blue"—provided with 256 processors working in tandem—whereas
until then they had been tied: one victory each and three stalemates.
Bad news, all the same, for mankind, which thought it could resist the
machine until the dawn of the third millenium! But how do you cope
with a technological monster that can calculate four million combina-
tions a second? In the meantime, it seems that the American data pro-
cessing giant beat its previous record when the New York Stock Exchange opened.

But there can't be only bad news: thanks to X-rays, a former Scot-
land Yard detective and a retired professor of neurology now possess ir-
refutable proof that Tutankhamen was indeed done in, treacherously,
either by the vizier who then took his place and ruled while helping
himself to his widow, or by the general of the armies who did not wait
long to succeed the vizier, and who, by dint of inveterate revisionism,
then tried to erase the name of the young pharaoh from all the official
lists of the kings of Egypt.

I wonder, dear Ophelia, you whose little head of a mummy or an In-
dian witch juts out over the body of an urchin, how you will be able to
survive for long in the heart of a world so cruel that the murders and
outrages of the past float up again among those of today.

"And so? It seems that *nothing in fact happened to you!*"

I jump as if that imperious summons to explain were addressed to
me. In fact, it is meant for a young woman who is sipping a Pinot des
Charentes at the next table, and the one who presented it is a regular
customer of the restaurant, an old beau of the inbred aristocrat sort.

Never mind: I tell myself that he has formulated a damn good question! For, if you think about it, wouldn't that be the worst thing for all
of us as we are: that at the end of ends, nothing, in fact, happened to us?

("What did I hear? God, could it be possible: nothing has really happened to you?" As if, in a country like ours, the assumption didn't already appear quite reckless. . . .)

Suddenly, I prick up my ears. Eager to pick up other messages.

"I love love very much!" confides one. "As for me, I need room to
breathe," says the other.

Among the group on my left, I hear: "I'm always afraid of choice . . ."
(How strange it is, I think: I've always been afraid only of everything
else.)

"The mistake of my life!" someone proclaims.

"My greatest disappointment": another one ups the ante.

What's wrong with them all?

I told myself as I listened to all those superimposed voices—that twittering of a miserable wife, that lament of a sick lover, claims of a betrayed mistress—that the murmur that would gather them would swell a choir whose solemn tirades would stand out, as if borrowed from Greek actors, only to sink into cacophony.

But before we stop here, in that comical and sinister apotheosis, let us listen to the sermon that an older woman is giving to a young man: "Just look at you! You're not even twenty-four years old, and what a state you're in! What will you look like ten years from now? I see what you're up to, and if you ask me, it's a little shady. You don't see where you're going? You've gone the whole way . . . backwards, if I dare say so. You know, what you're feeling is not even the shadow of a feeling. But I'm not about to recite your life to you. Anyway, it's no big deal. In two weeks, I'll have forgotten the whole thing. But why did I have to run into a guy like you, not healthy, neither one thing nor the other, always a little sick? I must be cursed! (She begins to cough.) I should have dug up someone safe, different, good, normal, you know what I mean? Basically, until now, there never was anybody. Now all I have to do is whistle and the guys come running, you have no clue. If I wanted, all of them would be at my feet. I can't help it, that's just how it is. At home, nothing but wandering hands and bulging eyes! And if the new guy happened to have some dough, so much the better! All this time I've slogged away with you—but that's not the main thing."

At another table, someone says in a smooth voice: "Yes, yes, heaven on earth! Eden . . . except for that awful ecological disaster . . ."

It seemed to be time to settle the check quickly. At high noon, the sun had dashed down a cliff of clouds and burst onto the city. The way a ball is sent into a net. Shit, I said to myself: this time, this was it, the girls were all going to become beautiful again at the same time, and maybe, then, a single one in the heap would have the common sense, the good idea to fall in love with me a little? The summer alone, solemn and definitive, would have the last word once more, and would release its loud noise at random! The ironmonger—"Iron, bronze, copper, tin!"—would utter the slightly plaintive shout of a stray muezzin . . .

I decided to spend the afternoon at the World's Fair swimming pool. (On the way, I think that, forty years later, they hadn't found the time or had the will to take apart the foundations, the pavilions, or the rides of that immense amusement park. Should we rejoice or complain about

it? Wasn't the whole country in that image? Ruins surviving in a pro-
liferating cemetery. Death reproducing itself.) In a gazebo in an open air
zoo, a Siberian tiger was yawning. On the paths, joggers were training,
like old boy scouts, for the marathon the following Sunday around the
capital, and during the race, as each year, the sweeper trucks would col-
lect those who had overestimated their strength.

When I discovered the glass enclosure of the pool, the warm steam
grabbed me by the throat. So did the hubbub, a deafening tumult of
divers, shouts of excitement, the vibration of diving boards, and above
all, that sound of the slap of bodies jumping on the end of the board or
flopping into the water. I thought I could even make out the swell of a
collective chant, an interrupted children's chorus, sometimes, through
the loud cries. I was dripping, unable to determine if it was the pervad-
ing mist or my own sweat that pasted my nylon shirt to my skin. Had
I come smack in the middle of an athletic event or a school swimming
fair?

As if nothing had happened, I thought. Everything was about to start
over again as before. In the past. This time, summer had certainly returned, celebrated in the pool as in an arena by couples playing and
yelling, and by children, especially children *living well*. Full of life,
even. Is there anything in the world so uniform and universal as those
children's choirs with interchangeable voices?

Well, that's what had hit me, and then grabbed me by the throat.
That and the call on the microphone with the airport voice: "Little
Jerome has lost his mommy: he's waiting for her in the cafeteria . . ."

Come on! So, *they* haven't killed them all, I muttered, finally mea-
suring the anguish and despair that had gripped me as I became aware
of their object.

I decided not to undress and went to have a drink at the bar. Through
the curved glass, you could see the blue sky and the swimmers. Memories assailed me.

Wasn't it last summer that the first corpses of children had been discovered, in the middle of the country, in cellars, near the mines that
were the burial site of the victims of the country's greatest mining disaster, which had occurred forty years ago, and had plunged the nation
into mourning? After decimating the miners, they had started on the
minors. Was that why the whole population wasn't mistaken? It had
not seen this new massacre of innocents as a simple, even if a particularly sordid, news item, but had lent it a political significance. (And ever
since then, every Sunday, thousands of people paraded spontaneously

in cities and villages, in silence, dressed in white, demanding an improbable justice, an impossible reparation.)

Yes: it must have been that and nothing else that had returned to my memory at the sight of the rowdy kids in the middle of the World's Fair swimming pool: how wouldn't I have felt a lump in my throat at the sight of those young people frolicking, unaware of the danger that threatened them, and at those games of little survivors—the sight of whom was no consolation? Weren't we now living in the land of no consolation?

"Caution! Children!" says the traffic sign in school zones. The formulation is ambiguous: should we fear for them or be afraid of their rage tomorrow? What do we know of the nightmares they've been fomenting in their beds for some time, all over this country?

All of that happened in the Land of the Unnamable . . .

What we are going to say here at first glance has nothing to do with that. But we certainly need to portray this lugubrious setting and never forget that it happened *here:* in a very small country burdened by enormous murders. The cannibal subsoil fertilized with the flesh of children. (Ultimately, we would even be scared to turn over the earth of our own vegetable plots: who knows what terrible secrets are concealed in our most suburban gardens?) The villages are called *Grace-H, Grace-B, Grace-M,* because it is precisely grace that they lacked and grace that was not granted the children murdered there like sheep in a slaughterhouse.

What are they hoping for, those who set out on Sundays dressed in white or carrying white balloons? They aren't wrong: they look a little like ghosts already. . . . And, when the processions break up, so many balloons still linger in the sky above their heads that the light no longer passes through them. They parade to convince themselves that they still exist: "I march therefore I am." They have invented *"le jogging de la pitié."* They have no voice: maybe they're right?

Even on television, nothing else could be shown anymore: only the disinterment of the martyrized little bodies; only the funeral marches that are organized immediately wherever the macabre discoveries occur. Later, a whole generation of children in our country may well remember only that, bombarded as they are with images of searches, exhumations, and then reburials, as people pulled out of the earth those they were going to rebury in it afterward.

Some of those young spectators must have believed at the time that it was all fake, a fiction, that it was just a television series like the American family sagas in which they had been steeped until then.

There was no longer any point in changing channels: odds were that the same sequences of excavation or funerals were circulating from one to another, in a continuous loop—interrupted only by commercials every now and then.

From one minute to the next, anyone could raise suspicions, become the suspect of the most recent crime, and be considered a dangerous and murderous "pedophile." (Strangely, they didn't say "pedophobe." But words, like things, were losing their meaning.)

Students in one class are questioned about the case. They all support the death penalty. One of them proclaims it with a nervous laugh. "Killing a murderer isn't killing . . . ," says another. "What if it's a sick person?" "Then he should be killed because he's sick . . ."

"What were you doing on the day of the 'White March to the capital?'" we are asked. I blush a bit because I wonder if, inadvertently, I wasn't making love with my girlfriend that day. And then, no, it comes back to me. "I was reading the text of my last libretto to the blind," I say. "That's my job . . ." But will such a use of time seem respectable enough?

I pity those of us who haunt this region: I really fear that death has invaded us so much that we almost need it. That every time yet another murder is revealed, we can't meet, united, except at the funeral, around one of those small coffins: soon we won't feel that we live together except when facing the sight of the most unfair, abject death. I sometimes believe, awfully—God forgive me!—that if death didn't exist, people from here would more than likely have invented it. I recall that, when the whole thing started, I was overcome by a diffuse, slimy terror. I was afraid all the time.

"Of what?" they asked me.

"Of the death of children . . . ," I answered, as though it were an obvious statement. But an obvious statement that could only have been formulated by a moron. "It's a little like being afraid of the Germans long after the war . . . ," I tried to explain, pitifully.

I also recall that the whole thing happened just as I was falling in love—when for so long, I didn't think I could anymore. And I had wanted to express the joy of that love in a libretto. But as soon as I started writing it, an insidious fear gripped me.

My God, when will we recover the sweetness of surviving? When will we have the right to it? The right to be happy in a country where such things happened that it could be tempted to die unto itself? So much so that we chose to silence the name of that country whose ignominy was sometimes such that it remained unnamable and unnamed, deciding to call it only *Innomie,* The Land of the Unnamable.

We still loved it, when our love for a woman was in its first moments, its first words. Now that there is no longer a country, only the woman remains. For how long?

"My love . . . ," I had murmured, even before really knowing you. "In this country where one has killed, where one has *unmade* children, don't you think we should make one? Make one *against the emptiness?"*

You don't say "no."

—Translated from the French by Barbara Harshav

ANTOINE TSHITUNGU KONGOLO

Colonial Memories in Belgian and Congolese Literature

This essay represents a deliberately and necessarily modest contribution to our understanding of an undeniably complex set of issues, namely, the ways in which colonial memories have been operating, both in Belgium and in the Congo, with a particular emphasis on the last quarter of the twentieth century.

One cannot deny that certain erosions of memory have been taking place on both sides. They have resulted in the burying of painful subjects under layers of silence, a phenomenon caused in no small measure by a legacy of guilt. Yet, there have also been signs of renewed interest in the colonial past in recent decades. This has had a noticeable impact on Belgian and Congolese literature, as well as on the parallel adoption of a genuinely critical stance.

These changes have left numerous marks on the fictional corpora of writers from both the North and the South. The intertwining of their discursive practices, a century after colonization was first set in motion, is of no little consequence. Indeed, whether one measures these writings according to the yardstick of their convergences or their differences, the fact remains that colonial memory and its weighty symbolic charge play an important role in each case.

In *Zakhor, Jewish History and Jewish Memory*, the American historian Yosef H. Yerushalmi sets as his objective "a specific examination of the dynamics of *Jewish* collective memory."[1] He purposely underscores the complexity of his argument, which consists in disentangling the ties that bind together memory and the writing of history in Jewish civilization. What allows Yerushalmi to grasp the intricacies of these entanglements is that they often seem to point toward the

1. Yosef Hayim Yerushalmi, *Zakhor, Jewish History and Jewish Memory* (Seattle: University of Washington Press, 1982), xv.

YFS 102, *Belgian Memories,* ed. Catherine Labio, © 2002 by Yale University.

same unusual paradox: "that although Judaism throughout the ages was absorbed with the meaning of history, historiography itself played at best an ancillary role among the Jews, and often no role at all; and, concomitantly, that while memory of the past was always a central component of Jewish experience, the historian was not its primary custodian" (xiv).

Not only is this question of vital importance in its own right, it also allows for a wider problematic to emerge, one that reaches beyond the Jewish world. Indeed, it touches on the ways in which group memories are constituted as well as on their subtle mechanisms, their internal and external dynamics, the receptacles that hold them, and their transmission channels. The observations made by the American historian can be seen straightway as containing many precious lessons. Writing, even for a people as literate as the Jews, has never been the only or even the only reliable repository of a group's memory. Liturgy and chronicles have played a fundamental role in the making of Jewish memory, and this to the detriment of historiography as such. What pertains to Jewish memory in particular, can, however, also be put to profitable use in the case of a more global approach to the study of the problematic relationship between history and memory.

The preceding remarks underscore that specific modes of memorial transmission obtain in the case of peoples who can claim the following double inheritance: on the one hand, the general habits of an orality whose roots go deep into an immemorial soil and, on the other, the Latin alphabet, which supports intellectual productions that are modern and have Western sources of inspiration. The latter include the writing of history as such and of those fictions that are more or less inspired by it. This dual memory is necessarily a source of conflict. Mythical time, which eliminates any kind of historical causality, lies behind oral accounts. Dates and events seem less important than their interpretation, which flows directly from the ancient myths. On the other hand, as soon as one deals with materials that have been cast in writing, a whole new set of expectations emerges.

Even this perfunctory comparison of the written and the oral—which can both be used to gather the sediment of Congolese collective memory—lets us catch a glimpse of a genuine asymmetry that cannot be elucidated by relying on second-hand ideas. Moreover, we ought not to "plead orality" or argue that an exception obtains when an ancestral orality and its schemata rule—especially when these are reduced to a handful of clichés—as we try to understand how historical events are passed on, particularly in the case of the events associated with Belgian colonization.

Finally, in addition to these general considerations, I would also like to underscore that colonial memory, an aspect of history that tends to spark fierce debates both in Belgium and in the Congo, seems subject to a complex array of factors inasmuch as it is structured in each case by "social frameworks . . . transmitted and sustained through the conscious efforts and institutions of the group" (Yerushalmi, xv).[2]

Why are some of the more painful episodes of the colonial and even the pre-colonial era expunged from collective memory? Why has the scourge of slavery left such infinitesimal traces in collective forms of representation? Why is the scandal of the "severed hands" (*"les mains coupées"*), which finally discredited once and for all Leopold II's colonizing venture, dealt with more frequently in works written by Westerners than in Congolese texts, even when one factors in all the different genres? Why, on the other hand, are some of the remnants of colonial paternalism now evoked in a rather favorable light? Why does orality have a kind of monopoly over some historically-laden themes about which writers maintain an oppressive silence that is all the more troubling for it?

COLONIAL MEMORY IN THE CONGO AND IN BELGIUM

In the Congo, what comes out of the crucible that is commonly referred to as "popular culture" includes a great many references that are overtly critical of the Belgian era. Such has not been the case with the elites, which have been far less inclined to deal with history proper. Nevertheless, some key members of the intelligentsia appear to have recently committed themselves, more so than had been done in the past, to throwing light on the colonial era. Their contributions are anything but negligible because of their willingness to adopt a critical stance. Indeed, though some people, in the decades that followed independence, had gotten into the habit of praising ancestral orality without investigating its contributions to history, the study of orality no longer seems to be divorced from the demands imposed by rigorous historical investigations. African history, to use the phrase of Thomas

2. Yerushalmi is here referring to Maurice Halbwachs's *Les cadres sociaux de la mémoire* (Paris: F. Alcan, 1925) and *La mémoire collective* (Paris: Presses universitaires de France, 1950).

Mpoyi-Buatu, must "return its ill-gotten gains," that is, it must now flow from a rigorous analysis of the vestiges and documents of the past.[3] This not-so-trivial mandate should allow us to triumph over sentimentalism, forgo judging on mere intent, and put a stop to attempts at mythification.

Jean-Louis Lippert's appraisal of Belgium's collective memory of its relationship to the Congo raises just as many issues: "Who a hundred years hence could possibly be expected to believe that a European province as small as Belgium had colonized the continent of the Congo? And that it had owed both its ephemeral existence as a prosperous kingdom as well as its spiritual insolvency to that continent?"[4]

Alternating between texts from the two traditions allows us to read and take note of the underlying processes that yield such epiphenomena as concealment, neglect, confusion, and even amnesia, independently of their selectivity or lack thereof or of whether these are deliberate or unconscious processes. On the Belgian side, I think in particular of Lippert's on-going career as a fiction writer and of his remarkable trilogy, *Maïak* (1900–98), though I also want to mention Albert Russo's *Sang mêlé ou ton fils Léopold* (1990) and Marie-Claire Blaimont's *Black Lola* (1994), whose literary investigations combine mythical and realistic dimensions in ways that are comparable to Lippert's. Lippert, however, goes as far as anyone can in his concomitant exploration of the historical and the private.

On the Congolese side, the impressive autobiography of V. Y. Mudimbe, *Les corps glorieux des mots et des êtres. Essai d'un jardin africain à la bénédictine* (1994) sums up the revitalization that has been taking place in the intelligentsia. Subjugated by the demands of a fairly radical nationalism, the intelligentsia's assessment of the Belgian period had previously been extremely negative. However, a growing awareness of the limitations this stance was imposing eventually made its members reconsider and distance themselves from hard-line nationalism. Mudimbe, for instance, offers a lucid and rigorous reading of Africa's past in its precolonial, colonial, and postcolonial phases while trying as much as possible to deal with facts objectively and to eschew the temptation to yield to the idealization of a romanticized past. At the same time, he removes the blinders of African ideologies, whose

3. Thomas Mpoyi-Buatu, "L'archéologie africaine. Préhistoire et paléontologie," *Présence africaine* 159 (1999): 98.

4. Jean-Louis Lippert, *Dialogue des oiseaux du phare. Maïak I* (Avin/Hannut, Belgium: Éditions Luce Wilquin, 1988), 194.

narrow definitions of identity he condemns as potentially leading to totalitarianism. The sentimental displays of historians more concerned with myths than with facts hardly find favor with him either.

Both sides dismiss amnesia and argue that one ought not to search the past without a heightened consciousness of history. Yet, their respective connections to a past that bears the stamp of colonization are not identical.

Immediately after the painful break that came with the Congo's independence, Belgium seems to have proceeded to bury its colonial past, which had ended in the throes of a traumatic separation. We have had to wait almost two decades before the publication of fictional works of any significance. One exception to this rule is *L'homme qui demanda du feu* (1977), in which Ivan Reisdorff evokes the twilight of the Belgian colonization of Rwanda-Burundi and deals with the subject of the Hutu/Tutsi dualism and its specific violence mechanisms. This novel demonstrates that critical distance was possible, even if it was not much in evidence in the first years of the postcolonial era, which was dominated by sensationalist reporting and the nostalgic tremolos of old-timers' memoirs.

The Congolese coming to terms with the history of colonization has been slower for a number of reasons. First, the Congolese doxa has always been reluctant to acknowledge the important role played by Belgium's colonization in the emergence of its economic, social, and even cultural modernity. At the cultural level, this stigmatization is unquestionable. As noted by Belgian writer Oscar-Paul Gilbert, the metaphor of the "empire of silence" can be applied to most of the analyses put forth by Congolese intellectuals.[5]

Interestingly enough, these same intellectuals refer obsessively to the situation in the French African Empire. In particular, they criticize the Belgian colonizer for, among other things, not having encouraged or promoted literary creativity in the immense territory placed under its tutelage both directly and indirectly from 1885 to 1960. By contrast, Belgian achievements with respect to the country's economic and social infrastructures, especially in the area of healthcare, seem to have made a bigger impression on the collective Congolese memory.

Congolese intellectuals have understandably drawn a line in the sand between the Belgian period and the postindependence era. Unfortunately, literary historiography is now paying the price of an overly

5. Oscar-Paul Gilbert, *L'empire du silence. Congo 1946* (Brussels: Éditions du Peuple, 1947).

systematic devaluation of the earlier literature. Indeed, the novelist Paul Lomami-Tshibamba and the poet Antoine Roger Bolamba are almost miraculous survivors of the Belgian era, which is generally likened to a cultural desert. This ideologically charged approach has led to the erasure, so to speak, of texts written in Congolese languages, which were the dominant form of expression in the first decades of colonization, even though these writings play as important a role in our understanding of the cultural processes that have been taking place in the Congo as the promotion of literacy by missionaries intent on "enculturating" the gospels.

These strata of local language texts are nevertheless essential to our understanding of the ways in which one passes from the oral to the written. In addition, they throw precious light on some of the key features of today's—and possibly even tomorrow's—literature. Unfortunately, the profoundly negative value assigned to the phrase "empire of silence," albeit justifiable in the context of a denunciation of a colonial system as such, does seem to have also been accompanied by the unfortunate elision of otherwise indispensable distinctions. Moreover, is it not paradoxical that the Congolese should constantly refer to a Belgian writer when they attempt to translate their perception of the colonial era?

BELGIUM: THE LAST THREE DECADES

Belgians' African memory has come unraveled rather spectacularly in the last three decades, primarily for the following reasons: it has been forgotten; the traditional points of reference have gradually become lost on new generations; and history has been subjected to increasingly biased perceptions. The total ignorance of the geography, culture, and history of that central Africa that was once Belgian is nevertheless part and parcel of a very complex crux of issues. Has this repression been caused by the historical culpability for erstwhile atrocities? Are the epiphenomena of a collective amnesia involuntary or are they knowingly put in place, as Lippert, that loud iconoclast, argues: "We had to put together an extraordinarily refined puzzle (*un puzzle impalpable*). Its pieces were made of things unsaid. Of blind thoughts. Of absent memories. Of a programmed amnesia. What had we gone to the Congo for? Why were we no longer there? Such mysteries were finer than the most refined sugar (*mystères plus impalpables que le sucre*)" (179).[6]

---

6. [Note from the translator: *sucre impalpable* (confectioner's sugar) is used more frequently than *sucre glace* in Francophone Belgium.]

Both hypotheses are no doubt partially admissible. If we are going to speak of a relative amnesia, however, we need to do so in the context of a particular era, including the domestic situation of a country pulled between its periphery and its center. Split in half, dragged into a spiraling federalism, at times even seduced by confederalism, all of which hurt an increasingly weakened central State, Belgium has progressively eliminated its common pool of historical and symbolic references. This has included, of course, that colonial past, which had in earlier times been one of the emblematic features of national collective memory.

The regionalization of such sensitive areas as education, including curricula, in order to obey the dicta of the new linguistic policies, has also helped to sever Belgium's ties with Congolese realia, which had invariably been a part of the now obsolete national curricula. It is undeniable, for example, that Flanders's legitimate desire to strengthen its own identity has resulted, intentionally or not, in the obliteration of colonial references, especially of a significant number of all kinds of texts that had been written in French. Such a mutilation, whose negative impact remains to be investigated, is particularly unfortunate when one remembers the important role played in the Congo by Belgian missionaries, most of whom hailed from the northern half of the country. The liquidation of the house of Belgium has not been without consequence with respect to its common historical heritage, including its colonial phase.

The implications of this loss are many. The media, for instance, put out utterly absurd interpretations of African tragedies that are replete with approximations, exotic clichés, and remarkable memory lapses. They thereby discount Belgium's historical responsibilities. Recent tragedies—and I am here, of course, referring to the Rwandan genocide—are portrayed as having inescapably resulted from an atavistic causality, a representation that utterly fails to factor in the nevertheless essential historical background. This tattered memory must be put back together little by little, not only if we are ever to reclaim the past, but also and more importantly if we want to be able to map a new future.

THE WORK OF FICTION

Not only can literary texts function as receptacles of human experience, their emotional charge also allows us to read about and see many otherwise invisible facets of the human journey, including its shadows and highlights.

Just as literature is able to name horrifying tragedies, however, it can also take its distance from them through the use of irony. Belgian writings of the last quarter of the twentieth century have carried large volumes of sediment of African memory along by functioning as repositories for a multiplicity of voices, bearing witness to conquering drives, and revealing the tensions, rifts, and cultural fusions that arise as horror is surpassed. Writers are increasingly able to put back together the pieces of a rather complex history. They are at last naming the horrors that punctuated the conquests, domestication, and exploitation of the territories of Central Africa. We can see this clearly in Lippert's work and in his patent contempt for Leopold II.

These new voices describe the avatars that come with culture shocks as well as the fascination induced by the discovery of the other and by its corollary, the humility that consists in actually listening to that other. Though Lippert focuses more on important historical figures like Leopold II, Lumumba, and Mobutu, Marie-Claire Blaimont and Albert Russo dwell more on the encounter with the other. All three share, however, a common desire to proclaim their ties to Africa and the belief that these can be sublimated through either cultural or biological *métissage*, or possibly both.

Born in Stanleyville in 1952, Lippert has published a number of works, under the alias Anatole Atlas, that put him squarely among the "Situationists." He is the author of a trilogy *Maïak*, which includes *Pleine lune sur l'existence du jeune bougre* (1990), *Mamiwata* (1994), and *Dialogues des oiseaux du phare* (1998).

In *Mamiwata* a young iconoclastic painter returns to the land of his childhood, the Congo, now Zaïre. Arrested by the security forces of the regime, he is subjected to an endless interrogation. This pilgrimage home takes place under the imaginary protection, on the one hand, of his deceased Portuguese grandmother, nicknamed Mamiwata, after the siren of the river Congo, and, on the other hand, of his grandfather, a former Congolese owner of uranium mines, who had later managed to carve for himself, on the strength of large reserves of cynicism, a global empire dealing with the control of images and telecommunications. Other characters include a Belgian minister of the interior, who is also godfather to the black sergeant who, some twenty years later, would take on the glorious title of Maréchal, after having served as the "secular arm" of his Belgian masters.[7]

7. Lippert is here of course alluding to Joseph Mobutu.

The mythical figure of Lumumba stands out against this gallery of masters and their acolytes. His arrest on All Saint's Day in 1959 and his imprisonment are the true leitmotiv of this ambitious and jubilant novel. Its Ariadne's thread is none other than the Congo's history, from the assassination of Lumumba to Mobutu's accession, followed by the meeting of the National Sovereign Conference (*Conférence Nationale Souveraine*), with Belgium in counterpoint, like some Lotharingian empire.

The immersion in the memories of an African childhood opens up with rare subtlety onto the theme of *métissage*. Indeed, the pilgrim claims both Europe and Africa for himself. He means to act as a bridge between the two continents in order to ensure the revival of the former and reassure the latter as to the relevance of its humanistic values, threatened by the mirages of northern consumer society. The appeal to popular African myths is particularly exemplary in that it distances itself from any facile exoticism.

Marie-Claire Blaimont was born in 1950 in Birnheim, Germany. Her peaceful childhood in the Belgian Congo was brutally interrupted by the serious troubles that rocked the Congo right after independence. After spending ten years in the Belgian Congo, from 1950 to 1960, her family was forced to return to metropolitan Belgium. Blaimont and her parents promptly closed this unfortunate parenthesis, however, and quickly returned to live in the Congo, where they stayed until 1963. After the family's definitive return to Belgium, she studied in La Louvière and Namur and received a degree in journalism from the Institut des Hautes Études en Communication Sociale (IHEC). She then moved to Charleroi, where she divided her time between sociocultural activities in underprivileged neighborhoods and freelance work for a variety of newspapers and magazines, before moving on to a brilliant career as a journalist for *La nouvelle gazette*.

The female narrator of *Black Lola* (Éditions du Cerisier, 1994), a journalist by trade, comes face to face with the plight of young drifters who are seeking refuge in drugs. The plot, set in Charleroi, refers continuously and alternatively to the emotions and memories associated with her African childhood. A quest for identity is here motivated in some measure by the mixing of two cultures that have finally been reconciled.

Albert Russo was born in Kamina, in the Katanga province in 1943, of a Belgian-Italian father and an Irish mother. He completed his primary and secondary education in the Congo before moving to South Africa, the United States, and finally France, where he is currently working for UNESCO. His anchoring at the crossroads of several cultures and languages—he writes in both English and French—has driven him to study the issue of *métissage* in some depth.

Sang mêlé ou ton fils Léopold (1990) is set in Elisabethville, the capital of the mining province of Katanga.[8] It tells the story of an orphan adopted by an American homosexual who has severed his ties to his native country and moved to the Congo after the Second World War. The relationships described in the novel are anything but uncomplicated. The adoptive father is single, yet his female housekeeper passes for his official concubine even though there is nothing sexual between her and her employer, who carefully hides his homosexuality. The young child, Léo Kitoko William, is of mixed race and has a name that is a third European, a third African, and a third American. What's more, his African name (Kitoko, which means "the beautiful one") is only a nickname. He is, moreover, the child of a nonexistent couple.

The adoptive father's servant showers Kitoko with affection and some authority. She is a watchful mother who surrounds her baby with what amounts to a cocoon of happiness. However, as Kitoko reaches the age of reason, he wonders relentlessly about his true identity. His growing self-awareness is made all the more painful by his discovery of the frightening divides of colonial society, with the privileged on one side and the mass of the excluded on the other. Among the latter group there is another young child, a friend of Kitoko's, who has trouble dealing with his Jewish identity. Whites and blacks live almost impenetrably partitioned lives.

One of Kitoko's friends is a young white boy who speaks Swahili better than he does, even though everyone thinks of Kitoko as Black or Congolese. The unveiling of his troubled and conflicted identity is dramatic, and further complicated by his discovery of his father's homosexuality. Kitoko, the child of mixed race, is nevertheless able to make a narrow escape and to move to his adoptive father's country as an adult. His father meanwhile dies during the troubles that take hold of the Congo during the country's move toward independence.

THREE EXEMPLARY DECADES FOR THE CONGO

Whether it deals with the different phases of colonization or even of the postindependence period, the Congolese collective memory is a devas-

8. [Note from the translator: *Sang mêlé* has been translated into English as *Mixed Blood* (Brooklyn, NY: Domhan Books, 2000)].

tated province buried under a chaotic rubble one would be hard pressed to map in any systematic fashion. Here again, the relationship to the colonial past hinges on a set of complex factors.

First, this past was subjected to a number of ideological attacks launched in the name of the *Authenticité* movement, which aimed to destroy all references to colonialism in order to foster, superficially at least, a cultural renaissance grounded in an exacting nationalism.

Colonial monuments were taken from their pedestals to anonymous backyards or were simply vandalized. Belgian-sounding place names were banned; Christian names were flushed out. Zairean authorities would later justify these actions, which were actually meant to pave the way for Mobutu's accession to his increasingly arbitrary power, by invoking the *mental decolonization* necessary for the so-called *return to Authenticity* (*retour à l'Authenticité*), an awkward idiom that was eventually replaced by the phrase *recourse to Authenticity* (*recours à l'Authenticité*).

In any event, no matter how seductive its nationalism, this movement was, at least in its rhetorical manifestations, hardly able to protect itself from references, unconscious or conscious, to the execrated period of "colonialism," as evidenced by some of its magical incantations and its myths.

"Happy the people who dance and sing for their chief." Did not this slogan, so emblematic of the inept propaganda of the time, ring a bell? Has not the atavistic love of dance—a truism transmitted ceaselessly and almost without ever being qualified, by everyone from the explorers to the missionaries, and even to those Belgian writers least infatuated with exoticism and colonialism—been one of those myths for which the Congolese have had to pay a heavy price? Such an example demonstrates that the interpretation of colonialism, its system, its imaginary, and its myths by the Congolese themselves in the name of nationalism, was not calling for the requisite rigor.

The rules of history have now inverted this tendency: the swift rejection of all that was rightly or wrongly suspected of any kind of atavistic connection to colonization is no longer a must. The bitter failure of African independence in general—and of Congolese independence in particular—has finally put an end to the earlier radicalism, to the point where colonization is now romanticized, turned into a paradise lost that is constantly invoked in a nostalgic vein.

Indeed, in the Congo as well as in Belgium, collective memory has made some unusual albeit highly significant selections. I would now like to address the question of what has happened in the case of Congolese literary texts.

Born in 1950 in Tielen in the Kasaï province, Thomas Mpoyi-Buatu has published a large number of critical studies and essays. *La re-pro-duction* is an original and ambitious work that plays with a variety of genres and temporal dimensions.

The novel attempts to give an account of the history of the Congo/Zaïre for the past hundred years or more. It begins with the age of exploration, which is represented by H. M. Stanley and serves as a preamble to Leopold II's colonization, first in his own name, then in Belgium's. It ends with Mobutu's coming to power and the story of his rule. The different historical layers are telescoped in a narrative that feeds on the soil made up of that collective memory the author is attempting to reconstitute in his own way. The tutelary figures of colonial history take a direct hit. These include Stanley, Leopold II, Livingstone, and many others. The author's destruction of the sacred aura surrounding these people reduces them to sinister-looking masks.

Seen from this angle, the Mobutu era duplicates the Leopoldian regime, at least by the yardstick of its intrinsic violence. Parallels are repeatedly drawn between some of the macabre episodes of the Leopoldian era and the excesses and crimes of the Mobutu regime. In particular, the novelist refers obsessively to the hanging of Prime Minister Evariste Kimbe and of his three companions in misfortune.

The thematic range of this text is as broad as its chronological and formal range (not only does Mpoyi-Buatu interpolate time periods, he also mixes genres such as poetry, essay, narrative, and dialogue, as well as styles). Among other things, the novelist deals with the pangs of acculturation, political violence in African dictatorships, various kinds of sexual deviance, wandering (*errance*), and feelings of abandonment. Nor does he neglect the rebellions that flared up in the Congo in the sixties. The eastern part of the country is bathed in a mythical aura as the launching pad of several important changes in the Congo's history. It is from the east that the explorers and, before them, the Arabs, had come. It is in the east that rebellions took place with a view to change the country's fate in a manner that was, to say the least, decisive. The author raises what amounts to a monument to the memory of P. E. Lumumba, fallen hero and antithesis to Mobutu, whose megalomania the novelist constantly denounces.

Among the key texts of the last ten years or so, we must make a special mention of the autobiography of V. Y. Mudimbe, born in Likasi in

1941, and who teaches in the United States. Indeed, *Le corps glorieux des mots et des êtres. Essai d'un jardin africain à la bénédictine,* an autobiographical narrative with very high literary and ideological stakes, is the latest link in an already very complex body of work. Beyond the strictly autobiographical dimension of the work, which is somehow justified by and duplicated in the multiplicity of genres deployed in the work, Mudimbe describes in great detail the whole colonial and postcolonial period, including its cultural, social, and economic dimensions, in order to bring out the most important changes that have taken place in the Congo, as well as the ways in which it has opened itself up to a variety of contemporary ideologies, no matter what their provenance (Africa or the rest of the world). The reader is invited to the demythification of the successive credos and loyalties that have shaped a life devoted to university teaching and to writing, first in the Congo/Zaïre and later in the United States, land of exile for a writer who became stateless because of his persistent refusal to serve Mobutu and his regime.

The book rests on a series of contradictions and builds on a foundation of fidelity: Mudimbe, a former Benedictine monk, takes a sudden turn from Catholicism to agnosticism but not without highlighting the moral and intellectual values of the Benedictine order, which have made a lasting impression on his character. The legacy of his Benedictine teachers is best summed up in the saying *Ora et labora,* which continues to shape the author's life in spite of himself. He admits he has no cause to complain, for this golden rule, which has left its stamp on his body and his mind, has given meaning to his existence.

Mudimbe combines the genres of the narrative and of the essay with breathtaking subtlety. Noteworthy for its scope, its form, as well as the positions the author takes, the text brings to light many of the precious links that have formed between Belgium and the Congo without relying on clichés and received ideas. Mudimbe even throws a new light on the colonial era, too often the object of wholesale resentment and rejection. Between the missionary legacy, be it ethnographic, linguistic, sociological, or other, and the specifically Congolese contributions, there is neither rupture nor compartmentalization. One finds instead continuity, interaction, extension, and even enrichment.

The cultural and scientific life of today's and tomorrow's Congo cannot be understood without taking yesterday's signposts into account. This is particularly true of the shadows and lights of the colonial past. Indeed, the colonial ideology has a stronger hold on mentali-

ties than one would care to admit. At the same time, the uses to which
the Congolese have put their legacy, particularly in the case of their
most deserving intellectuals and artists, have ensured that this legacy
remains at the heart of the historical, ideological, and creative processes.

MUST WE CONCLUDE?

Does it follow from the preceding sketches that Belgian and Congolese
memories are involved in a subtle game of mirrors and that similar
methods of selection and repression are in play? Nothing is less certain.
It is nevertheless patent that the literature of the last quarter of the
twentieth century, both by Belgian and by Congolese writers, is characterized by a remarkable immersion in history, including compulsive
returns to the era of Belgian colonization. In particular, one cannot help
but be struck by the clear-headed and critical analyses one finds in the
works of Mpoyi-Buatu (*La re-production*, 1987), Lippert (*Mamiwata*,
1994), and Mudimbe (*Les corps glorieux des mots et des êtres. Essai
d'un jardin africain à la bénédictine*, 1994).

With the benefit of hindsight, it is increasingly apparent that contrary to what has generally been believed, Belgian influence in Central
Africa in general and in the Congo in particular has extended far beyond
the erection of mining, industrial, and manufacturing infrastructures,
not to mention the disease prevention campaigns for which the era is
best remembered. Belgian influence seems to have generated remarkable cultural dynamics that go beyond acculturation. One can reasonably wonder, however, why collective memory has been steeped in
some issues rather than others. Needless to say, the selective character
of memory has a lot to do with this. In any event, nothing is written in
stone. Though the fate of the rejection of the colonial past seemed
sealed in the 1960s, for instance, such was no longer the case at the close
of the twentieth century, when the destitute state of the populations
led to an idealization of colonization, which was suddenly endowed
with all the virtues known to humankind and was almost mythified
into a new golden age, its intrinsic history notwithstanding.

We must further underscore that the sediment that constitutes the
collective memory of peoples is made up in part of clichés which most
of the myths of identity—be they ethnic or national—then build upon.
Needless to say, approximations, dead ends, omissions, and hyperboles
are part and parcel of this phenomenon. References to Belgium's colo-

nial medical policy, for instance, are a perfect example of hyperbolism; it is but an epiphenomenon caused by the unflattering comparison that can be drawn between the old efficiency and today's deficiencies. In such a case, we are dealing with the implementation of a reading grid that has little to do with the adoption of a critical perspective.

Today more than ever, the formation of collective memory must involve the destruction of the blinders that can distort people's perspectives. Only then shall we be able to mark out the signposts necessary for a clear-headed reading of history. This presupposes that we get rid of obsolete thought patterns, that we challenge monolithic methodologies, and that we be wary of going down the slippery slope of simplisms and their share of mirages. Because of its symbolic content, does not collective memory function as a lever for action?

The answer is undeniably yes. Hence the need to protect oneself as much as possible from ideological pollution and its consequences, which are often extremely damaging. A host of historical issues form the background to the war that is currently being waged in the Democratic Republic of the Congo, including questions pertaining to the nature and function of historical references. Indeed some of the protagonists' unstated yet operative aspiration to redraw borders left by colonization is based on an interpretation of the famous Berlin Conference of 1885 that is an approximation at best.

Though critical distance has been set in motion both in the North and the South, in the field of Congolese consciousness, the necessity of an intellectual reorganization based on accurate archival and bibliographical references must be reaffirmed. In the crucial phase through which the Congo is going now, this is not a luxury, but the very condition of a possible exit from the never-ending tunnel of a country in crisis.

—Translated from the French by Catherine Labio

SOPHIE DE SCHAEPDRIJVER

Death Is Elsewhere:
The Shifting Locus of Tragedy in
Belgian Great War Literature

SYNOPSIS

Belgian First World War literature (whether fiction or semifiction, memoirs, poetry, or drama) was, in its early phase, and like much of European war literature, overwhelmingly written in the heroic mode. This heroic mode represented the war as meaningful (if terrible), a crusade for civilization in which Belgium's role was an emblematically valorous one, that of civilization's first champion and martyr in 1914. But the heroic momentum proved hard to sustain over four years of attrition and mass death; and the end of the war proved a bitter anticlimax. The heroic mode gave way to a disillusioned mode of writing about the war, a mode that emphatically rejected the confident use of "1914" shibboleths (such as, precisely, civilization). The war—both trench warfare and life under military occupation—now came to be represented as a degrading experience. The disillusioned representation reached a peak around 1930. This was the time of the "war boom" in Western European literature generally, with disenchantment the dominant mode everywhere. Other Western European literatures however, replacing the heroic with the tragic, were able to persuasively recrystallize around the theme of the condemned generation. Belgian war literature was not. It never quite succeeded in formulating a lasting, compelling vision of doomed Belgian youth. Two factors—one international, one domestic in nature—may account for this elusiveness. The international element is Belgium's loss of status in postwar Europe. Belgium's relatively low death toll provided a jarring contrast to the argument of Belgian victimization that had bolstered the European mobilization rhetoric of 1914—a rhetoric that was now hotly repudiated. Belgium, as a result, utterly lost its tragic aura. The domestic factor is language. In postwar Flemish representation, the "war genera-

YFS 102, *Belgian Memories,* ed. Catherine Labio, © 2002 by Yale University.

94

tion" was re-imagined as split along linguistic lines, with no significant common experience to link Flemings and Francophones.

The Belgian literature of the war failed to stake out a Belgian locus of tragedy. It could not, therefore, serve as a relay-station in Great War memory the way that British, French, and German literature did; it could never become a *lieu de mémoire* [site of memory] in its own right. Consequently, in the present-day Belgian literary imagination, the drama of World War I has moved out of Belgium.

ABSENCE

Two years after the Armistice, Ypres was described by an English observer as "a terrible place still." In and around the devastated town, "death and the ruins completely outweigh the living. . . . There is a pull from the other world, a drag on the heart and spirit. One is ashamed to be alive."[1]

Three generations later, the otherworldly pull of the Ypres Salient, where some of the most deadly battles of the Western Front took place, still tugs at its more impressionable denizens. One of them is Tom Goegebuer, the protagonist of *Nooit meer terug naar Tipperary* (No Way Back To Tipperary), a 1995 semi-autobiographical novel by the Flemish author (and Salient native) Wim Chielens.[2] Goegebuer is both fascinated and suffocated by the intense element of mourning suffusing his home region. Unable to avert his thoughts, he is given to long cycling tours amid its 170 British military cemeteries. Cycling, for Goegebuer, is a form of penance: "The entire mass of the suffering of hundreds of thousands of soldiers seemed to hang from my handle-bar" (86). In his capacity as cemetery guide, Goegebuer one summer afternoon meets a young tourist by the name of Moira, whom to his surprise he finds not only utterly impervious to the solemn accoutrements of British Great War mourning—the Portland stone, the paper poppies, the Kipling epitaphs—but openly hostile to the very notion of *commemoration*. "Fuck your bloody war" reads her furious entry in Lyssenthoek Cemetery's visitors' book. It comes as no surprise to the reader that Moira is Irish. She considers the Irish volunteers of the Flanders campaign to have been, to a man, victims of British imperialism. Her

1. The British travel writer Stephen Graham, in *The Challenge of the Dead* (1921), reprinted in Jon Glover and Jon Silkin, eds., *The Penguin Book of First World War Prose* (London: Penguin, 1990), 82.

2. Wim Chielens, *Nooit meer terug naar Tipperary* (Groot-Bijgaarden, Belgium: Globe, 1995). All translations in this article are mine.

vehemence makes a deep impression on Goegebuer. As the two protagonists embark on a steamy liaison calling for much sampling of local draughts, Goegebuer faces his former ignorance: "For ten years I [used to be] one of those clever, smooth tour guides that sell stories that make no sense, clichés colored by (. . .) the British imperialist vision" (84). (This said, Goegebuer's take on the Irish-at-war tends to be more nuanced, more ironic, and, ultimately, more tragic than his lover's.) The story's dénouement, in which Moira turns out to be an IRA agent on a mission to assassinate the British ambassador, need not detain us here. Suffice it to say that the novel channels the familiar theme of outrage over soldiers' victimization in the Great War toward the case of the Irish, whose deaths represented a kind of apex of absurdity. Finally, and importantly, it should be stressed that, in this Belgian work of World War I fiction, the drama of '14–'18 is located on Belgian soil but not in Belgian experience. The locals—cemetery-guides, inn-keepers—are bystanders: the tragedy is not theirs. Nor, it is suggested, has it ever *been* theirs. The locus of tragedy was never Belgian. At least not rightfully so: Belgium's 1914 role of *casus belli* (to which I will return later) now merely—and mortifyingly—underscores the war's absurdity. "Billy Collins [of the Royal Irish Rifles] only lived to be nineteen, dying as he did one thousand kilometers and two seas away from home. And why? So that I might today be a free Belgian? Oh, pity the history manuals!" (26).

The '14–'18 drama in Xavier Hanotte's subtle, sophisticated 1998 *De secrètes injustices*—part crime mystery, part musing on victimhood and remembrance—is equally focused on the British experience on Flemish soil (minus the Irish element).[3] The novel's protagonist, Barthélemy Dussert, a Brussels police officer investigating a murder, in his free time explores British Great War memory: he translates Wilfred Owen's *Anthem for Doomed Youth,* and makes up biographies of the men buried at the Ramparts Cemetery in Ypres. Like Goegebuer, Dussert is transfixed by the drama of the British experience and by the haunting elegiac culture it generated. Like Goegebuer, he scoffs at the defense-of-gallant-little-Belgium theme that, in 1914, bolstered the British campaign for mobilization. "There are days when I really ask myself what we are doing here. I'm thinking for instance that the Jerries' atrocities must have been much exaggerated. 'Remember Belgium!' said the posters. Remember indeed! Our exchanges with the lo-

3. Xavier Hanotte, *De secrètes injustices* (Paris: Belfond, 1998).

cals tend to be restricted to the pound bills they filch from us for a few beers or cups of bad tea" (399). Thus a dead British soldier's fictional diary entry, which shows how Dussert excludes the Belgian experience from the tragedy of war. Yet, *De secrètes injustices* does offer a strong element of Belgian war drama. It is, however, located in the *next* war. Dussert's murder investigations lead him to the village of Vinkt, north of Ghent, the site of a May 1940 German massacre of Belgian civilians, an event that he discovers is barely commemorated: the memorial monument to the victims of Vinkt is a desultory, mute, and unvisited affair whose "empty symbols convey the absence of an intelligible message" (371). Indeed, one of the novel's characters, a German negationist by the name of Hubermann, sees the very desultoriness of the monument (contrasting so sharply with the urgency of places such as Oradour or Lidice, which are "real *lieux de mémoire*") as proof of Belgians' rightful "malaise" over the Vinkt "myth"—as is the general Belgian amnesia regarding the event (454–58). Dussert is led to question this amnesia. He eventually links the oblivion surrounding Vinkt to the disintegration of the Belgian polity—to the fact that "Belgium" is no longer regarded as a community of fate, and is, moreover, retrospectively redefined as never even having *been* a community of fate. Hence the erasure of all memory regarding the confrontation, which took place at Vinkt, between the *Wehrmacht* and a contingent of *Chasseurs ardennais* (elite Walloon troops). This skirmish caused a small German setback, for which the civilian killings were a retaliation. Hubermann, who is intent on redefining the killings as the *Wehrmacht*'s "just punishment" of local civilian snipers, dismisses the *Chasseurs* episode as myth: given Belgium's artificial nature, it is absurd to imagine Walloon willingness to fight and die on, and for the defense of, Flemish soil (455). And yet, Dussert muses, the *Chasseurs* really did see action in this Flemish village—which may not have asked for it (309). At any rate, they have been forgotten even more than have the civilian dead. A memorial in their honor has unceremoniously been dumped on a street corner, its French inscriptions duly erased; and the street named after them has since been rebaptized Peace Street, a blameless, sanitized name, tasting of oblivion (378).

1914

Given *De secrètes injustices*' main tropes—civilian massacres, World War I, the distortion of memory—what stands out is the absence of references to civilian massacres *in* World War I. This absence reveals the extent to which World War I Belgium has sunk to the status of *non-lieu de mémoire,* even in this novel, which so inspiredly problematizes Belgian war amnesia. Yet, in terms of the circumstances surrounding them, the mass shootings of Belgian civilians by the invading German army in 1914 bear some striking resemblances to the 1940 murders at Vinkt. (Moreover, the interbellum German campaign to justify the killings by allegations of Belgian civilian sniping "prefigures," so to speak, the negationist mission of Hanotte's fictional character Hubermann.) And the 1914 massacres had been, at the time, the Great War's first *cause célèbre.* They vastly enhanced Belgium's international reputation, even in the eyes of those commentators who, like Romain Rolland, refused to credit the war with meaning: Rolland hailed "the heroism of this nation which has uncomplainingly sacrificed itself in order to save its honor" as a sign of the continued existence of idealism in modern times.[4]

In so rhapsodizing, Rolland was in tune with a chorus of contemporaries. The Belgian government's decision to defend the state's neutrality was hailed in Entente discourse (with strong echoes in neutral countries such as the U.S.A.) as a principled defense of the sanctity of international law, and, by extension, as a stand on behalf of civilization itself.[5]

Belgian literary circles in turn were enthralled by the world's admiration. In Brussels in early September, the literary patron Edmond Picard gave a dinner party during which one of the guests recited British parliamentary speeches in praise of Belgium. Greatly moved, Picard briefly entertained the idea of publishing these speeches in brochure form, to be distributed free of charge so as to acquaint the Belgian masses with "the grandiose image of what we have so modestly done

4. In *King Albert's Book: A Tribute to the Belgian King and People from Representative Men and Women Throughout the World* (London: The Daily Telegraph, 1914), 107. On the 1914 massacres and their memory, see the brilliant monograph by John Horne and Alan Kramer, *German Atrocities 1914: A History of Denial* (New Haven: Yale University Press, 2001).

5. Sophie de Schaepdrijver, "Occupation, Propaganda and the Idea of Belgium," in Aviel Roshwald and Richard Stites, eds., *European Culture In the Great War: The Arts, Entertainment, and Propaganda, 1914–1918* (Cambridge: Cambridge University Press, 1999), 267–69, and "Deux patries. La Belgique entre exaltation et regret, 1914–1918," *Cahiers d'histoire du temps présent* 7 (2000): 17–49; see also my *De Groote Oorlog. Het koninkrijk België tijdens de Eerste Wereldoorlog* (The Great War: The Kingdom of Belgium during the First World War) (Amsterdam: Atlas, 1997), 71–72, 87–88, 110–11.

for the honor of Justice and the cult of Liberty!"[6] Three weeks later, Brussels was occupied, and Belgian patriotic discourse was forced underground. The task of representing Belgium's tragic apotheosis fell to Belgian refugees. Among those, the Flemish poet René de Clercq, who had fled to Holland, hit a particularly exalted tone, pushing the theme of Belgium's sacrifice to its soterial limits. In *De zware kroon* (The Heavy Crown), a collection of poems published in early 1915, de Clercq likened Belgium to the Saviour, around whose "crown of thorns" the entire world "in admiration and affection/weaves a laurel crown."[7] The poem *Als de Heiland* (Like the Saviour) specifies the analogy:

> Young and fair
> You have let Yourself be nailed on the Cross
> To Save the World.
> Beads of Your pure blood glisten
> In Your Black crown of thorns,
> O Belgium, God's dearest son!
> . . . .
>
> Yet woe, horrible woe, the fiendish band of torturers,
> . . . standing guard around the corpse.
> The third day you will rise from the grave,
> Young and fair and glorious. [28]

The metaphor of sacrifice and resuscitation also colored Émile Verhaeren's evocation of Belgium's plight. Exiled in France, Verhaeren put his vast international reputation to national service in an intense lecturing and publishing campaign on Belgium's behalf (which ultimately was to cause his death in a 1916 railway accident). In Verhaeren's war prose (as in his poetry), the invasion became "our bloodied Easter feast" ("notre Pâques sanglante"), a moment of national resuscitation. "We simply did our duty and were thereby renewed." The nation's very victimhood elevated it: "Bloodied Belgium ("Belgique sanglante"), may you be loved in all your wounds!"[8] On a less transcendental note, Verhaeren revised his world-embracing lyrical humanism to exclude Germany in his essay "Germany the Uncivilizable" (*Belgique sanglante,*

6. Edmond Picard, *La guerre européo-allemande (4 août 1914–30 juin 1915),* 2 September 1914 (Brussels, *Archives et Musée de la littérature,* AML 2229), vol. 1, 56.

7. René de Clercq, "Belgisch Volkslied" (Belgian National Hymn), in his *De zware kroon* (The Heavy Crown), poems (Bussum, The Netherlands: C. A. J. van Dishoeck, 1915), 50.

8. Emile Verhaeren, "L'âme moderne," in *La Belgique sanglante* (Paris: Nouvelle revue française, 6th ed., 1915), 82–83.

93–104). To Verhaeren, the one-time believer in humanity's radiant future, Germany's main crime was that it had betrayed modernity, representing as it did a throwback to a "feudal" way of thinking, an unenlightened amalgam of obsequiousness and authoritarianism, fear and brutality, characterized in "L'âme moderne" by "the submission of all thought and desire to some putatively sacred end" (*Belgique sanglante*, 150). To this mentality, the *modern* spirit, fresh, future-oriented, inquisitive, critical, and ever eager for renewal and experiment, "made of dignity and freedom, of humane clarity and terrestrial joy, of contagious and nobly dangerous emotion . . . is irreducibly opposed" (151). And the task of defending this modern spirit against "regressive but formidable Germany" had fallen to Belgium, which had risen to the occasion with "simple heroism." (151–52) Retrograde Germany, then, is posited as contrast to Belgium's radiant identity of liberalism's champion/martyr.

This duality was dramatized in a three-act patriotic play by the Nobel Prize laureate Maurice Maeterlinck, titled *Le bourgmestre de Stilmonde*. The play was written in 1917 (possibly in order to revive flagging international indignation over Belgium's past sufferings), premiered to some acclaim in Buenos Aires in 1918, and went on to be produced in Spain, Britain, and the U.S.A., where it was hailed as "the Great War-play."[9] It is set in the small Flemish city of Stilmonde, which is being invaded as the play starts. Its authorities have taken the precaution of confiscating all local weaponry. Still, within hours of the imperial troops' arrival, a German lieutenant is shot. An elderly gardener found in the vicinity is arrested and charged with the murder, of which he is innocent; it is suggested that the officer has been killed by one of his own men in exasperation over the brutal discipline of the German army. The German commander, however, wants retaliation, and threatens to execute the gardener at the end of the day unless the "real" culprit is found. At this point Stilmonde's mayor, a sexagenarian with a passion for horticulture, steps in to vouch for the gardener's innocence, demanding to be executed instead. In a particularly dramatic twist, one of the German officers turns out to be the mayor's son-in-law. He is, however, prevented from intervening on his father-in-law's behalf by the rigidity of the army's rules, to which he ultimately adheres. Inexorably, the valiant burgomaster is executed. His daughter's ensuing, horrified rejection of her German husband elicits a disparag-

9. Maurice Maeterlinck, *Le bourgmestre de Stilmonde* [The Mayor of Stilmonde] (Paris: Edouard-Joseph, 1919), 9.

ing remark from the latter's commanding officer. "You [i.e., the son-in-law] have done your duty . . . It's no use trying to understand . . . These people are all more or less crazy . . ." (178).

And on this note the play ends. It is, of course, a note of utter incompatibility of outlook. *Le bourgmestre de Stilmonde* posits a duality in which Germany is the repository of perniciously retrograde values—aristocratic arrogance, cynical pursuit of power at all costs. By contrast, Belgium, in this drama with its reminiscences of the Burghers of Calais tragedy, embodies liberal, bourgeois ideals. Belgium possesses an unassuming elite whose paternal devotion to its charges and moral rectitude render it worthy of its status, an elite personified by the saintly burgomaster. It is held together not by the quest for dominance, but by the cohesive values of work, exemplified in the mayor and his old gardener's shared love for the patient growing of precious crops such as orchids and hybrid (!) grapes. (Note how this theme obliquely likens all of Belgium to a garden—a luscious garden, admirable yet vulnerable, requiring loving and united tending-to, and, of course, exciting neighbors' greed.) Belgium, finally, signifies a modest but unyielding devotion to honesty and to keeping one's word, which German culture is unable to comprehend. (Or, as the mayor's son-in-law stammers after having witnessed the farewell scene between burgomaster and gardener: "I do not understand any of this . . . A rage for martyrdom, that's all it is . . .," only to be told that what he has seen is no more than a sample of homegrown decency [131].)

Maeterlinck, Verhaeren, and de Clercq were voices in a larger Belgian discourse of war—a discourse that intended to sustain the symbolic momentum of the "Belgian moment" of August 1914, defined as the moment when Belgium, repository of all that was admirable in European civilization, sacrificed itself *for* European civilization. ("Belgium," the historian Godefroid Kurth wrote in 1915, "was, until the third of August of 1914, the garden of European civilization—today, it has become its graveyard."[10]) International admiration could not be allowed to fade. (Its fickleness was foremost in Belgians' minds. "Let's hope it sticks," as Edmond Picard gloomily noted in his diary.[11]) Nor could Belgians be allowed to sink into despondency by ceasing to relate

10. In a polemic study on Germany's attack on Belgian neutrality, posthumously published under the title *Le guet-apens prussien en Belgique* [Prussia's Belgian Trap], with a preface by Cardinal Mercier (Paris: Champion; Brussels: Dewit, 1919), 1.

11. Picard, *La guerre*, vol. 2, 337 (2 December 1914).

their wartime sufferings—whether at the front, in exile, or under occupation—to the 1914 decision for sacrifice. Nor could the heroics of
1914 retrospectively appear as an epiphenomenal outburst. They had
to be shown to obtain over time. Hence the emphasis on continuing
Belgian civilian resistance to the occupying powers. Hence the highlighting of the Belgian army's uphill struggle, from the defense of Liège
to the stand on the Yser.

Meanwhile, among the other belligerents, and especially in Britain,
"Belgium rhetoric" was increasingly made to serve the mobilization
campaign. Indignation over Belgium's plight was kept alive by means
of atrocity lore spiked with gruesome details meant to place Germany
firmly beyond the pale of "civilization," and in which the abstract notion of Germany's "rape" of Belgium's neutrality was replaced by
more rousing stories of Germans' rape of Belgians. Belgium, then, was
symbolically used, so to speak, to "other" Germany; and "Belgium
rhetoric" became part and parcel of the culture of war. But as the body
count increasingly overshadowed the war's original themes, that culture of war came to be rejected, and "Belgium rhetoric" with it. By the
time of the Versailles Treaty, "Belgium," once shorthand for the moral
issues of the war, had become a by-word for war propaganda. At best,
"Belgium" seemed as irrelevant as the notions of bourgeois honor it had
embodied in 1914.

Many Belgians were painfully perplexed by this sudden loss of international prestige. Some responded with indignant attempts to remind the world—or, that failing, their fellow citizens—of Belgium's
past valor. A particularly shrill note was struck in the prize-winning
1921 children's tale *Belgelette.*[12] Its eponymous heroine, a blond little
girl ("not a very little girl, but not a big one, either" [5]), lives quietly
and diligently in her well-tended garden, undisturbed by her uncles/
neighbors, all of whom have pledged never to trespass on Belgelette's
territory—just as she herself has promised never to let anyone through.
Yet one day, uncle Teut, a gloomy woodman who wants to have it out
with garrulous uncle Gaulin, demands to take a short-cut through Belgelette's garden. The little girl refuses and bravely stands up to the
bully. In the process, she is cruelly beaten, and only belatedly joined
in the fight by Gaulin and by the phlegmatic uncle Britt. A long night
of bitter struggle ensues, in which little Belgelette does her bit by

12. A. Misson, *Belgelette. Conte pour les petits belges et pour les grands alliés et pour
vous aussi les boches* [Belgelette: A Tale for Little Belgians, Big Allies, and for You, too,
les boches] (Brussels: Vromant & Cie, 1921).

valiantly chewing away at Teut's ankles. The struggle eventually ends with the entry of formidable Yank. Teut is chased from the garden of Belgelette, who imperturbably resumes her knitting. She receives no comfort from any of her uncles: "You may have thought that this tale would end differently . . . [with] the three grown-ups . . . helping the little girl to rebuild her house and her garden. . . . But each has his own worries and thinks them worse than those of others . . ." (19). Still, Belgelette is no longer the little girl she once was; she has grown into a young woman pinning her blond tresses into a proud *chignon*—and she has become a neighbor to reckon with: "All the world now knows her story, and no-one says, as before: Belgelette . . . who's that? Now they say: here is the spot where she hit Teut full in the face with her little wooden shoe" (22). And so the story ends. The author's bizarre anthropomorphic representation of the world war may serve as an indication of how far meaninglessness had encroached upon the once-confident rhetoric of heroic Belgium.

TWILIGHT

It was a rhetoric that fewer and fewer Belgians wanted to hear. Maeterlinck dismissed his own *Le bourgmestre de Stilmonde* as "only a war and propaganda drama" (Maeterlinck, 9). His compatriots concurred. The play was barely produced and soon forgotten. By common consent, the late Verhaeren's wartime writings were excluded from his literary legacy. (In avant-garde circles, these writings earned him the nickname of "the Belgian Déroulède," a withering quip attributed to André Breton, which rather unfairly placed the late Socialist and internationalist on a par with the French founder of the rabid *Ligue des patriotes*.) Postwar Belgium, to be sure, produced a steady stream of hagiographic writings, which fueled a cult of civilian resistance heroes. But few of these narratives managed to articulately link their protagonists' sufferings to any wider cause of Belgium-at-war. Some fondly imagined the occupation as an ennobling experience, teaching Belgians the values of solidarity, patience, and abnegation, and giving a hitherto materialistic culture a taste of "an internal joy, derived from our voluntary sacrifice, and more intoxicating than all our past satisfactions could ever be."[13] (Note how the terms "internal" and "intoxicating" suggest

13. The novelist and literary critic Georges Rency (pseudonym of Albert Stassart), *La vie matérielle de la Belgique durant la Guerre Mondiale* (Brussels: Bertels, 1920, 2nd. ed., 1924), 381.

a kind of regeneration for its own—and not for Europe's, or civilization's—sake.) Views like these were contradicted by narratives that chose to highlight, by contrast, the myriad compromises and cowardices of life under German rule. A famous example is the 1920 novel *Dans les ténèbres* [In the Shadows] by Alex Pasquier (a lawyer and Picard's protégé), which portrays a well-meaning but weak young officer's wife left to fend for herself in occupied Brussels, described as a place where poignant (but possibly pointless) courage co-exists with war profiteering swathed in patriotism. *Dans les ténèbres* caused something of an uproar over its portrayal of the occupation as essentially a degrading experience, and of occupied Belgium as a cutthroat instead of a harmonious universe.[14]

Like the invasion and the occupation, the Belgian front experience inspired a fair number of narratives written in the heroic mode, works that presented the Belgian campaign as essentially partaking of the 1914 momentum—as essentially a "joyous crusade," after the title of a 1916 memoir by the Antwerp journalist Fritz Francken.[15] Francken described the war as an adventure, embarked upon in a spirit of chivalrous indignation, a spirit sustained even in the face of danger and death, and bolstered by a kind of irrepressible gaiety that Francken imagined as essentially Belgian. Yet Francken's crusade had nothing to say on life in the trenches. More generally, Belgium's heroic front narratives avoided dealing with the immobility of the Western Front following 1914. A 1917 novel with the (telling) title of *La glorieuse retraite* [The Glorious Retreat], written by the poet Maurice Gauchez,[16] presents the swashbuckling tale of the hero's Liège-to-Yser exploits, with, toward the end, a tinge of bafflement over the stalemate.[17] The same inability to imagine trench warfare in the heroic mode characterizes a 1922 memoir entitled *Mes cloîtres dans la tempête*, whose narrative largely ends after the first eight months of war.

Whether in spite or because of this, *Mes cloîtres dans la tempête*

14. Alix (pseudonym of Alex) Pasquier, *Dans les ténèbres. Roman* [In the Shadows: A Novel] (Paris: Eugène Figuière et Cie, n.d. [late 1920 or early 1921]).
15. Fritz Francken (pseudonym of Frederik Clijmans), *De blijde kruisvaart* [The Joyous Crusade] (Antwerp: Janssens, 1919).
16. Maurice Gauchez (pseudonym of Maurice Gilles) in early 1915 enjoyed a fleeting moment of international glory as the author of the very first (though not exactly the best) published battle narrative: *De la Meuse à l'Yser, ce que j'ai vu* (Paris: Fayard, March 1915, with a preface by Henri de Régnier of the Académie française).
17. Maurice Gauchez, *La glorieuse retraite* (London: Librairie moderne, 1917).

[My Cloisters in the Storm] was by far the greatest publishing success ever achieved by a Belgian war book; indeed it was the twenties' most popular war memoir in French. (Among French-language war books, it was outsold only by three novels, Barbusse's *Le feu* [The Fire], Dorgelès' *Les croix de bois* [Wooden Crosses], and René Benjamin's *Gaspard*.)[18] The reason for this popularity may be found in the book's exuberant mix of mysticism and bellicosity. Its author, Martial Lekeux, was an artillery officer turned Franciscan monk turned officer again at the outbreak of the war, and brought both backgrounds to bear on his representation of the war in terms of both self-immolation *and* adventure. Lekeux followed up on the triumph of *Mes cloîtres dans la tempête* with the 1931 *Passeurs d'hommes* [Smugglers of Men], the theme of which is the smuggling line that spirited young men out of occupied Belgium to the Yser army. (Written in an equally dramatic vein, the book was widely read, and even adapted for the cinema.) *Passeurs d'hommes* was expressly intended to counteract the antiwar mentality fueled by the phenomenal success of Erich Maria Remarque's 1929 *All Quiet on the Western Front*. The war, as Lekeux stated in his introduction, had not, *pace* Remarque, been essentially ugly. It had also been an elevating experience, and the present epoch—Lekeux described it as an age of "bars and sports"—was quite mistaken in deriding "four years of idealism" as a waste of time.[19]

1930

Lekeux's "age of bars and sports" was also the time when the Belgian front novel reached what has been described as "a point of pessimistic intensity,"[20] with a small cohort of books written in the disillusioned mode that characterized the 1929–1930 "boom" of war books all over Europe. Some of these Belgian war books had been published earlier to little interest and were presently rushed back into print. The two best-known such reprints are Lucien Christophe's *Aux lueurs du brasier* [By the Light of the Embers] (first published in 1921) and Max Deauville's

---

18. Jean-Norton Cru, *Témoins. Essai d'analyse et de critique des souvenirs de combattants édités en français de 1915 à 1928* (Paris, 1929; reprint Nancy: Les presses universitaires, 1993), 349.

19. Martial Lekeux, *Passeurs d'hommes. Le drame de la frontière 1914–1915* [1931] (New edition with an additional epilogue, Paris: Plon, 1932), 5.

20. Robert Gilsoul, "Le roman historique et le roman de guerre," in Gustav Charlier and Joseph Hanse, eds., *Histoire illustrée des lettres françaises de Belgique* (Brussels: La Renaissance du livre, 1958), 520.

La boue des Flandres [The Mud of Flanders] (first published in 1922).
Both memoirs expressly deal with the experience of stalemate. They
represent different points on a continuum of earnestness-to-sarcasm.
Christophe's tone tends toward the exalted, Deauville's is almost un-
remittingly ironic. Christophe's war is a purifying, Deauville's a pol-
luting experience. For this reason, *Aux lueurs du brasier* has generally
been defined as a more "patriotic," and *La boue des Flandres* as a "paci-
fist" memoir. This perspective, while accurate, overlooks the similar-
ities between both accounts: both find themselves at a loss to define
the purpose of suffering, while not quite being at a point where they re-
ject the Belgian cause as absurd.

The memoir by Christophe, a wartime infantry lieutenant who was
27 when the war ended, starts with notes taken in 1917—a year when
the purpose of Belgium's sacrifice had largely disappeared from sight.
Aux lueurs du brasier tries valiantly to instill a sense of purpose in
trench warfare by likening it to the admirable if unsung task of "keeping the house in order," or to the diligent activity of beavers. (As in *Le
bourgmestre de Stilmonde*, "work" is presented here as Belgium's specific form of honor.) Purpose is sought in the defense of certain intan-
gible values, vaguely defined in terms of bourgeois life-styles: "the
solidity of recognized duties, the polished sweetness of custom, the respect for propriety and habit, cleanliness and decency, the sugar-tong
and the slippers."[21] Christophe, like so many of his contemporaries,
was no longer able to firmly tie wartime suffering to the defense of liberal burgher values, confidently and precisely expressed—such as, for
instance, the rule of law, Belgium's past great cause. As meaning evap-
orates in Christophe's memoir, the Belgian community of sacrifice dis-
integrates. In one dramatic episode, a former volunteer seizes an opportunity to leave the front and join a mission to China. Christophe
does not allow this discouraging development to alter the notion of sacrifice: no, he reassures himself, "one's duty is never done" (173–81,
251). But the wider purpose of "doing one's duty" remains hazy, and
sacrifice becomes its own justification: one must—as Christophe
quotes Baudelaire—be a saint *for one's own sake.* (179, 253)

Max Deauville, a war volunteer like Christophe, though ten years
his senior, saw nineteen months of front-line action as a battalion surgeon before being categorized as an invalid and sent to a Breton hospi-

21. Lucien Christophe, *Aux lueurs du brasier (1917–1920)* (Paris: Albin Michel; Brussels: Labor, 1930), 61.

tal in February 1916. There, he arranged his notes into a memoir of the Belgian campaign between the outbreak of war and November 1915. The resulting book was published in 1917 under the title *Jusqu'à l'Yser.* Its tone of stoic testimony and its attention to detail caused the formidable Jean-Norton Cru, stern critic of war literature, to declare it one of the genre's masterpieces, both from a literary and from a documentary point of view, and by far the war's best testimony by a medical doctor (Cru, 117). In his overview of three hundred French-language war books, Cru ranked *Jusqu'à l'Yser* among the twenty-nine "excellent" ones, and declared that the three best-selling war books in French put together (the aforementioned *Le feu, Les croix de bois,* and *Gaspard*) were not worth Deauville's memoir (570). Meanwhile, as Cru noted with dismay, *Jusqu'à l'Yser* remained virtually unknown in Belgium, where, by Deauville's own admission, it sold a grand total of twelve copies between 1917 and 1937.[22]

The sarcastic tone of Deauville's later memoir, *La boue des Flandres*—a tone Cru deplored as pandering to a postwar taste for antiwar sarcasm—was more appreciated in Belgium,[23] where the book was reprinted to acclaim in 1930. (*Jusqu'à l'Yser* was not.) A special edition of the literary journal *La Nervie,* dedicated to Deauville, opened on this note of praise: "His Muse is a daughter of irony."[24]

La boue des Flandres does indeed, quite trenchantly, skewer the main *bêtes noires* of the disenchanted canon: shirkers, staff officers, uncomprehending civilians. Deauville subverted the heroic mode's awe-filled reference to war volunteers (VDG, or *Volontaire De Guerre*) by using the troops' mocking reference to the conscripted as *Volontaire entre Deux Gendarmes,* "Volunteer between Two Gendarmes."[25] The rhetoric of war is lambasted with equal force. Here, Deauville detects an element of additional irony: the Belgian army's linguistic duality. More than two-thirds of the Yser troops were Flemings with, at best, a

22. Max Deauville (pseudonym of Maurice Duwez), *Dernières fumées* (Brussels: La Renaissance du livre, 1937), 274; Cru, 427.

23. At the time of its first publication, *La boue des Flandres* sold little, but it was awarded a literary prize that, absurdly, it had to share with *Belgelette,* the patriotic children's tale mentioned earlier (Deauville, *Dernières fumées,* 270). The prize committee's decision probably meant to convey impartiality, but instead betrayed the general bafflement of the immediate postwar years as to the meaning of Belgium's wartime experience.

24. Benjamin M. Woodbridge, "Max Deauville," *La Nervie. Revue illustrée d'arts et de lettres, numéro spécial consacré à Max Deauville* (1931): 1.

25. Max Deauville, *La boue des Flandres* (Paris: Librairie Valois, 1930), 17. (*La boue des Flandres* was published in José Germain's famous "Combattants Européens" collection.)

smattering of French, which rendered the Yser army a rather stony soil for the flowering of military eloquence. One scene deftly shows an officer's harangue in high-flown French ("mes braves") being pithily dismissed in unbowdlerized Flemish: "Wa' zegt hé?" "Kom, Jef. T'es niks. Da's allemo kluterij." Loosely translated, this reads: "What's he saying?" "Let's go, Jef. It's nothing. It's all bullshit" (68). Throughout, Deauville returns to the theme of mud, signifying a bogging-down of initial momentum: "Ah! Cursed be the Yser mud, in which our heroism, our enthusiasm, and our loyalty lie dying, the mud in which Belgium's honor rots away together with the one hundred and fifty thousand credulous idiots (*poires*) that defend it" (281, see also 330). This is a telling statement, for it betrays another sentiment besides sarcasm: Deauville has not yet distanced himself from said "honor," for all that he wishes to strip away its aura of glory. And—in very effective shifts from the mode of irony to that of pathos—he invokes a community of soldiers, held together by misery, a disenchanted sense of duty, and a bond with the dead, a community whose claim on the future is couched in Barbussian terms: "Beware. . . . [A] day will come when the trumpets . . . will sound the real war, the holy war of those who have suffered too much" (319).

The ranks as a community of suffering, the soldiers as a community of fate: did a new community come to replace the heroic notion of "Belgium, champion of civilization" once it no longer proved viable? Did the Belgian war generation become a trope in interwar literature?

It was not to be. First of all, the "front generation"—Deauville's *poires*—represented a smaller percentage of Belgian men than it did among the other Western belligerents. As a result of the suddenness of the German invasion, the closing-off of the occupied country, and the difficulties of conscription among the refugees, fewer than 20 per cent of military-age Belgian men were ever mobilized (as against an estimated 54 per cent in Britain, 86 per cent in Germany, and 89 per cent in France). Among the mobilized, losses were fewer than in other armies (a little over 11 per cent, compared to 13 per cent among the British, 14 per cent among the German, and 17.6 per cent among the French mobilized).[26] The Belgian army, to be sure, suffered major losses from the Liège through the Yser battles, and again during the liberation offensive. But during the war of attrition (which in the European post-

26. R. Olbrechts, "La population," in Ernest Mahaim, *La Belgique restaurée. Étude sociologique* (Brussels: Maurice Lamertin, 1926), 3–66, specifically 14–15.

war imagination had come to epitomize the entire conflict), the Belgian front, though hardly a refuge, remained relatively calm. The Yser front was not the theater of "holocausts" such as the Somme, Verdun, or, for that matter, Passchendaele, fought on Belgian soil, but not by Belgians. (Once during the postwar reparations talks, an exasperated Lloyd George saw fit to throw the number of British soldiers buried in Flanders in the face of the Belgian delegate.[27]) More generally, the discrepancy between the "Belgian sacrifice" hyperbole of 1914 and the extent of actual Belgian losses was not lost on international opinion. Belgians duly registered this loss of world respect. By 1917, as Christophe's memoir noted, the acclamations had died down. Worse, the Belgians were considered the shirkers (*embusqués*) of the Western front, a charge which *Aux lueurs du brasier* persistently refutes, positing time and again the specificity of Belgian misery and the importance of Belgian sacrifice. The Belgians-at-war, as Christophe forlornly explains, only *seem to be* shirkers because, cut off from their homefront as they are, they are, quite simply, more visible when at rest. "A Belgian, wherever he is, people will ask what he's doing there" (26). Present exile derives from past sacrifice. "Back then, we had the honor of dying first. And ever since, we have been the vagabonds of our sacrifice. But how do you expect foreigners to understand this if we ourselves have forgotten it?" (31).

But *Aux lueurs du brasier*'s efforts to define a specifically Belgian category of heroism/misery were ultimately doomed to pale in the face of the crushing fact that France—Christophe's spiritual homeland— had lost one out of six men of military age; Belgium, one out of fifty. The disproportion was known in postwar Belgium.[28] Christophe's reactions to it are not documented. But his later work signifies a shift away from the Yser, and away from the Belgian war generation: in the person of Péguy, "proud fighter whose voice counsels me still" (204), Christophe found a locus of tragedy and of literary inspiration.[29] Péguy became the ageing Christophe's ultimate trope of heroism. "He liked

27. Sally Marks, *Innocent Abroad: Belgium at the Paris Peace Conference of 1919* (Chapel Hill, N.C.: The University of North Carolina Press, 1981), 187.

28. The figures are from Mahaim, *La Belgique restaurée*.

29. As evidenced in *L'ode à Péguy* (Brussels: Éditions des artistes, 1942), an essayistic trilogy in prose and verse written between 1915 and 1941. See also *Le jeune homme Péguy. De la source au fleuve, 1897–1905*, and *Les grandes heures de Charles Péguy. Du fleuve à la mer 1905–1914* (Brussels: La Renaissance du livre, 1964). Christophe also wrote the introduction to the catalogue of a Péguy exhibition held in Brussels in 1958 (Auguste Martin, *Charles Péguy* [Brussels: Laconti, 1958]).

to say that the cult of Péguy had been his life's honor," as Christophe's biographer recalls.[30] Killed in 1914, Péguy eternally partook of what was remembered as that year's idealist purity, unsullied by attrition and doubt. And his death in a field of beets on the Marne offered an image of the entire French front as one immense stretch of sacrifice, not so much dwarfing the Yser as rendering it irrelevant as a site of mourning per se.

Meanwhile, to the extent that the Yser was indeed considered relevant as a site of mourning, it was as an *anti-Belgian* site of mourning. The year 1930 was also the year of the inauguration (in Diksmuide, the former Belgian front's most dangerous sector) of a concrete monument known as the Yser Tower. Fifty meters high, it loomed dramatically over the Yser plain. Its cruciform top bore the inscription AVV/VVK, an abbreviation of the slogan "Alles Voor Vlaanderen—Vlaanderen Voor Kristus" ("Everything for Flanders—Flanders for Christ"). Another dedication quoted verse by the priest-poet Cyriel Verschaeve: "Here lie their remains, like seed in the sand/Hope for thy Harvest, Oh Flanders Land." The message of the memorial was clear: it posthumously removed the Flemings among the Belgian dead from Belgian commemoration. Moreover, it redefined their deaths as sacrifices for Flanders, with that sacrifice's "harvest" necessarily spelling the end of Belgium. In short, the Yser Tower was as bluntly an anti-Belgian memorial as could be devised by the fiercely separatist Flemish-nationalist culture of that time. This was a minority culture to be sure, even within Flanders, but it commanded a dedicated following among the small-town Catholic middle classes. This culture owed much of its *Belgica delenda est*-vehemence to the influence of a particular milieu that had emerged during the occupation. This was the milieu of so-called "activism"—a movement that had chosen compliance with the occupation regime so as to further the Flemish-nationalist program. (Incidentally, the aforementioned patriotic poet René de Clercq "crossed over" to activism in the course of the war, and in so doing substituted Flanders for Belgium in his poetic image of the Saviour.[31]) Because of its radical anti-Belgian slant, the Flemish-nationalist commemoration of war derived its heroic momentum from the memory of collaboration, rather than from that of the front. This is very clearly expressed in a bestselling 1927 novel with the title of *Eer Vlaanderen vergaat* (Before

30. Marcel Lobet, "Lucien Christophe (1891–1975)," in *Nouvelle Biographie Nationale de Belgique* (Brussels, 1990), vol. 2, 85.

31. De Schaepdrijver, "Occupation," 291–92.

Flanders Perishes), written by the former gunner Joseph Simons. In this novel, the war is imagined as a kind of moment of truth for embattled Flanders. The novel's protagonist, a young Flemish aristocrat named Florimond van Laar, discovers the Flemish cause in the trenches, and urges revolt. But it is the declaration of Flemish independence in occupied Belgium by the activist "Council of Flanders" (in reality, a puppet government set up by the occupation authorities) in February 1918 that stings van Laar into action: "Now or never!"[32] He presses his fellow Flemish soldiers to cross the lines to join activism, which he defines as the only movement that shows the world "that there are still Flemings, that there is a Flanders in Belgium" (225). But van Laar's fervent harangues to the "Yser Flemings" to "crawl out of the mud of the blood trenches" to join the "light" that is activism (231), are defeated by his fellow soldiers' pusillanimity. And so, as a prophetic chaplain (possibly modeled after Verschaeve) explains at the end of the novel, "One chance has been passed up. . . . But the activists have sown the seed of independence in Flanders, which the enemy will never be able to destroy" (325).

This redefinition of the war as a "Flemish moment" (if a failed one) did not become the dominant Flemish view overnight, given the bitterly contested nature of its recasting of collaborationism as revolutionary idealism. Nor was the step from language to separate mourning an unproblematic one: the majority of Flemings, in the interwar years, still more or less shared in a "pan-Belgian" war memory, not heeding the Yser Tower Committee's call to commemorate the Flemish dead *qua* Flemish dead. In the less political works of Flemish front literature, the issue of language discrimination in the Yser army merged into a more general Belgian—indeed European—theme of soldiers' victimization. The radical nationalist myth of Flemish soldiers' dying because they did not understand French orders and signs—such as "Danger de mort"—is not echoed anywhere in Flemish veterans' literature.[33]

Still, the vexations of language at the Belgian front were present in all but the most blithely cheerful Flemish accounts—and absent from even the sharpest Francophone ones. No account ever bridged this gap in perspective. Nor did translations enable the Francophone reading

32. Joseph Simons, *Eer Vlaanderen vergaat* [1927] (Turnhout: Van Mierlo; Brussels: Gudrun, 1936), 196.

33. Frederik Deflo, *De literaire oorlog. De Vlaamse prozaliteratuur over de Eerste Wereldoorlog, Kreatief* 32/3–4 (October 1998): 64–65, 68.

public—overwhelmingly ignorant of Dutch—to acquire a view across the language barrier: not a single item of Flemish First World War writing ever made it into French.[34] Language, then, ultimately contributed to the impossibility of durably imagining the Belgian war generation as a community of fate.

SILENCE

At one point in Xavier Hanotte's *De secrètes injustices,* Inspector Dussert's murder inquiries lead him to the home of an elderly *Chasseur ardennais,* eyewitness to the 1940 massacre at Vinkt. The old man smiles ironically at Dussert's disapproving suggestion that "no great fuss was ever made" over Vinkt. "This country has no history, monsieur Dussert. All it has is a few snippets of folklore, a multitude of particular little myths that do not interlock. It lives in a kind of perpetual present. No wonder, then, that it possesses no memory, either" (339).

The memory of Belgium's Great War experience partakes of this disintegration. Constructing a coherent memory of the war has, to be sure, proven a daunting task for all of the cultures involved, and an impossible one for some. In his study of World War I as a shift in European culture, Modris Eksteins has noted postwar historians' incapacity to, so to speak, memorialize the war, defeated as they were by the bewildering disproportion between massive suffering and minor stakes. It was up to literature, Eksteins states, to break the silence; literature transcended bafflement by defining the war generation as tragic.[35] In thus erecting a memorial for the war generation, the literature of World War I subsequently grew into a *lieu de mémoire* of its own.

The Belgian literature of the war, however, never grew into what might be called a "relay-station" for Belgian Great War memory. And it certainly did not enter the European '14–'18 canon, despite, or rather because of, the reverberations of "1914," a moment never successfully redefined as tragic (as opposed to heroic), and hence a memory irrecuperably caught up in the repudiated hyperbole of war culture. Even the unique experience of occupation failed to engender a distinct voice: no Belgian narrative of "life inside" ever reached the complexity of Maxence Van Der Meersch's *Invasion 14,* a 1935 novel of life in the occu-

34. Although Simons' novel, not surprisingly, was translated into German under the title of *Flandern stirbt nicht. Das flämische Fronterlebnis* (Flanders Does Not Die: The Flemish Experience of the Front) (Wolfshagen: Westphal, 1937, with a reprint in 1942).

35. Modris Eksteins, *Rites of Spring: The Great War and the Birth of the Modern Age* (London-New York: Bantam, 1989), Chapter 9, "Memory."

pied French North. Georges Eekhoud, one of the most prestigious Belgian novelists of his time, briefly considered collaboration as the subject of a war novel: "What a beautiful book, beautiful yet majestically bitter, satiric, poignant and tragic, one could write under the title of 'The Activists.'"[36] But Eekhoud ultimately retreated to prose of a more "picaro-romantic and deliberately anachronistic" (his words) nature.[37] And as to the Belgian front generation: it did not, in the postwar imagination, rise to the status of a remembered community of fate, because it was considered neither, so to speak, sufficiently *fated* nor enough of a *community.*

Contemporary Belgian literature on 1914–1918, consequently, tends to seek its tropes of tragedy outside Belgium. This holds even for the comic strip, the alleged Belgian form par excellence, as evidenced by *Henry's Diary,* a dramatic antiwar story by the young Belgian comic strip artist Philippe Glogowski, which narrates the front experience of a British infantryman in the Salient.[38] Xavier Hanotte's latest war novel, the 2000 *Derrière la colline,* is a tragic tale of friendship and mourning centered on the battle of the Somme, seen from the point of view of a fictional poet enlisted in a "Pals' Batallion" from Salford, Lancashire.[39] Wim Chielens and his brother Piet, who directs the In Flanders Fields Museum in Ypres (the name, of course, hails from the John McRae poem), in 1996 published a knowledgeable literary guide to the Salient, written as a kind of epistolary commentary on British war literature. There is no equivalent guide to the Belgian front.[40] As a last, and particularly dramatic, example of the absence of the Belgian war experience in a modern Belgian novel, I want to cite Pierre Mertens' highly acclaimed 1987 *Les éblouissements.* This semifictional biography of the expressionist poet Gottfried Benn, though it dwells on the German occupation of Brussels, sees it uniquely through the lens of Benn's experience—as a lesson in futility and hence a major way-station on the poet's journey inward.[41] (Occupied Brussels was a "rest and

36. Georges Eekhoud, *Journal,* 24 November 1918 (manuscript, Brussels, *Archives et Musée de la Littérature,* AML 2954), notebook 19, 48.

37. Mirande Lucien, *Eekhoud le rauque* (Villeneuve d'Ascq: Presses Universitaires du Septentrion, 1999), 193.

38. Philippe Glogowski, *Henry's Diary* (Marche: Editions Vanther/Ypres: In Flanders Fields Museum, 1999). This album has been published in French, Dutch, and English.

39. Xavier Hanotte, *Derrière la colline* (Paris: Belfond, 2000).

40. Piet and Wim Chielens, *De troost van schoonheid. De literaire Salient (Ieper 1914–1918)* (The Consolation of Beauty: The Literary Salient [Ypres 1914–1918]) (Groot-Bijgaarden: Globe, 1996).

41. Pierre Mertens, *Les éblouissements* (Paris: Seuil, 1987).

recreation" area for the German troops; Benn, a dermatologist, was in charge of army venereal inspection. In his capacity as military surgeon, Benn conducted the post-mortem examination of Nurse Edith Cavell, executed in 1915—another exercise in alienation.) In addition to Benn's journey inward, the chapter on his occupation years offers a kind of inventory of modern foreign writers' passages through Brussels, enumerated during a conversation between German literati. A genuflection to the past presence of Verlaine *et les autres* that ultimately suggests Brussels' *raison d'être* to be the need for external literary confirmation. Even Mertens' own literary persona as a Belgian writer—an identity imagined as rewardingly ambiguous by nature of its Belgianness—appears to need some kind of outside sanction, as evidenced by Mertens' Musilian identification as a failed "inhabitant of Kakania."[42] At the end of the day, in the Belgian literary imagination, even ambiguities reside more interestingly—more *tragically*—elsewhere.

---

42. Vincent Landel, "Pierre Mertens ou le roman hors-la-loi," *Magazine littéraire* 273 (January 1990): 66.

MARC QUAGHEBEUR

The Sixteenth Century:
A Decisive Myth

Historical approaches to the study of a literary corpus take into account, among other things, its handling of universal and local myths as
well as individual depictions of actual persons. In this respect the evocation of the sixteenth century occupies a rather privileged position in
Belgian letters. In particular, the role played by someone as important
as emperor Charles V in the imaginary of the country's Francophone
literary production is quite remarkable, sitting as it does on the border
between, on the one hand, the kind of mythologization that obtains in
the case of prominent individuals who are customarily viewed as having failed in some way—as with Charles V's grandfather, Charles the
Bold,—and, on the other, the indexing that occurs independently of any
imaginary fabulation when a person's name is routinely used as a ref-
erent to a glorious past—as with other "successful" personages like
Philip the Good in the old Netherlands and Leopold II in modern-day
Belgium.

The reason behind this is that the century of Charles V (1500–1558)
gave birth to two very different moments. The first was the apogee of
the old Netherlands to which he gave, thanks to the Transaction of
Augsbourg (1548) and the Pragmatic Sanction (1549), the means of their
autonomy, including constitutions we would now refer to as federal,
and a unified system of dynastic succession. On the other hand, the century also witnessed, and did so very quickly, the breakup into northern
and southern Netherlands of the Circle of Burgundy, which had fulfilled both their greatness and their century-old struggle against the
ambitions of France.[1] This conflict then set against each other Philip

---

1. [Note from the translator: The Circle of Burgundy included the ten southern and
the seven northern provinces of the Netherlands.]

YFS 102, *Belgian Memories*, ed. Catherine Labio, © 2002 by Yale University.

II, legitimate son of the old emperor, who had been raised in Spain, and William of Orange, a prince whom Charles V had trained in his *pays de par deça* during the last twelve years of his reign and on whose shoulder he leaned as he walked down the ancient hall of the palace of Brussels at the time of his abdication.[2]

When came the nineteenth century, with its nationalistic subspecies of romanticism, it is from the well of their memory of the sixteenth century that Belgium's literary imagination, its collective imaginary, and a significant share of its national historical investigations drew one of the myths—if not the central myth—crucial to the making of its national identity. This occurred both before and after the revolutionary days of August and September 1830, which saw Belgium spoil the Treaty of Vienna's attempt to recreate between France and Germany a space roughly equivalent to that which had been occupied by the patrimonial Estates of the seventh Duke of Burgundy.[3]

THE MYTHIFICATION
OF THE SIXTEENTH CENTURY

This emergent and dynamic myth was meant to promote liberty and affirm its popular roots. Yet, it had to do so while laboring under the constraints of a necessarily manichean logic. It did, on the one hand, sometimes celebrate the Netherlands (*Pays d'en bas*) of the turn of the sixteenth century as a kind of earthly paradise.[4] Such a characterization reflected the wealth of the Netherlands, the density of their population, and their remarkable economic, political, and artistic development. The myth also made it possible for the persona of the Belgian—known as the *gueux* (beggar)—to emerge.[5] The *gueux* is a fearless and intractable rebel with a noble and generous soul. He is deprived of the means of repression and cares about the freedom of his own people.

2. [Note from the translator: *pays de par deça* was a quasi-official way of referring to the old Netherlands]

3. [Note from the translator: namely Charles V, who was proclaimed Duke of Burgundy in 1515.]

4. [Note from the translator: *Pays d'en bas* is an old synonym of *Pays-Bas*. It refers to all of the old Netherlands, from Arras and Luxemburg to Friesland.]

5. *Gueux* is the name supposedly given by Comte de Berlaymont to the aristocrats who had come to give a petition dealing with the Inquisition—the so-called Compromise of the Nobles—to Margaret of Parma, eldest daughter of Charles V, and regent of the Netherlands. This label, which they then chose to claim for themselves, also designates the heroes of the combats that took place later, on sea and land, against the Spanish army and eventually resulted in the independence of the northern Netherlands.

Conversely, however, the myth of the sixteenth century also conjured up, quite logically, the image of the tyrant and his henchmen. The targets of this execration are, of course, Philip II of Spain—whose reign saw the rebellion and partition of the old Netherlands—and his illustrious second-in-command, Ferdinand Alvarez de Toledo, Duke of Alba.

The reader will immediately have gathered that the figure of Charles V intersects with—and serves as a counterpoint to—this complex set of images. Not only was he the last natural prince to have been born in what is now Belgium before the birth of the future Leopold II in 1835, it was also under his reign that the old Netherlands and their symbols, the towns of Antwerp and Brussels, would know their greatest splendor.[6] At the same time, he was also the father of Philip II and the defender of that Catholic faith in whose name his son would intend to punish.

The nineteenth-century glorification of independence and the rapid and extraordinarily successful industrialization of the new Belgian state made nineteenth-century elites want to project themselves back into an earlier era, also characterized by expansionism, growth, and wealth, and of which Charles V was seen as a symbol. Needless to say, this intensified the ambiguity of this mythical figure since these same elites also tended to interpret the political and religious conflicts of the sixteenth century in light of nineteenth-century struggles for or against democratic freedoms and freedom of thought. This complex set of circumstances led people to modulate some of the emperor's features. By contrast, the image of Philip II would always be confined—unequivocally and for all Belgians—to the stock narratives and clichés of his legend.

It is equally clear that Belgians came out of this mythical reconstitution of the past looking above all like the victims of an unjust and fanatical larger foreign country. This image would be recycled freely and abundantly during World War I, sometimes by means of a simple reworking of the texts and images that had grown out of the tragedies of the sixteenth century. One of Maeterlinck's earliest writings, "Le massacre des innocents" (1886), was thus reinserted in 1916 in Les débris de la guerre by the man who had won the Nobel Prize for literature in 1911. The first nineteen paragraphs of the narrative have disappeared.

6. [Note from the translator: Charles V was born in Ghent in 1500 and died in Yuste (Spain) in 1558.]

The new version begins with the arrival of a troop of armed men, "the Spaniards," who are surrounding their leader, "an elderly man with a white beard," which is a customary description of the Duke of Alba.[7]

Spain was the Other of nineteenth-century Belgium. It was the incarnation of disaster and oppression, and of the tyranny inflicted upon a people who were only asking to live and enjoy life to the fullest and cared not a whit for the historical stakes that had entrapped them. Such representations, from which fictional texts freely drew—often by exacerbating this dualism in the most extreme manner possible—can by and large also be found in the writings of nineteenth-century historians, both Catholic and Voltairian. This overwhelming convergence between the scholar's discourse and the writer's fable demonstrates what an intense hold these representations had on the Belgian collective imaginary, traces of which it retains to this day.

As a result, the image of Spain in Belgian letters necessarily came to be dominated by the so-called "black legend," an image that pervades nineteenth-century European perceptions of the Iberian peninsula. In its specifically Belgian version, however, it was also accompanied by the celebration of Belgium as the land of milk and honey (*pays de Cocagne*), by explorations of the differences between the time of Charles V and the reign of Philip II, and by the exponential growth of the iconic figure of the *gueux*.

BEFORE INDEPENDENCE: A HISTORIAN MAKES FICTION COME ALIVE

The specifically Belgian version of this imaginary, collective, and literary dynamic—especially as it pertains to the myth of the *gueux*—played itself out as early as 1827, i.e., three years before the independence of Belgium, in *Les gueux de mer* by Henri Moke (1803–1862), a historian and university professor whose publications would later include his *Histoire de la Belgique* (1839–1841). The subtitle of this good historical novel is a story unto itself: *Ou la Belgique sous le duc d'Albe.* The following year, Moke struck again with a tale that was less accomplished, but had the merit of focusing on another facet of the rebellion. This work, *Le gueux des bois ou les patriotes belges de 1566*, is set in the woods that sheltered protestants and others. The main ingredients of the myth of the sixteenth century are already clustered in this diptych.

7. Maurice Maeterlinck, *Les débris de la guerre* (Paris: Charpentier, 1916), 131.

Moke's prefaces are rather understated. In the introduction to *Les gueux de mer* he remarks that his goal is to present readers with a work devoted to an earlier "glorious era for Belgium" and to either remind or inform them of the excesses of the oppression inflicted upon the unhappy provinces by a foreign government.[8] Concerned with "historical probability" in his portrayal of important figures, Moke wished to avoid being overly partisan. He believed that all parties were guilty of excesses and condemned them equally vehemently. Moreover, he also clearly stated his intention to treat "virtuous men of all persuasions and faiths" fairly, in part in order to make his depictions of Philip II, the Duke of Alba, and William of Orange all the more interesting.

The *Introduction* to *Le gueux des bois* (1828) is more learned and partisan. It is also remarkably indicative of the difficulties Belgians encountered when they tried to make themselves heard in the concert of the European nations. Moke reminds us that in the sixteenth century, the Netherlands showed the world

> a sight such as [it] had never seen: that of a free, opulent, peaceful, and respected state. When a sovereign, whose name shall forever be odious and who steeped half of Europe in blood, decided to substitute his despotism for national laws, he met with a surprising form of opposition from the Belgians, inasmuch as it was first and foremost deferential and reasonable and was always lawful. Europe understood only dimly the nature of the slow and deliberate course of action adopted by this free people. Europeans could grasp the concept of armed rebellion, but they could not conceive of such an unusual form of opposition, which relied on political representation, acted without moving, and was grounded in patriotism.[9]

As a result, this preliberal revolution remained "hidden under an impenetrable veil," its heroes "utterly misunderstood" by Schiller in spite of the fact that he was himself a liberal (12). Moke's goal was instead to remind his readers of the greatness of these Belgian heroes by relying on the writings of one of their adversaries, the Italian jesuit Strada.

Because of this evenhanded writing, of which one finds other examples in *Le roman d'un géologue* (1874) by Xavier de Reul (1830–1895) and in *Dom Placide* (1875) by Eugène Van Bemmel (1824–1880), the clarity of Moke's condemnation did not tip over into the kind of

8. Henri G. Moke, *Les gueux de mer* (Brussels: Office de Publicité, 1927). All the quotes in this paragraph are from pages v–vi.

9. Henri G. Moke, *Le gueux des bois* (Brussels: Lebègue, 1898), 11.

phantasmagoric intensity that would eventually set Charles De Coster's style apart. Moke's work was much more nuanced. His Duke of Alba is not just a man whose features "revealed his pride, ambition, and bloodthirstiness" and whose "bulging lip had something livid and hideous about it" (148). The Duke also shows affection for Don Alonzo, who is an illegitimate son born of Alba's love for a black Christian woman and who dies while fiercely defending two women from a band of drunken soldiers.

Moke's subtler portrayal accounts for the surprising episode at the end of the novel. As Louis de Winchestre, grandson of Jean de Bruges and Lord of Gruthuyse (one of the most important families in the service of the House of Burgundy), and a declared ally of the prince of Orange, is about to marry Marguerite de Waldeghem, the Duke of Alba suddenly appears on the scene.[10] Knowing that Louis tried, chivalrously yet unsuccessfully, to save Don Alonzo, Alba asks him about his son's final moments. Louis, we are told, "felt sorry for [Alonzo's] father, but did not blame him" (225). Alba then adds that he knows Louis both as a rebel and as the man who was once dear to his son. He then grants Louis his freedom, but not without demanding that he cease to bear arms against Philip II. A short while later, the newlyweds meet the Duke in the Hainaut, as he makes his way to Italy. He hopes they will be able to stay in the "*belle patrie*" he has been unable to keep for his king and adds that no one will succeed where the king's greatest general has failed. This allows Moke to launch into a grand finale in favor of the House of Orange and its liberal and patriotic king, to whom Belgians would, in one of those twists and ironies of history, mete out a fate comparable to Philip II's only three years later.

This is not the most significant aspect of the work with respect to the question of myth formation. Whereas Moke tries to humanize the man who has done Philip II's dirty work, the king is represented as utterly repulsive and spineless. This is characteristic of the way in which Philip II has been remembered throughout the entire history of the Belgian literary tradition, a phenomenon that emerged precisely at the time when what one can reasonably call a national consciousness was beginning to take shape.

All the scenes in which Philip II appears are highly colorful and con-

10. In an earlier scene, Louis, disguised as a sailor, had grabbed and tossed out the window a glass raised by the Duke of Alba as he toasted the humiliation of the prince of Orange and the capture of Flessingue. Instead of revealing his identity, Louis declares: "I am Belgian . . . ; this word alone can justify my behavior" (*Gueux des bois*, 25).

tribute to his denigration.[11] This is true of the scene in which Louis de Winchestre saves the Queen of Spain from being murdered by henchmen intent on assassinating her because of her alleged involvement with heretics, of the descent into the cellars of the Inquisition, and of the torture of an innocent elderly monk carried out in the king's presence. In every instance, the king of Spain is defined by the harsh accents of the black legend, or, more accurately, by those features and those features only, which bring out, in counterpoint, the nobility of the Belgian(s).

THE EARLY DAYS

While dreaming of Belgium—as the word was understood in its sixteenth-century Latin version and as it was briefly configured in nineteenth-century Netherlands—*Les gueux de mer* put together the episodes, figures, and topoi of the sixteenth-century myth on which an independent Belgium fed, a phenomenon that eventually led to the publication of De Coster's masterpiece some forty years later. Moke worked from his own liberal and national perspective. This accounts for the care he took with historical accuracy in his depiction of important figures as well as for his inclusion within the fabric of the narrative of novelistic touches that were meant to affect readers (the pure yet cheerful maiden; the bold and sincere young man, and so on). The presence of older characters, who bear witness to the world of Charles V and to an earlier age of happiness without lacking in either courage or lucidity, adds another touch to Moke's double framework.

We find similar elements, along with a correspondingly complex depiction of the religious situation of the time, in the writings of Baron Jules de Saint-Genois (1813–1867), including *Hembyse,* a three-volume novel published in 1835 and one of the literary successes of the years immediately following Belgium's independence. This time the story takes place in Ghent between 1577 and 1584. It depicts the troubled period that stretches from the Pacification of Ghent to the Peace of Religion to the Spanish recapture of the city by Alessandro Farnese in 1578.[12] It retraces the fortunes of the first magistrate of Ghent, Jonc-

---

11. Moke underscores, in a note to chapter 30, that most of the words spoken by Philip II in the novel come from historical sources, especially Gregorio Leti's *La vie de Philippe II.*

12. [Note from the translator: the Pacification of Ghent (1576) was an agreement reached by the southern provinces of the Netherlands and the provinces of Holland and Zeeland, aimed at driving the Spanish from the country. The Peace of Religion (1577) was

ker Jan Hembyse. He is portrayed as close to Protestants and as having stood for town freedoms (*libertés communales*) at one point, but also as someone who is spiteful and highly ambitious. He is eventually exiled, then called back when the time comes for the Spaniards to go home. Old secret negotiations are discovered before he is able to regain his power, however, which provokes the anger of the people, who have him decapitated. All this takes place the same year that William of Orange was murdered and the Duke of Anjou, heir to the throne of France, was poisoned.

De Saint-Genois ends his narrative on a critical turning point in the history of the southern Netherlands, the era during which the future that would eventually give birth to Belgium in the modern sense took shape. He makes sure to include a meeting between Hembyse and one of his brothers, who has come in vain to offer him some poison before his execution. His exhortation takes up the topoi we have already located in Moke's work: "Brother, remember your ancestors and their unblemished reputations, remember your son, the *gueux de mer*, who bravely threw himself into the sea, saying: 'I would rather perish thus than lose my life shamefully by the hands of the executioner.'"[13] What we are witnessing here, of course, is the defeat of the southern Netherlands, but not the annihilation of the noble spirit that had sustained the rebellion. De Coster will remember this.

Fifty-five pages of notes and historical documents are included in the third volume of *Hembyse*. They validate the decision to situate "the novel in a historical context, fiction in reality, invention in truth" in the manner of "Walter Scott" and "Jacob, the Bibliophile" (1:xi). Additionally, as with Moke or Scott, the narrative also relies on fiction by including a story of pure love.

This combination was also used by Felix Bogaerts (1805–1851) in his novel, *El Maestro del campo* (1839), in which fiction plays a more significant role. The narrative is also set in Ghent, this time toward the end of the pivotal year 1567, i.e., at the height of the repression by the Duke of Alba. The relative ambiguity of his representative, the Maestro of the title, stems from his affection for Don Juan, a son no one knows of and who serves under him. Don Juan falls in love with Maria Hernandez, the daughter of an excellent old man, who is originally

---

an agreement, reached between Catholics and Protestants, that lay the groundwork for religious tolerance.]

13. Baron Jules de Saint-Genois, *Hembyse* (Brussels: J. P. Méline, 1835), 3:135.

from Aragon. Robbed some time ago of his possessions, he had temporarily settled in Antwerp to make up his losses by taking advantage of the economic opportunities it offered. The old man despises "the wretched prejudice that forbade nobles to engage in commerce, under penalty of degradation."[14] His participation in the "brilliant speculations whose yields had brought Antwerp to the height of prosperity since the beginning of the sixteenth century" have enabled him to accumulate a new fortune and leave "the Corinth of Belgium" for Ghent, where he is forever engaging in acts of charity (12–13). Long on close terms with Count Egmont, he has adopted the same principle Egmont had during the troubles: "although he was a Spaniard, he could not bear the despotism the Madrid Court was practicing and wanted to maintain in our country; he ardently wished for all to have the right to freedom of conscience and was very vocal in his condemnation of the absurd and cruel rigors of Philip II" (13–14).

A poet's rather than a historian's novel, Bogaerts' fiction no longer hinges on the demonstrated authenticity of a series of events or characters. Against a background less rigid in matters of historical verisimilitude than his predecessors', he means to test fiction's limits and to engage in an intense and fantastical evocation of something tradition will eventually identify as "the Spanish fury" in reference to another episode in Flemish history. For the first time, Bogaerts' novel depicts a devouring process that sweeps even the best people away and does not have any kind of happy ending. Still, this book endows the major Spanish characters with genuine complexity and highlights the wisdom, strength of character, and physical vigor of the old men Maeterlinck would turn into a freestanding myth some fifty years later. It also brings back the figure of Count Egmont in a *pas de deux* with that of William the Silent, whose distant descendants would be driven out of Belgium after the revolution of September 1830.

The year is, after all, 1839. William of Holland is finally ratifying the independence of Belgium in exchange for the retrocession of the future Grand Duchy of Luxembourg and the Dutch province of Limburg. The heyday of unionism is coming to an end now that the alliance between Catholics and secularists has lost some of its *raison d'être*. During the phase that followed in domestic politics—a phase marked by a succession of liberal governments and that lasted, minus some significant interruptions, from 1847 to 1884—not only would the myth of

14. Felix Bogaerts, *El Maestro del campo* (Antwerp: J.-M. Jacobs fils, 1839), 12–13.

the sixteenth century endure, it would also generate its first great literary accomplishment. The birth of De Coster's masterpiece, *La légende d'Ulenspiegel*, would, however, be preceded by the publication of a number of other texts that drew heavily on the same material and inflect it in ways we shall come across again in *La légende*. The publication of these texts is contemporaneous with the exceptional work done by historians at the time, work that gave rise to numerous publications, including a number of primary sources.

Two plays appeared in the years before the publication of *La légende*. The first, *Philippe II et Don Carlos* by Clément Michaëls fils (1821–1887), already in 1863, that is, some forty years before the publication of Verhaeren's own *Philippe II* of 1901, dealt with the theme that Schiller had popularized and that Verdi would immortalize four years later. In the brief preface, Michaëls argues that the damned person of the whole affair is not the king, but Antonio Pérez, his secretary and confidant. This, however, is not necessarily accompanied by a positive depiction of Philip II, who is portrayed as a vain political puppet. The picture of the king accentuates features we have already spotted in the works of other writers: extreme indecision, endless paranoia, vanity, will to omnipotence, and submission to the Church and to the most nefarious advisers. The play shows us a king who is weak and sly, easily manipulated, not completely inhuman perhaps, but a prisoner of his own representations nonetheless. He is always double and false, even as he "trembles when he thinks that tomorrow perhaps their doubly dear blood [Don Carlos's and the Queen's] will have reddened [his] hand."[15]

At about the same time, Charles Potvin (1818–1902), a liberal with a great love for national literature, published a tragedy entitled *Les gueux* (1864). In this work, Potvin focuses on the other side of the myth of "black Spain." He links the names of Charles V and Egmont by contrasting their ethos implicitly to that of Philip II and of his Belgian and Spanish henchmen, de Noircarme and Alba, and by highlighting their common fate as children of the *pays de par-deçà*.

In this patriotic drama, Potvin also attempted to synthesize the themes of the *gueux de mer* and the *gueux des bois* that Moke had illustrated separately, and to present them together as emblematic of free thought. The author has an aristocrat, Larmarck, stand in for them on

---

15. Clément Michaëls fils, *Philippe II et Don Carlos* (Brussels: Veuve Parent; Paris: Lecuir, 1863), 140.

the stage. The chorus represents them as well, as can be seen in the case of a rather emblematic hymn sung by the *gueux de mer:*

> God made our conscience free
> Priests are our enemies!
> Let us drive the executioners out of the country
> Ours the head that thinks, ours the heart that vibrates
> God made our conscience free
> Man is not a subject of the pope
> Heaven is not a tributary of the Tiber![16]

In the Epilogue, an imaginary "Monument dedicated to the martyrs of the sixteenth century" is unveiled after a speech delivered by the King of the Belgians, who is being cheered by the crowd and has the King of Holland by his side. Two coryphaei, bearing the Belgian and Dutch flags, then launch into a hymn to the two people who had once fought for the same freedoms.

These various elements resurface, completely transformed by his genius, in De Coster's *Ulenspiegel.*

LITERARY AUTONOMY OF A MYTH

Far more poetic and more fundamentally esoteric, the penultimate chapter of Charles De Coster's (1827–1879) masterpiece, *La légende d'Ulenspiegel* (1867), ties the solution of the enigma that runs through it, i.e., the quest for the Seven, to the as yet to be invented fate of the northern and southern halves of what Charles V had referred to as his *patrie.*[17] The answer comes at the end of a cosmic and historical maturation process that results in the recreation by bourgeois, secular, and progressive modes of thought of seven life forces that have been corrupted by absolutism.

In the songs of *La légende,* De Coster insists that: "Amid the dung May saps arise; / If Seven's ill, yet Seven's well."[18] Toward the end of

16. Charles Potvin, *Les gueux,* in *La revue trimestrielle* (1864): 57.

17. *La légende d'Ulenspiegel* is a sweeping five-book novel that borrows from all the following traditions: historical, picaresque, esoteric, initiatory, epic, and comic. It is immersed in the turbulent history of the Netherlands of the sixteenth century and traces the transformation of an impish child called Tyl Ulenspiegel into a hero of the rebellion against Spain and a herald of unconditional freedom after the death of his father, condemned to be burned at the stake. De Coster created a dual-purpose hero who was not involved with any form of power and wrote a foundational myth that was highly unusual for the nineteenth century.

18. Charles De Coster, *The Legend of Ulenspiegel and Lamme Goedzak and their Adventures Heroical, Joyous, and Glorious in the Land of Flanders and Elsewhere,* trans.

the book, will-o'-the-wisps turn the Seven that have weighed on the destiny of the main characters to ashes. A river of blood flows. Seven new shapes then make a sudden entrance. Pride becomes Noble Ambition; Avarice Economy; Wrath Vivacity; Lust Love, and so on. Ulenspiegel and Nele, his beloved, now hear the sweet singing of a chorus of men and women:

Quand sur la terre et quand sur l'onde	When over land and sea shall reign
Ces sept transformés règneront,	In form transfigured all these seven.
Hommes, alors levez le front:	Men, boldly raise your heads to heaven;
Ce sera le bonheur du monde.[19]	The Golden Age has come again.[20]

Spirits then immediately embark on another, equally important, hymn, which focuses on the northern and southern halves of what is occasionally referred to as the lands of the deltas. Their words echo, poetically this time, the finale of Potvin's *Gueux:*

Quand le septentrion	When the north
Baisera le couchant,	Shall kiss the west,
Ce sera la fin des ruines:	Ruin shall end;
Cherche la ceinture. . . .	The girdle seek. . . .
Septentrion, c'est Neerlande;	North, 'tis the Netherland;
Belgique, c'est le couchant;	Belgium is the west;
Ceinture, c'est alliance;	Girdle is alliance;
Ceinture, c'est amitié. (451–52)	Girdle is friendship. (2:349)

These excerpts demonstrate both the literary originality of De Coster's work, which cannot be discussed here, as well as its insertion in a specific cultural tradition. Such an observation takes nothing away from the fact that De Coster managed to turn the myth of the sixteenth century into a myth that is highly personal and, at the same time, whose collective impact was such that one can speak of Belgian literature in terms of *before* and *after La légende.* It is with this in mind that I would now like to turn my attention to the preface of the work, "La préface du hibou" ("The Owl's Preface").[21]

F. M. Atkinson, lyrics trans. John Heron Lepper, 2 vols (Garden City, NY: Doubleday, Page & Company, 1922), 2:348.

19. Charles De Coster, *La légende et les aventures héroïques, joyeuses et glorieuses d'Ulenspiegel et de Lamme Goedzak au pays de Flandre et ailleurs,* ed. Joseph Hanse (Brussels: La Renaissance du livre, 1996), 450.

20. *The Legend,* 2:349.

21. [Note from the translator: Ulenspiegel means owl's mirror.]

Not only is the Preface written in the burlesque manner typical of the book—thereby opening up important new avenues for the creation of Francophone, as opposed to French,[22] works—De Coster does not shy away from discussing the narrative choices that could potentially be held against the work in the name of the historical record or the existing contours of the myth. He chooses to defend quite loudly instead his "unremitting opposition" between a "detested" and cruel foreign king and a people who are "heroic, jovial, honest, and hardworking," as well as his portrayal of both Charles V and Philip II as executioners of the old Netherlands.[23]

Though the figure of the emperor, to whom the author grants a certain degree of manly courage and a strong sense of humor—he is, after all, a child of the Netherlands—is to that extent more ambiguous than his son's, the Charles V of *La légende d'Ulenspiegel* is by and large the by-product of a Manichean aesthetic. De Coster generally prefers to lay the blame on Charles V *qua* statesman and likens the emperor's power to the absolute power fought by the progressive nineteenth-century forces opposed to the monarchical Europe of the Treaty of Vienna. As a result, De Coster's characterizations of Charles V do not rely on any sort of historical nuance. Rather, they echo narrative strategies traditionally found in folk and poetic tales and exalt the people in their fight against tyranny. Though *La légende* prolongs to some extent part of the material that De Coster's predecessors had been molding since Moke, both on the historical and the fictional level, it does so by favoring what one ought to call the "saga of the sons." In so doing, it opens up a specifically Belgian imaginary and symbolic literary space.

In short, De Coster both takes up and transmogrifies this material in order not only to give it a shape that suits his own genius, but also to convey—even at the cost of "visionary" distortions—the history of an old land that has not met the fate normally reserved for the Nation-States that came out of the fifteenth and sixteenth centuries.

Not only is its history relatively incongruous, Belgium, which does not have a language of its own, relies to some extent on the language of

---

22. The end of "La préface du hibou," devoted to the situation of the "provincial poet" is both exemplary and prophetic in this regard. It does not hesitate to refer back to Rabelais and the old French language in order to remind the reader that the classical tradition is not ontologically necessary. It is the product of a policy that has been successful, but does not necessarily suit the cousins of the French.

23. *La légende*, 3. [Note from the translator: the "Owl's Preface" is not included in the Atkinson translation; translations from the preface are mine.]

the quintessential Nation-State, France.[24] At the time De Coster was writing, of course, France was ruled by Napoleon III, whom the writer abhorred, both because of his regime and because of his imperialism, which posed a threat to Belgium. Here, too, the ironic preface to *La légende* allows us to appreciate that a multilayered reading needs to be brought to bear on the text. Such a reading would provide at least a partial explanation for the writer's atypical representation of Charles V: "Do you not worry that an attentive censor will seek allusions to illustrious contemporaries in the belly of your elephant?" (2)

The more creative and innovative features of De Coster's work either perplexed his peers or made them jealous. They also left the public speechless. Additionally, his portrayal of the sixteenth century drew on historical and literary traditions, but radicalized them by transcending the traditional dualism that opposed princes and people, even though De Coster came down hard on all princes, with the exception of William the Silent. In particular, De Coster's narrative is full of digressions and historical recollections. It is also fundamentally picaresque, carnivalesque, *farcesque*, poetic, fantastic, and esoteric. Indeed, history weighs less heavily on *La légende* than it had on works published in the previous fifty years. Its central characters belong to the realm of legends and the balance between the historical and the literary is tipped in favor of the more fictional aspects, which are also in this instance somewhat different from the ones that historical novels had traditionally relied upon. The principles that guide popular narratives are here joined to a specific world view and to the subtlety of a nonlinear poetic structure where everything is symbolic in its own way.

We find an exemplary illustration of this phenomenon in the forty-second chapter of the first book, where the traditionally good-natured and Rabelaisian descriptions of the emperor do not in any way lessen the charge that De Coster levels against him, even at the time of his abdication. Needless to say, none of De Coster's predecessors had treated this episode like a scene from a masquerade. By contrast, the abdication scene of *La légende*, which incorporates a host of verifiable historical particulars, allows the writer to put the last touches on a carnivalesque and Manichean portrait of two royal accomplices who are solely preoccupied with their own gain. In chapter 58, Charles V goes

24. I have studied this specific aspect of *La légende* in "L'invention en français d'une forme non française," *Letteratura di Frontiera* 2:2 (1992): 65–75 and "Pour transcender la nation impossible: *La légende*," in *La légende de Thyl Ulenspiegel* (Bologna: Clueb [Beloeil 2], 1991), 211–42.

so far as to exclaim in front of Philip II that: "If the princes of Germany had been Catholic, I would have been Lutheran and confiscated their goods" (1:154).

De Coster is hardly kinder to Egmont. Nor, needless to say, does he tone down his portrayal of Philip II. In the twenty-fourth chapter of book III—which comes on the heels of a scene in which Ulenspiegel has managed to fool Alba—we observe the king in a scene that takes place during the last few months of Don Carlos's life. Neither wine nor fire can warm him. Unlike most other works, but in keeping with its treatment of Charles V, *La légende* tars father and son with the same brush: "Those who served King Philip and his son Don Carlos knew not which of the twain they ought to fear the most; whether the son, agile, murderous, tearing his servitors with his nails, or the cowardly and crafty father, using others to strike, and like a hyaena, living upon corpses" (2:71).

This scene takes place in the Escurial, another mythical place. Historically, however, the tragic events referred to in the text cannot possibly have taken place there since the construction of the palace was far from complete at the time. Similarly, the "mother" who cries over Don Carlos's death, Isabelle de Valois, is actually his stepmother. Historical accuracy is not what is at stake in De Coster's book. *La légende* develops and embroiders the historical elements it reworks by exaggerating and isolating specific features in a dialectic that is both moralistic and comical and which can be described as Manichean and/or dualistic. Relying on key features of the history-laden myth, it invents a completely new literary myth that brings together elements from both popular and scholarly traditions. At the same time, since the central figures of the work are not historical actors but legendary beings who are not constrained by the laws of time, De Coster is able to take full advantage of the liberties fiction allows and to make readers laugh.

This innovation both justified and became emblematic of the strange existence of the southern half of the Netherlands within the European States over a two-hundred-and-fifty-year period. No matter what difficulties this presented at the time of the triumph of the supposedly homogeneous Nation-State, De Coster's inventiveness bestowed upon Belgians a mythical image that was both plausible and original, even though it meant taking some very strong liberties with history, not to mention with a language that had already been standardized along a specific set of French norms. These liberties seriously handicapped the writer for the rest of his life. On the other hand, they also earned him recognition when the time came for the fin-de-siècle generation to take center stage.

AN INFLUENCE OF ALMOST
LEGENDARY PROPORTIONS

This generation consisted primarily of creative writers. Fascinated by the art for art's sake movement, they took pains to shake up the somewhat stilted tutelage exercised by earlier generations—whose creative writers had often also been historians, scholars, or polygraphs—by liberating the imaginary and working on language itself. They consequently came to see themselves in *La légende,* which they literally had to dig from its grave and which they called their "patrial" book. Did it not provide a model for writing in French but according to non-French norms? Was this not a text where the imagination came unhinged in the service of a good cause? *La légende* accordingly became part of the new literary and mythical common body of knowledge. It also harked back, in its own way, to a historical tradition that was still growing and was becoming more sharply delineated, especially in the works of Henri Pirenne.

The great generation of Leopold II's reign occasionally immersed itself quite openly in this imaginary inheritance, especially once it had won its artistic struggle, and the conviction that a national literature did exist began to take hold. In 1901 the public was particularly struck by Emile Verhaeren's (1855–1916) *Philippe II.* The poet's play has significantly fewer characters than Michaëls's play. It focuses on the king and his acolytes on the one hand and on Don Carlos and Countess de Clairmont, his alleged mistress, on the other.

One notable character operates between these two groups: Don Juan of Austria. Don Juan, an illegitimate son of Charles V, is remembered first and foremost as the hero of the Battle of Lepanto, an epic victory, in which his half-brother, Philip II, did not take part. The mere presence of Don Juan enables Verhaeren to oppose a noble and heroic creature to a careful and devious king. Once again, the play is set in a "rigid and black" Escurial.[25]

Verhaeren's Don Carlos, who was raised with Don Juan and Alessandro Farnese after the emperor's death, wants nothing more than to rule over the Netherlands. In a typically Oedipal pattern, his speeches pit Philip II against his father and his son. Don Carlos's dreams also re-

25. Emile Verhaeren, *Philippe II* (Paris: Mercure de France, 1901), 11.

volve around dynastic continuity and the exaltation of the Netherlands, two key elements of the myth of the sixteenth century:

> Ghent, Brussels, and Antwerp will belong to me as they had belonged
> to Charles V. O! Don Juan, do you hear the frightened steeples, the bel-
> freys, the clamors, and the Triumphal Entries in the heart of the beau-
> tiful Flemish country? I will make it love Spain by soothing it. Philip II
> wants to kill it to subdue it. We shall be as firm as he is, but we shall
> make might shine forth like lightning in the hands of our right. At the
> very least my words will be clear and direct. I shall not lie. I shall give
> my rebellion against the king as pledge of my vows! [30]

Georges Eekhoud (1854–1927) took up the torch in 1912 with *Les
libertins d'Anvers* [The Libertines of Antwerp], which is based on the
history of a libertarian sect founded by Eloi le Couvreur in the first half
of the sixteenth century. Well documented, the book allows the writer
to plead *in petto* for sexual freedom and social justice and adds up to a
hymn to the splendor of the southern Netherlands, which are not yet
torn asunder by fratricidal wars between Catholics and Protestants.
Eekhoud dismisses them both for their puritanical and intolerant
views. His Antwerp is characterized by that luxury and freedom that
had stunned contemporaries and had unsettled more than its share of
Spaniards. As a result, Charles V's solemn entry (*joyeuse entrée*) into
Antwerp, a scene witnessed by Dürer, epitomizes the elation associated with life in the sixteenth century.[26]

The fascination with the sixteenth century did not abate after the
end of World War I, a time marked by the completion of Henri Pirenne's
(1862–1935) monumental *Histoire de Belgique* and by the start of the
publication of Eugène Baie's (1874–1963) multi-volume summa, *Le siècle des gueux*, in which he portrayed Egmont as a "vulnerable" man.[27]
(Baie's description of Egmont's premature death was colored by the
events of 1914–18.)

Forgotten because of his conduct during World War II, Horace Van
Offel (1878–1944) published *Le gueux de mer*, a short historical novel
in 1936. Van Offel combined elements from a variety of sources, including the works of Potvin and De Coster. Remarkably, however, this
novel betrays no nostalgia for a greater Netherlands, but takes note instead of the events of 1585 by focusing on Farnese, a prince who is a de-

26. Michel de Ghelderode staged the same scene thirty years later in *Le soleil se
couche,* a play whose title echoes Charles V's famous "the sun never sets on my do-
mains."

27. Eugène Baie, *Le siècle des gueux* (Brussels: Librairie Vanderlinden, 1947), 1:247.

scendant of Charles V, and who proves to be worthy of both his ancestor and his country. Of course, Van Offel was writing in the 1930s, i.e., when Belgians were aware of the pressures that were building and no longer felt carried forward by history.

REFLECTIONS OF MYTH AND COUNTRY

One writer did take matters further. Not only did he propose several versions of the sixteenth century in many of his works, he turned it into a fantasy, to the point where it became the imaginary space of reference of his entire oeuvre and glorified a country that was somehow more real than the one in which he was living on a daily basis.

Michel de Ghelderode (1898–1962) made his entrance on the literary scene with a work dedicated to De Coster, *L'histoire comique de Keizer Karel* (1922). This work drew on the popular traditions that had been revived and distributed for centuries in the form of chapbooks. These traditions had seized on the character of the emperor and turned his life into a mock medieval epic in which it was hard to distinguish between the archetypical situations that belonged of necessity to this kind of Rabelaisian narrative and the references to authentic episodes from the life of Charles V. Ghelderode's preface to the second edition of his book (1923) makes a point of reminding the reader that *"cet empereur de farce"* might well be "the incarnation of the people themselves" and that his legend, which has wended its way alongside Ulenspiegel's, "was the only literature to which the people had access."[28]

Ghelderode's portrait of Philip II in *Escurial* (1928) stands in sharp contrast to this, but is in keeping with the mythical tradition of "black Spain." The title of the play refers to the emblematic presence of the king, who is never actually named, but who is described in very familiar ways. In *L'école des bouffons* (1942), Ghelderode brings back the character of Folial, the jester, who serves as the king's double. This time, the king is mentioned by name. However, he only intervenes by means of a letter read by the jester. The games of doubles (*dédoublements*) dear to the playwright and the ties to the sixteenth century become ever more complex.

A year later, as World War II was reaching its obvious turning point, Ghelderode wrote a play, *Le soleil se couche,* that integrated the three sides of the myth ("black Spain," *pays de Cocagne, gueux.*). This play

28. Michel de Ghelderode, *L'histoire comique de Keizer Karel* (Brussels: Les Éditions du Carrefour, 1943), 13.

was also a will and testament and fulfilled the author's destiny as a writer. Not only did it put together ironically the purest elements of the myth of the land of Brueghel and "black Spain," it also took up and fused all the elements that mattered to Ghelderode as a play-wright. Charles V, who has retired to Yuste, and his double, Messer Ignotus (who also stands in for Ghelderode) are the central focus of the play.

In Ghelderode's play everything, starting with their respective ti-tles, sets the emperor and the king apart. The latter's double is Fray Ra-mon, who is the archetypical figure of the fanatical Spanish monk. He is matched with Fray Pascual, a bawdy monk who is fascinated by the emperor and his country of origin. Fray Pascual asks Charles V whether it is true that "in his southern Netherlands, tables are as beautifully and richly set" as the table in Yuste, and if such is not the case only with princely tables. The emperor answers: "Yes, this is a land of plenty and of happiness. Master Gonorius Becanus, a doctor from Antwerp, claims that it had once been, originally, the earthly paradise. One is willing to believe it. Will it remain as the genius of its inhabitants have made it, however?"[29] Dismissing comments by Fray Ramon that herald Philip II's policies, the emperor goes on: "Was I to decimate in one fell swoop the people of the richest State the West had ever known—and from which I drew more treasures than from the Americas? I transferred it intact to my son. Indeed! I enlarged the inheritance left to me by the Grand Duke. It would be miraculous if it did not fall apart in more pi-ous but less flexible hands than mine" (18–19). The two images that have grown out of the historical myth with which Charles V is associ-ated are here so closely linked that they now find themselves well and truly dialectically, even consubstantially, related to one another.

The play also brings this "double people" (27) to life in a puppet show. Play within the play, it holds up a small mirror to Ulenspiegel's century. The mythical hero meets Saint Michael, emblem of the House of Burgundy and patron of the city of Brussels (not to mention patron of the name chosen for himself by the author). Having come down from his pedestal atop the town hall tower, Saint Michael tells Ulenspiegel that he has "lost his devil."[30] To which the jolly fellow responds by ask-ing whether he would not be satisfied with a Spaniard, who could eas-

29. Michel de Ghelderode, *Le soleil se couche,* in *Théâtre* (Paris: Gallimard, 1979), 5:15.

30. [Note from the translator: the statue of Saint Michael that sits atop the Brussels town hall shows him standing on top of the dragon he has slain.]

ily be found in the Palace, now that "the good genius that dwelt there," i.e., the emperor, "has departed from it" (34).

Charles V's jester makes a sudden entrance. Distraught because of the departure of "the old-fashioned knight" (36), he admits that the people of the Netherlands did recognize themselves in him. Ulenspiegel then decides to play the devil's advocate and talks about the new Caesar. The emperor finds the symposium "lively" and "natural" (37) until Ulenspiegel suggests that "Charles ruined the *Patrie* before handing it over to the foreigners" (39). Imitating Folial, the emperor refuses to remain a spectator any longer. He asserts that he was "a good father to a bad son" and that he wanted to deliver his lands from their "local *patries*" and their "outdated laws" in order to offer them "a prestigious empire" and to open "the doors of the world and of the oceans" to them (39). At this point, the jester confesses that his subjects do regret him and that his "was a grandiose reign" (40). In one of Ghelderode's signature moves, however, the devil appears at this particular juncture and asks if he has been summoned by Michael. The emperor examines the cloth structure that surrounds him. His double is projected onto it: it is the puppet master. At this point an extraordinary dialogue begins between Charles, who tosses his sword away, and his masked double, Ignotus, who comes out of the theater crushed. Ignotus later dubs and frees the emperor, in order to answer the pleas Charles is issuing "to the chimeras that pass before his eyes" (48).

In another phantasmagorical scene, Philip II is praying and following a Maid who is being led by monks to her execution. She is wearing a torn dress in which one can detect "a weave of discolored heraldic lions," i.e., an allegorical representation of the Netherlands, the *Patrie*, and Life (49). At the end of this scene, in which the real itself is brought into question, Ignotus/Ghelderode is able to give Charles V the title he had renounced when he had given up his sword: "Imperador—Verily I proclaim you" (51). The emperor now lives on for eternity, a survival he owes to the writer who had granted it to him and to whom he in turn grants the power of his own mythical aura.

This literary survival took place as Ghelderode put his pen down, just as, long ago, the emperor had laid his scepter down. Their common country, then under the Nazi heel, was going through some very dark years that would change it profoundly once again. With Ghelderode's play, however, the myth demonstrated its strength and its ability to incorporate issues pertaining to the theater and to writing. And it managed to do so in a crepuscular atmosphere. One had not witnessed such a synthesis since De Coster's *Ulenspiegel,* which had been written when people had great hopes for the future.

Historians were also focusing on this tutelary and incantatory figure of the father at the same time as Ghelderode. They included Ghislaine De Boom, author of *Charles Quint, prince des Pays-Bas* (1943), and John Bartier, who wrote a remarkable biography of Charles the Bold, Charles V's much admired ancestor. This historiographical work was pursued by and large until 1958, year of the quadricentennial of the emperor's death and of the Brussels world's fair. By contrast, as far as literature proper was concerned, the neoclassical aesthetics and the denial of the existence of anything specifically Belgian in Francophone literature that took center stage between 1945 and 1960 tended to consign to oblivion the myths of the *gueux* and the *pays de Cocagne* and to put a stop to the taking of liberties with the French language. Such distinctive features were thought to underscore too uncomfortably Belgium's difference vis-à-vis France. Only the avant-gardes, excluded from the official literary scene, rediscovered the playful attitudes and guerrilla tactics that remind us, metaphorically at least, of the *gueux* of old. They eventually came together under the banner "savage Belgium."

BEYOND THE MYTH

Once the triumph of the neoclassical school had passed, the sixteenth century made a gradual comeback in literary texts, albeit in a differed or metaphorical manner. In Paul Willems's (1912–1997) *Warna* (1962), for instance, a theatrical fable is set in a castle lost in the middle of a country in ruins. It immerses the spectator or reader in more ancient times, more immemorial even—roughly those of the disasters of the sixteenth and seventeenth centuries. In keeping with the rules of magical realism, these disasters are not named. We are here dealing on the whole with the technique used by Maeterlinck in "Le massacre des innocents," except that Willems's legendary images are even more ahistorical. Many postwar Belgian writers would give priority to the immemorial over the historical, just as they probably also dreamt of a Belgium that the events of 1940–45 had not catapulted out of the myths it had built for itself and in which it thought it would indefinitely be able to find itself again.

These myths did manage to live on, albeit outside the strict confines of literature. One need only think of the lyrics of Jacques Brel (1929–

1978) and of the Belgian comic strip school, as, for instance, in *Le fantôme espagnol* (1949), a volume from Willy Vandersteen's (1913–1990) famous *Bob et Bobette* series, and in *La révolte des gueux* (1954) in the *Tijl Uilenspiegel* series by the same author.[31]

The century Belgians have thought of as their *grand siècle* has not been the object of sweeping and all-encompassing historical Francophone studies in the last three to four decades. Works of this scope seem to have favored the fifteenth and eighteenth centuries instead. A similar shift has taken place in the literary field. The myth of the sixteenth century seems to have given way to that of Charles the Bold and to the cycle of Thebes, which represent radically different ways of coming to terms with failure. The sixteenth century has not completely disappeared, however, even though the myth itself no longer seems supported by the heroic and identitarian vision that had existed in the one hundred and fifty years prior to the 1960s, nor by the unique affirmation of the community that had formed around it. The recurring structural play of the characters has either disappeared or been modified, while that of the myth's three great components ("black Spain," *pays de Cocagne*, and *gueux*) has either subsided or been shifted to another context.

This has clearly been the case in the work of Marguerite Yourcenar (1903–1987), a writer who belongs only tangentially to the field of Belgian literature, but whose family history partakes in great measure of the history of the old Netherlands and of modern-day Belgium. The sixteenth century in which *The Abyss* (*L'oeuvre au noir* [1968]) is steeped fits the broader European context of the Renaissance in all its complexity. The work actually revolves around characters who are emblematic of the century in its inventive grandeur as well as its failures: first there is Zeno, a doctor, philosopher, and alchemist, whose life begins and ends in Bruges, and who stands for premodernity and reminds us of Erasmus; second, there is the equally singular figure of his friend, the prior of the Order of the Cordeliers in Bruges, who is a Christian humanist and an opponent of torture; finally, there is Zeno's half-brother, Henry Maximilian Ligre, a cultured soldier from Bruges who is very keen on adventures. The writer is here quite indifferent to any romantic or postromantic notion of fate and has no use for nationalis-

31. [Note from the translator: *Le fantôme espagnol* was originally published in Dutch as *Het Spaanse spook*, and *La révolte des gueux* as *De opstand der geuzen*. The original title of the *Bob et Bobette* series is *Suske en Wiske*.]

tic heroes or Manichean figures of good and evil. This does not, however, signal the absence of ethical preoccupations.

Yourcenar was careful not to resort to the kinds of anachronisms characteristic of many of the historical novels of the nineteenth and twentieth centuries. She unfurled her material on the basis of a more modern and distancing variety of historical knowledge. Nevertheless, the fact remains that she immersed herself in the sixteenth century by building on characters who stemmed in significant measure from the Southern Netherlands. As the "Author's Note" at the end of the work makes explicit, her objective was to view the sixty or so decisive years of the century through the lens of Zeno's life. These years

> close to 1510, [witnessed] the scission of what remained of ancient medieval Christianity into two parties, theologically and politically opposed. On one side, the failure of the Reformation, turning into Protestantism, and crushing what could be called its own left wing; on the other, the corresponding failure of Catholicism, encasing itself for four centuries to come in the iron corselet of Counter Reformation; the great explorations turning more and more into sheer exploitation of the known world; the sudden advance of capitalist economy concomitant with the beginning of the monarchic era.[32]

These comments take us far from the nineteenth century's dualistic vision, which had more or less tended to associate progress with Protestantism. They take us equally far from any exaltation of the Belgian nation, even though its misfortunes are described explicitly elsewhere. We are not dealing with the glorification of the *pays de Cocagne*, but with the memory of something essential, which has been lost, but which had once come to life in the well-to-do lands south of the border that had split the old Netherlands. Moreover, as had been done since the nineteenth century in most of the works dealing with the sixteenth century, Yourcenar insisted on the historical foundation of her commentary. She did so, however, from a certain kind of distance—some might say coldness. Her uses of history contrast sharply with our earlier examples and their reliance on chronicles and historians as proofs. In Yourcenar's work, history always remains something of an enigma. It is neither teleological nor theological.

Some ten years later, Dominique Rolin, born in 1913, tackled the

---

32. Marguerite Yourcenar, *The Abyss*, trans. Grace Frick in collaboration with the author (New York: Farrar, Straus and Giroux, 1976), 367.

sixteenth century in a diptych she wrote after the death of her father, Jean Rolin. In the novels she wrote at the time, she attempted, as she had done since the early sixties, to resume control of her own life and to find a place for her Belgian childhood in her work. In this instance, she tried to do so without immersing herself in a northern imaginary, as she had done in *Les marais* (1942), and without denying the years she had spent in France immediately after the war.

The opening of the first of these two books, *Dulle Griet* [Mad Meg] (1977) is quite telling. The narrative moves from Venice, the "foreign city," to the "short illness" and "end of [her] father."[33] These events take place in what Rolin henceforth refers to as "the other country," France, the other term of an alterity in which Venetian Italy is the site of the exotic other and of happiness. In order to express her innermost truths, her struggles and her strength, the writer reworks the tall and lanky female figure in the foreground of Pieter Brueghel's famous painting of war, apocalypse, and phantasmagoria (*Dulle Griet*, c. 1562). As the back cover of the book notes, "by merging with the visionary woman stepping forward toward the mouth of hell, [Rolin] passes through the body of memory in order to study its organism and its function with scrupulous cruelty. At the cost of the destruction of lived space and time, she manages to put back together a free and dark autobiography in which both dreams and day-dreams, intuitions and memories are filtered by a light that has a magical precision and belongs to her native country."

In one respect, we are far from the myth. In another, we are dwelling at its very core, in its most perfect decantation. Was it not through the sixteenth century and the most original painter of the old Netherlands that the novelist was able to reconnect with and express her origins? And had not the most emblematic artist of sixteenth-century Netherlands[34] chosen to paint what he had the way he had in spite of his trip to Italy and the Renaissance's fascination with the southern peninsula? Had this not enabled the artist to bear witness even better to the atrocities that had befallen his century and the devastation that had descended upon his country?

In the imaginary biography Rolin has devoted to Brueghel, *L'enragé* (1978), the painter, who is near death, looks back on his life. Remembering his journey north from Italy through France, Brueghel exalts the subtle aggression to which colors subjected him the moment he arrived

33. Dominique Rolin, *Dulle Griet* (Paris: Denoël, 1977), 7–8.
34. Hence Ghelderode's neologism of "Breughelande" for the *pays de Cocagne*.

in his native land: "Brutal in Italy, [colors] were here assailed by a careful, almost prudish light, under a sun that resembles the sky's great root. They connived with the atmosphere in order to melt into it and to die there after having drunk from its altar before being altered by it."[35] The painter's view of France during his stay in Paris is just as significant: "Tyrannical power and submission of a people resigned to the worst humiliations. People did not react here the way they did in the Netherlands. Their laments were mean. Their mutual hatreds petty."[36]

Alba's arrival and the atrocities that followed are of course integrated into the narrative. However, contrary to what we find in nineteenth-century narratives, these events are not given pride of place. Yet Rolin's strokes are no less biting for their greater subtlety. Their emphasis simply shifts. In Rolin's work, the painter is working on *The Magpie on the Gallows* (c. 1568)—a work to which Ghelderode has also devoted a play—when he learns of the arrest of his benefactor, the man whom the myth is usually content to name without dwelling on him: the Count of Horn. The account of his execution—given by the maidservant—takes up no more than a page. The die is cast from the start by the metaphor of the gallows, a key image of sixteenth-century Netherlands.

In an unpublished play, *Erasme* (1995), Michèle Fabien (1945–1999) focuses on another emblematic sixteenth-century figure. This time, the author, who has so admirably revisited the figure of Jocasta and who would complete her literary wanderings with a play devoted to *Charlotte* (of Belgium and of Mexico), embarks upon the story of a bastard and a genius rather than that of a princess.[37] At the end of his life, however, Fabien's Erasmus sees himself as one of his century's losers, in spite of the fact that he has remained the most important symbol of all its promises.

It is once again around a historic figure seen as an individual—that of a man who has elected to retire and is now looking back on a life that

35. Rolin, *L'enragé* (Paris: Ramsay, 1978), 137.
36. *L'enragé*, 136. Here the novelist, who had made some very harsh comments in the fifties about her own country and considered France to be the only possible *lieu de l'esprit*, clearly allows one element to surface that the myth rarely mentions, even though it is a very essential part of its genesis: the relationship to France.
37. I have studied the gift for speech in a character who has traditionally been spoken of but who rarely speaks in "A l'heure de la belgitude, Jocaste parle. L'invention de Michèle Fabien," in *Passerelles francophones I*, ed. B. Chikhi (Strasbourg: Vives Lettres No 10), 55–92.

is ending—that my own *Nuit de Yuste* (1999) revolves. The work highlights the true meaning and the relative failure of Charles V's reign.
Though one can see the years of real power go by, the text focuses on
other aspects of his life: the woman he cherished and the insane mother
in whose shadows the emperor once ruled; painting—Renaissance
painting, that is, Titian especially; the countless temporary residences
that suited an emperor incessantly on the move and served as his secret anchors; the great dream at Europe's core; and, finally, the deep
mark left by the Netherlands on the mentality and imaginary of this
prince. *La nuit de Yuste* lets Charles V speak as a man, whereas the
myth only lets him speak as an emperor. Of William of Orange, Charles
V says, for instance: "for this child of adoption, Caesar has circum-
vented his rigor. None of the fruits born from the womb of Isabella has
had this privilege: severity has been broken. William has even had access to the closed book of our weariness."[38]

As we have seen, though their presence is less dominant than it once
was, the sixteenth century and the Netherlands of old are nevertheless
far from absent from the literary landscape of postwar Belgium. They
seem to have become personal, rather than collective, re-anchoring
points for Belgian writers, however, or even sites of very distant memories—albeit with that relatively soft focus one often notices in a country where symbolism has been much more than just a phase.

The European dimension of the history of the sixteenth century and
of the crucible that was the old Netherlands is now woven more openly
into the fabric of narratives. Alba and Philip II no longer play the central roles. Figures like Egmont are elided. Though the image of "black
Spain" does not disappear altogether, it no longer carries the shrill
connotations one finds in hero-worshipping texts. Fictional works no
longer seek to affirm first and foremost the singularity of a people.[39]

38. Marc Quaghebeur, *La nuit de Yuste* (Brussels: Le Cormier, 1999), 32.
39. We should now carry out a similar research project for the Dutch-speaking corpus of Belgian literature in order to be able to distinguish between what is properly Belgian and what is unique to each of its cultures (the theme of the sixteenth century, its
splendor, and its rebellion inspired most notably the great nineteenth-century novelist
Hendrik Conscience). We shall necessarily be confronted with the relative malleability
of a myth that deals with such a distant past, but also with its continued currency in the
contemporary period, the historical variables that exist in the North and South of the
country, as well as with the often chiastic comparative history of the two literatures.
Shortly after the publication of Rolin's two books, for instance, the great Flemish writer
Louis-Paul Boon published *Het gueuzenboek* (1979). Buttressed by a solid historical apparatus, the great fresco of the rebellion that took place in the sixteenth century is once
again in the foreground.

They proceed from it and seek to recollect it in depth. They therefore continue to feed on the "strangeness" of a history that has been internalized, but that still often hesitates to proclaim its authenticity, specificity, and difference. The myth continues to fuel the imagination, however, and has morphed into a history, in which the question of the Nation-State and its fantasies no longer occupy center stage.

There are many more instances than those mentioned in the present essay of rereadings and mythifications of the sixteenth century as the historical foundation of a community and a literature. This period has left significant traces in our literatures, paintings, and monuments. It belongs to a kind of "infraculture" that is often unconscious and of which we find evidence in the still common references to the theme of "black Spain" or to the bacchic and melancholy Belgian character.

This picture-perfect dualism has the merit of referring us back to the unique failure of the sixteenth century, which manifested itself as something other than a cut and dry annihilation.[40] This failure opened the doors to a history to which Belgian life somehow, somewhere continues to bear witness. At the time of romantic nationalisms and in the language that belongs to the quintessential Nation-State, the mythical phrasing of this past owed it to itself to hold on to those features that underscored its sense of loss and its strangeness and also to insist on a libertarian vitality that could transcend the vagaries of history, particularly of that History that was being turned into myth by the discourses that gave Nation-States their momentum.

—Translated from the French by Catherine Labio

---

40. We cannot insist strongly enough on the fact that De Coster's Ulenspiegel is as thoroughly melancholy as Philip II.

III. "Sights" of Memory

SERGE TISSERON

Family Secrets and Social Memory in *Les aventures de Tintin*

Remarkably enough, tiny Belgium and the vast United States share the distinction of having produced the two most prolific comic strip schools of the twentieth century. The most famous of the Belgian story lines have to be the *Aventures de Tintin et Milou*, drawn by Hergé over almost half a century and reflecting the crises Europe experienced after 1930, particularly those having to do with racism and anti-Semitism. Hergé can, of course, be accused of having shared this particular mindset, but he can also be credited with having had the courage of his convictions: he never tried to appear "politically correct" and always expressed his opinions without worrying about their reception. For instance, he used the character of Capitaine Haddock to portray alcoholism as no other cartoonist had dared to do. At the same time, one can also leave aside a moral reading of the work in favor of a consideration of its internal logic. Indeed, since Hergé never traveled, he did not depict situations he had actually witnessed abroad, but rather what was said or shown around him. A quick survey of the iconography of the turn of the century does indeed demonstrate that when it came to racism, he faithfully reproduced the xenophobic mood of his time, especially in *Tintin au Congo.* Unfortunately for him, as it were, most of these documents have sunk into oblivion, while *Les aventures de Tintin* have remained. From *Le lotus bleu* on, however, Hergé resolved not to be guided only by what he saw and heard around him, but also to refer to reliable documents, to the point where Lévi-Strauss could praise the precision and ethnological accuracy of the places and objects presented in these works. What is not so well known is that Hergé had the same kind of large file cabinet in his office as the commander of the citadel in *L'affaire Tournesol*, and that it was filled with photographs clipped from newspapers. Most of these pictures were taken with the

YFS 102, *Belgian Memories,* ed. Catherine Labio, © 2002 by Yale University.

lens generally used by press photographers before the war, that is, the "50 mm," which comes closest to replicating the view produced by the human eye. *Les aventures de Tintin* definitely mirror their own era, but do so through the filter of the social images that were most widespread at the time. And, since many press photographers were using twin-lens reflex cameras, Tintin's adventures were drawn from the point of view of a child whose eye level was three feet from the ground!

This essay aims to go beyond these sociological and aesthetic aspects of Hergé's work. The memory of Belgium—and thus in part the memory of the world—is indeed presented in it through the ideology to which most of his fellow citizens did subscribe—even if the best of them did not—and by the graphic transcription of the photographic iconography then in vogue. And yet Hergé also fleshed out in the *Aventures de Tintin* a unique perspective on family memory that is of interest to us all.

A FAMILY SAGA

Les aventures de Tintin are a paradox. All its characters are about the same age, they never grow old, and yet they appeal to all ages. This is because a secret history runs through all the comic books, recounting the twists and turns of a family secret over several generations.

I discovered this secret thanks to a close study of the twenty-two comic books of *Tintin*,[1] all easily available for purchase, at a time when Hergé's biography, published only in 1987, was totally unknown.[2] But why did I embark on such an analysis, with what ulterior motives, and what hopes? In fact, this project was an integral part of an important clinical discovery I was making at that time: children draw the family secrets they are not allowed to talk about.[3] After collecting important material on these situations as they involve children, I decided to apply the same hypothesis to a professional artist. Might not an adult who chooses to devote himself to drawing also be attempting to get around

1. Serge Tisseron, "Haddock et le fantôme du chevalier. La question du père dans les aventures de Tintin," in *Les fantômes de la psychanalyse, Cahiers confrontation* 8 (Autumn 1982): 35–50; reprinted in *Tintin chez le psychanalyste* (Paris: Aubier, 1985).

2. Thierry Smolderen and Pierre Sterckx, *Hergé. Portrait biographique* (Tournai: Casterman, 1988). See also, Hervé Springael, *Avant Tintin. Dialogue sur Hergé* (Brussels: Hervé Springael, 1987).

3. My research on family secrets has since been published in several works and particularly in *Nos secrets de famille* (Paris: Ramsay, 1999).

the ban on talking about a family secret by drawing it? Hergé's work, which I knew and appreciated, seemed to be the ideal ground for that exploration.

THE SECRET OF A PRESTIGIOUS LINEAGE

For the reader to have a clear grasp of the reasoning that has led to the present argument, I must specify first of all the ways in which images function with regard to secrets, and particularly in drawings and comic strips. An image can make visible not only the literal but also the figurative sense of a word. To the extent I was guided by the search for a secret, I was naturally interested in the figurative meaning of the images, and specifically in the comic book that contains the word "secret" in its title, that is, *Le secret de la licorne*. As it turns out, this secret is eventually revealed in the next volume in the series, *Le trésor de Rackham le Rouge*: a treasure was—quite literally—hidden in the foundations of the castle of Moulinsart. However, if we take the words "treasure" and "foundation" in a figurative sense, the same images convey a completely different message: something very precious (a "treasure") is hidden in the ancestry (the "foundations") of the one who owns that castle, that is, the Chevalier de Hadoque. In other words, there is among the ancestors of the Chevalier, and thus among those of Capitaine Haddock, his descendant, an illustrious ancestor—an aristocrat, perhaps even a king (Figure 1). This ancestor did not acknowledge his progeny, but the hidden treasure—which, keep in mind, is "worth ten times a king's ransom" in Hergé's own characterization—is destined to commemorate him and his secret.

In 1983, I demonstrated that there are many clues in *Tintin* that indicate that the Chevalier de Hadoque had been a bastard son of Louis XIV, who had never recognized him legally. This illegitimate son would have hesitated between loving his father or secretly cursing him. Moreover, this dilemma would not only have burdened the life of the Chevalier, but also that of subsequent generations, especially Capitaine Haddock, his descendant, contributing in particular to his alcoholism.

The major difficulty of such an interpretation resided, of course, in the absence of an explicit representation of any "father," legitimate or not, in *Tintin*. Should that absence of a father figure be taken as the sign that a father had remained hidden to Hergé? Or was it not quite simply the sign that Hergé was not interested in problems of filiation and that

Figure 1. Hergé, *Le secret de la Licorne* © Hergé/Moulinsart 2002

I myself had invented them out of whole cloth? My hypothesis was that Hergé's decision not to include any *image* of a "royal father" in the *Aventures de Tintin* did not mean that he had given up on recording the presence of that father, but that he had done so in the *text*, specifically in the form of a phonetic sequence associating the three letters K, A, and R. These three letters do recur in most of the proper names that Hergé has imagined in *Tintin:* La Castafiore, of course, the gorilla Ranko in *L'ile noire*, Alcazar, Ottokar, the "Karaboudjan" (the cargo ship Haddock captains in *Le crabe aux pinces d'or*), Rakham le Rouge, Rascar Kapac (the mummy of the *Sept boules de cristal*), Huascar (the high priest of the sun in *Le temple du soleil*), the sherpa Tharkey of *Tintin au Tibet*, Carreidas (the childish billionaire of *Vol 1714 pour Sydney*) and, of course, the Picaros, to mention only the most important instances. Thanks to these various puns, the word "King" is present throughout Hergé's work in the guise of an encrypted signifier: KAR—as revealed to us in *Le sceptre d'Ottokar*.

Indeed, imagine my surprise when a few months later I discovered, upon rereading *Le sceptre d'Ottokar*, that Hergé himself had given us the meaning of those three letters! In this volume the legitimacy of a royal dynasty is subjected to a yearly test. Once a year the king must parade in his coach, while brandishing the royal specter. Should he ever be unable to perform this rite, he would be deposed and lose all legitimacy. This obligation, Hergé explains to us in a tourism brochure included in the comic strip, had apparently been imposed by the founder of the royal Syldavic dynasty, somebody named "Muskar," and Hergé provides the etymology of this word—an utterly fanciful one, of course, since Syldavia never existed: Muskar was created, the foldout tells us, by combining two Syldavic words: "Musk," which meant "value," and "KAR," which meant . . . "king"!

This foldout thus functions along the lines of what the science of hieroglyphics calls a "determinative sign." It does not provide narrative information, but is intended to specify the meaning to be given to another sign, which, in this instance, is precisely the "KAR" sign present in almost all proper names created by Hergé.

I consequently ventured the hypothesis that one can find in Hergé a problematic identical to the one he portrayed in Haddock: that of a male ancestor not recognized legally by his father, but who received material gifts from him—like the castle of Moulinsart granted the Chevalier by King Louis XIV—and was forced into silence. It seemed impossible to go any farther until the sensational turn of events of 1987.

THE SECRET OF THE REMI FAMILY

In 1987, heretofore unpublished documents revealed that Hergé's father had been born to an unknown, but probably aristocratic father. Hergé's father had also had a twin, born to the same unknown father, and both brothers' education and clothing had been provided by a real countess living in an honest to goodness castle, while their mother—named Marie Dewigne—was only a humble chambermaid! This revelation sheds a very different light not only on all the *Aventures de Tintin*, but also on the pleasure we take in reading them. Hergé's construction of the secret of a royal but inadmissible lineage can now be seen as the exact transfer of a secret to be found in his own family. And each of the characters he imagined represents one of the successive generations implicated in the secret (Figure 2).

There are two women at the birth of this story: Marie Dewigne and the mysterious Countess de Dudzeele. Both can be found in the two facets of the character of La Castafiore. Then, in the secret's second generation, we have the twin brothers, Alexis and Léon, Hergé's father and uncle. The personality and mannerisms of the Dupondt brothers are the precise transposition of the difficulties encountered by these two men. Finally, in the secret's third generation, there is Hergé himself, the oldest son of Alexis Remi: the difficulties he encountered throughout his life are portrayed through three thoroughly complementary characters: Tintin, Haddock, and Tournesol.

LA CASTAFIORE

La Castafiore appears in the comic book *Le sceptre d'Ottokar* at the same time as the only royal character portrayed in all the Tintin volumes. By appearing in the same comic book, La Castafiore and the royal ancestor are shown as belonging to the same generation. By the same token, La Castafiore also appears at the precise moment Hergé gives the crucial explanation of the meaning to be granted the three letters, K, A, and R, which are intended to indicate the presence of the enigmatic royal ancestor. Finally, to complete this parallelism, at this first appearance, and for the first and last time, she is wearing an "Astrakhan" cloak, whose name contains the famous three letters K, A, and R!

But there are still more surprises with La Castafiore. As soon as she appears, she is represented as a double character, sometimes identified with a capricious and frivolous diva, and sometimes with Marguerite,

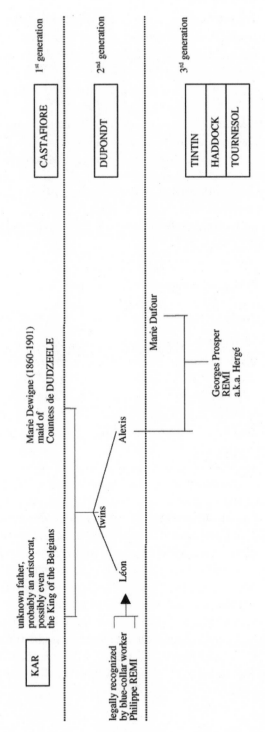

Figure 2.

the heroine of Gounod's opera, a role she will bear down upon with gusto in virtually all the remaining *Tintin* volumes. Interestingly enough, *qua* diva, La Castafiore undoubtedly stands for the Comtesse de Dudzeele, as Hergé—who never knew her, of course—could dream her up; Marguerite, on the other hand, unquestionably represents Marie Dewigne.

Marguerite is a woman from a modest background who falls in love with a handsome young man she mistakes for a prince. Alas, he is actually Faust restored to youth by the diabolical Mephisto. The latter hides a box of jewels in Marguerite's garden. When she discovers the jewels, she adorns herself with them. The famous aria ("Ah, I laugh to see how lovely I look in this mirror") signals her intense happiness, which comes from her conviction that she will be able to seduce Faust. She goes on with her singing:

> This is the daughter of a king,
> To whom everyone bows as she goes past.
> Ah, if only he were here,
> If only he could see me thus!

As the opera continues, Marguerite becomes pregnant by Faust—out of wedlock, obviously—and is eventually accused of killing her child before going mad. Is this fate not a dramatized version of Marie Dewigne's, Hergé's paternal grandmother, seduced and abandoned by a man in a social situation far above her own?

But let us return to La Castafiore as "diva." Because of her appearance and her public success, she stands in for the mysterious countess herself, the "second mother" of Hergé's father and uncle. But might she not also be the real mother of the twins? We are here getting on to a new version of the fantasies Hergé may have spun upon encountering the family secret that was hidden from him, perhaps as he followed his own father's dreams. The enigmatic Countess de Dudzeele would then be the real mother of the twins, whose upbringing she would have entrusted to her maid, Marie Dewigne. This new version of the fantasy takes into account the couple formed in *Tintin* by La Castafiore and her maid, the famous Irma. Indeed, the name Irma is an inversion of the syllables of the name "Marie," as in Marie Dewigne, just as Hergé's own pen name (Her-gé) was created by inverting his initials ("G" as in "Georges" and "R" as in "Remi")! Further, in *Les bijoux de la castafiore*, Marie/Irma is suspected by the Dupondts of stealing her mistress's jewels; in other words, if we adopt the equation, jewels = children, of stealing the twins!

Finally, Hergé also added to La Castafiore another characteristic that Marie Dewigne and the Countess de Dudzeele shared. Just as those two women never revealed the name of their father to Léon and Alexis, La Castafiore never succeeds in reproducing Haddock's name, that same Haddock, who, as Hergé has told us, is the character who stands in for the author himself. She calls him in turn Paddock, Bardock, Karbock, Harrock, Kappock, Koddach, Mastock, Kosack, Kolbackh, Harnack, Hablock, Maggock, Medock, and Kaspstock . . . but never Haddock!

THE SECRET'S SECOND GENERATION: THE DUPONDTS

Hergé's father and uncle, Alexis and Léon, were twins, who always dressed alike. They even took care, according to Hergé, to add the same accessories to their similar costumes: same umbrellas, same pocket handkerchiefs, etc.

As for the Dupondts, it is important to note, first of all, that the question of the name lies at the core of their identity. What is the name of the father of the Dupondts? Is it Dupond or Dupont? Might not the twins have two fathers after all? Behind the different spellings of their two family names, it is not hard to see the visual staging, as in the workings of a dream, of the family secret around the "two fathers" of Alexis and Léon, the secret father and the blue-collar worker Remi who recognized them legally when they were eleven years old.

Let us now turn to the mannerisms of the Dupondts. They are, as everyone knows, police inspectors. These inspectors, however, are intellectually challenged and invariably wrong. Now, a close examination of the obstacles faced by the Dupondts reveals that these obstacles are very often verbal pitfalls, while their investigations are always governed by an unfailing respect for the letter. Hence their use of empty formulas such as: "Nobody leave," "We shall proceed with the usual investigations," or "For me, this a very simple matter," etc.

Similarly, eager to go unnoticed in a foreign country, the Dupondts mistake the everyday clothes of its inhabitants with their traditional dress and end up attracting everyone's attention (Figure 3). Here is another case of an identity one wants to hide, but that is revealed by one's

Figure 3. Hergé, *Le lotus bleu* © Hergé/Moulinsart 2002

clothing. Moreover, isn't the experience of the Dupondts as they are being pointed at equivalent to that of the twins, Alexis and Léon, who must have stood out, not only because they were identical, but also, quite probably, because of the beautiful outfits, the *beaux vêtements*, given to them by the countess, and which, by signaling a disparity with their modest origin, could have branded them "bastards"?

Finally, the Dupondts are constantly confusing the literal and figurative meaning of words. For example, having decided, in *Le temple du soleil*, to rely on dowsing to look for their companions, the Dupondts decide to go down into a coal mine when their pendulum indicates that Tintin and Haddock have "reached bottom," and they elect to go on a Dodgem ride in an amusement park when the pendulum tells them that Tintin and Haddock are "very shaken"!

Inasmuch as all these "symbolic confusions" ultimately echo the mystery of their two family names, the Dupondts represent Hergé's father and uncle, who were condemned to a life of ignorance and wandering because they lacked access to the symbolic world that would have been theirs had they known their true identity.

THE SECRET'S THIRD GENERATION:
TINTIN, HADDOCK, TOURNESOL

Tintin, Haddock, and Tournesol seal their friendship in *Le secret de la licorne* and *Le trésor de Rackham le Rouge*, at the end of which Haddock also acquires—thanks, what's more, to Tournesol's money—the castle of Moulinsart, where all three will end up living. In other words, the trio that will eventually become an inseparable threesome coalesces around the genealogical quest to track down the Chevalier de Hadoque. We shall now see how Tintin, Haddock, and Tournesol each represent one facet of Hergé as he grappled with his family secret. Or, if you prefer, and since Hergé was able to give a mythological dimension to his characters, each of these three heroes represents one aspect of the possible stances that can be adopted by a child confronting a parent's secret.

First, Tintin is above all a child lost in a world of adults and who does his utmost to understand its secrets. Unlike the Dupondts, however, he succeeds and even excels at it. No enigma is beyond him. He can solve images like rebuses (as, for example, in *Le secret de la licorne*, when some sparrows pointed out to him then put him on the track of the Loiseaux [birds] brothers). Conversely, he can also detect the import of figurative meanings. In *Les bijoux de la Castafiore,* for instance, he translates literally the title of the opera of La Castafiore's triumph— the "Gazza Ladra" or "The Thieving Magpie"—in order to uncover that a magpie has stolen the jewels.

Tournesol, the second character of the Hergé trio, is a deaf scholar. Now, a child too can be come both deaf and smart when confronted with a family secret and the wrong he imagines as its source. In a way, a child who hears certain things he senses he should not be hearing is indeed under the impression that he is being asked to be "deaf." Tournesol's deafness is the metaphoric enactment—as in a dream—of the mandate given to a child and which consists in saying: "You have heard nothing of what you have actually heard; you must remain deaf to those things you must not know." Tournesol's deafness is a way of saying that no one is guilty of having hidden anything from him since it is he himself who doesn't hear anything! Such a prohibition can turn a child into an idiot, but it can also make him become a "scientist," i.e., someone who chooses to devote his life to the only line of work where searching for the truth is not only a recognized right, but even a duty: the pursuit of scientific knowledge. This way the child who is forbidden to search for the family truth can still preserve the idealized image of his parents along with the quest for truth that motivates him. Tournesol is thus the Hergé character who pushes farthest the search for a reconciliation with those very parents who have withheld such an essential truth from him. He exemplifies the docile and obedient child. What is more, in *Les bijoux de la Castafiore,* he creates in the utmost secrecy a white rose he names La Castafiore and offers it to her in a great outpouring of love.

Finally, Capitaine Haddock epitomizes the child in the continual throes of a secret. In *Le crabe aux pinces d'or,* he is an impulsive, alcoholic, suicidal, and at times homicidal character, who even tries to kill Tintin twice. This is because he is the victim of a secret that he finally solves with the help of Tintin and Tournesol in *Le secret de la Licorne* and *Le trésor de Rackham le Rouge.* Later, once the mystery is solved, he will feel much better and will come to be perceived by all as "that dear old captain," as Tintin calls him.

First and foremost, however, it is important to note that Hergé staged the impenetrable matter of his own origins around the character of Capitaine Haddock. Both text and images clearly portray the captain as the descendant of an illustrious man. Let us start with the text. The name Hergé chose for the captain is that of a fish, a "haddock." But the synonyms of "haddock" in French are "*aiglefin*" or "*aigrefin*," which, figuratively mean "swindler" or "crook," and even . . . "captain of industry." Thus, the family name of the character Hergé has said represents himself evokes both an illustrious man and a cheat, the perfect name for the enigmatic and illustrious grandfather, who had seduced and then abandoned Marie Dewigne!

The second sign of the secret lineage that links Captaine Haddock to an illustrious man is not a word, but an image. On page two of *Les sept boules de cristal* (Figure 4), we see the coat of arms that decorates the pediment of the entrance gate of Moulinsart. This coat of arms, seen only once in all the *Aventures of Tintin*, represents . . . a crowned *dauphin!* This drawing is like a graphic slip. There is, indeed, no overt reason why the castle of Moulinsart, given, Hergé tells us, by King

Figure 4. Hergé, *Les sept boules de cristal* © Hergé/Moulinsart 2002

Louis XIV to the Chevalier de Hadoque, should bear such a royal insignia! On the other hand, this coat of arms takes on its full meaning once we imagine that this meaning escaped Hergé the one time he ever traced it out in his work. This coat of arms is emblematic of his own secret desire, i.e., that his father Alexis had been acknowledged by his illustrious and perhaps aristocratic father, Hergé's famous and enigmatic grandfather. If such had been the case, it is Hergé who would be entitled to exhibit the family coat-of-arms.

HISTORICAL REALITY AND
PSYCHOLOGICAL REALITY

The reader undoubtedly still has a few questions. Is the history of an illustrious father that one can infer from *Les aventures de Tintin* the true story of Hergé's family? And, more importantly, was Hergé at all aware that he was putting into his work all that we have found there? The answer to both these questions is "no." The hidden story that runs through the Tintin volumes is, first and foremost, a story Hergé told himself when he was five or six years old in order to answer his own questions. Later, very probably weary of not getting from his parents the answers to the questions he was asking about his grandfather, he buried that story in a small corner of his mind. Once he had grown up and become a graphic artist, he then found the way back to it through his creation. At that point these erased memory structures became partially conscious once again as, for example, when he drew inspiration from his father and his uncle in order to create the two Dupondts. Yet other aspects of these childhood constructions clearly inspired his graphics without his being aware of it. It is hardly likely, for instance, that he was conscious of the coincidences of dates that suggest that the chevalier is the bastard son of Louis XIV, or of the importance of the letters KAR in the proper names in his work. Since Hergé is telling us the stories he told himself when he was five or six years old, his narrative does not encompass his family reality: his grandfather could have been an industrialist who was just passing through, an attorney, or even an utterly commonplace figure. Countess de Dudzeele's concern for the twins could indeed point to "services" rendered by Marie Dewigne, and of which we know nothing. Human complexity being what it is, this hypothesis is still conceivable, even if not highly plausible. In any case, what matters is not this "historical truth" we will probably never know anything more about, but rather the way this family secret was the crucible of the daydreams that eventually structured Hergé's work. His own oedipal desire to be the offspring of an "illustrious" father resonated with a family history that allowed uncertainty to persist regarding an aristocratic grandfather, a convergence which then produced the fantasy of a royal birth displayed in the secret kinship of the Chevalier de Hadoque and King Louis XIV.

Les aventures de Tintin therefore do not tell the history of a family; they narrate instead the tales a five- to eight-year-old child can come up with when a crucial feature of that history has been condemned to secrecy. Strictly speaking, the secret in question was not the child's, since it had been his grandmother's first. However, like every child faced with a family secret, Hergé appropriated it, or rather, he reinvented it on the basis of what he had heard and imagined.

This might finally provide an explanation of Hergé's ideological stability through the turmoil of his century. Because this secret forced him to stay in the mental world of his childhood, Hergé also remained loyal to the ideological choices of the adults who had surrounded him. The world of Tintin thus reflected, until the death of its creator, the ideological choices of the Belgian lower middle class of the early twentieth century, while everything around Hergé was changing. By the same token, Les aventures de Tintin managed to bear witness both to a family's unspeakable secret and to a generation's guilty ideology, which had been shamed and silenced by the defeat of the Axis powers. Family memories that remain frozen because of a family secret will sometimes succeed in freezing social memory as well. And that is also why Les aventures de Tintin have a beautiful future: they are at the crossroads of something unspeakable that is both familial and social and that discourages in a way every attempt to give them either an exclusively "social" or an exclusively "psychological" reading. Little reporter Tintin, who incidentally never reports to any newspaper, is a kind of investigator of a family memory stuck in another age because of its own private secret. And, as in a fairy tale, everything around it was also frozen, yet with the secret and mad hope that, someday, everything might be set in motion again—history, the ideology that went along with it, and the hidden secret.

—Translated from the French by Barbara Harshav

PHILIP MOSLEY

Anxiety, Memory, and Place in Belgian Cinema

Modern Belgium came into being in 1830 as the result of a need to create a buffer-state between the European powers of the time. The fusion of ethnolinguistic differences in the interest of a unified nation-state began a historical process that has subjected the Belgian people to prolonged anxieties over their identity, the role of their ruling class, and the policies adopted by their successive governments. While such periodic anxieties belong to the histories of any nation-state, chronic doubts about the validity and legitimacy of nationhood have always accompanied the troublesome Belgian case, occasionally destabilizing national unity to an extent that threatened the continued existence of the state. These anxieties have manifested themselves in various momentous historical issues whose import at one time or another has been primarily political, social, moral, religious, and even geophysical (holding the line of internal and external frontiers). These issues have included imperialism and colonialism, wartime collaboration, the role of the monarchy, state versus religious education, languages, unemployment, and immigration.

The volatile Belgian national condition has been somewhat defused in recent years by a steady movement toward a form of federalization via constitutional revisions, but at the cost of a weakened unitary state. This widespread loss of confidence produced a moral panic precipitated by a series of traumatic events, beginning in the late 1980s with a wave of urban terrorism, followed by the Dutroux pedophile murders in 1996, and the Agusta-Dassault corruption scandal in 1998. This panic brought huge numbers of citizens onto the streets to express their outrage at the apparent collapse of governmental authority and the corruption of the Belgian establishment.

Since the concept of national identity depends heavily on a tradi-

YFS 102, *Belgian Memories*, ed. Catherine Labio, © 2002 by Yale University.

160

tion of collective memory, these anxieties have also raised questions of public remembering and forgetting. Discussion of certain issues—for instance, the imperial-colonial projects in Africa and wartime collaboration with the Germans—has remained quite sensitive, especially at official levels. Since control of collective memory directly affects both self-image and power relations within society, it follows that suppression, elision, and revision of history may occur. As Jacques Le Goff reminds us: "To make themselves the master of memory and forgetfulness is one of the great preoccupations of the classes, groups and individuals who have dominated and continue to dominate historical societies. The things forgotten or not mentioned by history reveal these mechanisms for the manipulation of collective memory."[1]

Historiographers now generally accept that memory, while an individual cognitive act, is nonetheless at the same time also a social construct, since we remember and forget things within a context of belonging to social groups and engaging in communal patterns of behavior. Furthermore, as Maurice Halbwachs's pioneering work suggests, we construct the framework of social memory largely by a sense of place: "We situate what we recollect within the mental spaces provided by the group. But these mental spaces, Halbwachs insisted, always receive support from and refer back to the material spaces that particular social groups occupy."[2] As an art that represents both time and space, cinema is particularly able to explore such relationships between society, memory, and place.

*   *   *   *   *

Belgian cinema, affected in its own historical evolution by the fact of ethnolinguistic division, has nonetheless found ways to articulate national and subnational anxieties in a variety of film forms. Some films function as allegories of national identity problems, despite revolving around fictional (auto)biographies of individual characters. This is true, for instance, of Jan Bucquoy's *La vie sexuelle des belges* (1993) and especially of Jaco Van Dormael's *Toto le héros* (1991), which ingeniously relates a lifelong anxiety over the mistaken personal identity of the hero against a backdrop, as in Bucquoy's film, of Belgian social and cultural history from the 1950s onwards. Similarly, we may compare the

1. Jacques Le Goff, *History and Memory*, trans. Steven Rendall and Elizabeth Claman (New York: Columbia University Press, 1992), 54.
2. Paul Connerton, *How Societies Remember* (Cambridge: Cambridge University Press, 1989), 37.

strong satirical content of Bucquoy's film to that found in other national visions, such as the political dystopias of Robbe De Hert's *Camera Sutra* (1973) or Alain Berliner's *Le mur* (2000).

The four films I have chosen to discuss in this essay—*La promesse* (1996) and *Rosetta* (1999) by Luc and Jean-Pierre Dardenne, *Bruxelles-Transit* (1980) by Samy Szlingerbaum, and *Een vrouw tussen hond en wolf* (Woman in a Twilight Garden) (1979) by André Delvaux—are equally powerful transmitters of aspects of social memory. They are also deeply rooted in place. One way in which a Belgian sense of place has been determined officially is by the three semi-autonomous regions (Wallonia, Brussels, and Flanders), the institution of which reflects the development of political, economic, and ethnolinguistic interests within contemporary Belgium. In considering these films we will travel, so to speak, across these three regions, carrying with us an interweaving tracery of anxiety, memory, and place. Alongside these official designations of identity there exist multiple counterimages, based more closely on popular memory and frequently mobilized as oppositional views of place—as, for instance, in polarized opinions of Brussels as an old, "popular" city to be preserved or as a new "Europolis" to replace it.

My juxtaposition of these four films invites a number of comparisons and contrasts. The Dardennes and Szlingerbaum engage distinctively with issues of displacement, immigration, and unemployment, while Delvaux deals specifically with Flemish collaboration during World War Two. All four films represent significant creative cooperations. The Dardenne brothers usually work together, generating a peculiar understanding reminiscent of other fraternal filmmaking teams like Joel and Ethan Coen or especially Timothy and Stephen Quay, whose fantastic-surrealist cinema shares a sensibility deeply embedded in Belgian culture. Szlingerbaum (d. 1986) worked together with his mother, and Delvaux (d. 2002) with Flemish author Ivo Michiels.

*   *   *   *   *

A major Belgian anxiety during the last half-century, especially for the citizens of Wallonia, has been the declining industrial and agricultural power of that region. This anxiety has been exacerbated by a concurrent increase in Flemish prosperity and influence that, despite a Francophone majority in Brussels, has steadily transferred economic ascendancy in Belgian life from the French- to the Dutch-language region.

Several films by Walloon directors—notably Jean-Jacques Andrien,

Thierry Michel, and the Dardenne brothers—have addressed this post-industrial condition, its social and psychological effects. Jacques Dubois discusses Andrien's impressive work elsewhere in this volume. Michel has been instrumental in the construction both of a recognizably Walloon cinema sensitive to these issues—as in his dramatization of a failed general strike, *Hiver 60* (1982)—and of a postcolonial cinema, tackling equally prickly subjects in a series of documentaries such as *Les derniers colons* (1995) and *Mobutu, roi du Zaïre* (1999). The Dardennes began in documentary video, graduating to fictional features with *Falsch* (1986) and *Je pense à vous* (1992), both dealing very differently with questions of history and memory. Basing *Falsch* on a play by Belgian writer René Kalisky about displaced Jews' memories of the Holocaust, the directors switch the setting from New York to an anonymous airport. The film is a bold if highly stylized effort to confront issues of alienation and memory through the uncomfortable reunion of the Falsch (false) family at the airport. Set amid the abandoned factories of Seraing, near Liège, where the Dardennes grew up, *Je pense à vous* is more typical of their realist aesthetic in its portrayal of a man made redundant by the declining steel industry. However, an uneven script and mise-en-scène limit the filmmakers' success in fusing the psychological dynamics of a personal drama with a broader social and historical analysis.

The Dardennes honed their vision finely in their next two features, *La promesse* and *Rosetta,* both prizewinners at the Cannes festival. *La promesse* concerns a teenage boy, Igor, caught up in his father's opportunistic exploitation of a group of illegal immigrant workers. When one of them, an African named Amidu, falls from a construction site scaffold, he asks Igor with his dying words to promise to look after his wife and child. Igor's filial bond gradually weakens as he turns his youthful energies toward the keeping of his promise. Torn between his new commitment and the continuing demands of his father, who conceals Amidu's death from both his widow and the authorities in order to protect his own clandestine operation, Igor is forced into an ethical awakening.

Rosetta tells of another teenager from the same depressed urban milieu faced with equally difficult choices. Engaged in a desperate struggle to survive a hopeless existence caring for her alcoholic mother in a bleak trailer park, Rosetta wants nothing more than a "normal" life and a "real" job, neither of which appear remotely possible in her present circumstances. Though painfully vulnerable, Rosetta steels herself to be fiercely assertive and even unscrupulous in her dealings with others. Success in her terms is measured by selling a home-sewn dress to a clothing store or doing menial work for the owner of a chain of waffle stands.

La promesse reveals the uneasy coexistence of native Belgians and immigrant workers in an area where unemployment currently runs between twenty and thirty percent. A long history exists of immigration to the Sambre-Meuse industrial area to fill jobs in the coal mines, steel mills, and other factories. For instance, the life of the Italian mining community has been shown in Paul Meyer's neorealist-inspired *Déjà s'envole la fleur maigre* (1960)—which has belatedly received the recognition it deserves—and more recently in the films of Loredana Bianconi, such as *Avec de l'Italie qui descendrait l'Escaut* (1993). Since the 1960s, following the decline of the heavy industries and the decrease in immigration of the earliest ethnic groups (Italian, Polish, and Czech), Belgium has become more "an amalgam of peoples who bear the marks of postcolonial relocation, the Jewish diaspora, and general post-war mobility: it is a mosaic of different groups of people, for whom Belgium is a place rather than a nation."[3]

An increase in illegal immigration—corresponding to the present climate of Eastern European displacement, global labor mobility, and the relaxation of border controls—provides a means for Igor's father to earn a living by trafficking in alien workers. The opening shot of *La promesse*, showing a convoy of transient workers climbing down from an automobile transporter in front of an abandoned factory, powerfully contrasts this postindustrial society with its predecessor. Igor and his father believe that their "enterprise" employing these aliens cheaply will reward the two of them in a community where steady jobs in traditional workplaces have all but disappeared. This exploitation of others for personal gain and the disposal of Amidu's body suggest a chilling parallel to the Dutroux murders, which occurred in the Charleroi area of Wallonia and for many Belgians were symptomatic of a general breakdown of social and moral values. Charleroi is also the setting for a comparable recent film, *Les convoyeurs attendent* (1999), a first feature by documentarist Benoît Mariage. In following the fortunes of a similarly dysfunctional family unit, for whom this kind of bricolage has become a virtual way of life, the film takes the struggle for eco-

3. Lieve Spaas, *The Francophone Film: A Struggle for Identity* (Manchester and New York: Manchester University Press, 2000), 8.

nomic survival in *La promesse* and *Rosetta* to an absurdly humorous point.

In the context of a magazine interview, Jean-Pierre Dardenne guides dramatist and fellow Seraing native Jean-Marie Piemme on a walking tour of familiar parts of the town. The dialogue between the two artists explores their sense of memory and place as they agree on the crucial role of physical space in structuring mental space. Both consider public spaces—such as squares and bridges, where large communal gatherings occurred in their youth—to represent the most important places of memory, especially in their symbolic connection with the expression of collective will and power by a formerly proud, defiant, and often militant Walloon working class. Both also perceive a "double scenography" in the landscape of present day Seraing, an aspect the Dardennes sought to capture in *La promesse:* "To film in places built to last and in temporary places next to them. To try to show this evolution."[4] If we may attribute the first of these places to the solid architectural and social fabrics of industrial plant and traditional working-class life, the second is clearly in accord with the fragile, adaptable, disposable quality of postmodern space and the expedient, dislocated culture of late capitalist society that spawns it.

Jean-Pierre Dardenne explains that his and his brother's three most recent features, like their earlier Armand Gatti-influenced documentaries, continue to illuminate the crisis of Walloon decline but now emphasize storytelling and characterization over ideological statement. These later films particularly explore how individuals deal mentally and physically with an uneasy hiatus between old and new ways of life. Thus in *La promesse* and *Rosetta* the Dardennes foreground the bodies of their young protagonists, seemingly always in motion, as determinants of the visual style of the films. This is especially true of the close-up, hand-held camerawork in *Rosetta*, where shot composition and editing rhythm are dictated by the relentless, repetitive physicality of Rosetta's daily routine. While the postindustrial landscape of the Liège conurbation functions more than before as an emotional correlative to dominant trajectories of narrative and character development, the "double scenography" of Seraing continues to haunt every shot, however cursory, of boarded-up windows, grey streets, derelict lots, concrete jungles, and high-rise buildings. Igor and Rosetta literally embody

---

4. "Café des citoyens. Un dialogue entre Jean-Pierre Dardenne et Jean-Marie Piemme," *Le carnet et Les instants* 101 (1998): 23. All translations from this source are my own.

that environment. In every word, gesture, movement, and expression on their curiously innocent yet worldly faces, we see the visible traces of social history and memory. As Piemme astutely observes, "The body is the habitat of history" (*Carnet*, 24).

Lieve Spaas is of the opinion that *La promesse* and *Rosetta* differ from *Falsch* and *Je pense à vous* in that they offer no sense of the past, abandoning memory for "a new cinematic language to express a new paradigm, where identity emerges in the present" (40). While it is true that neither film makes any direct reference to the past, either in script or flashback form, the continuing engagement with a sense of the past expressed in the Dardenne-Piemme dialogue would seem to support my view that both films carry the unconscious weight of memory, one that is often buried or repressed. I suggest this in the spirit of Marc Bloch's "prudently retrogressive" historiographic method, whereby the past cannot be understood without a sense of the present, and vice versa. If past and present coexist within the flow of "real" or "lived" time (a basic tenet of "new" history), then memory is always present in conscious or unconscious forms. If, as Piemme suggests, "every dive into the past is a reconstruction made from and for the present" (*Carnet*, 26), then do not all present representations in turn depend upon an implicit or explicit sense of the past?

*   *   *   *   *

As we move northward from Wallonia to Brussels, we remain nonetheless in familiar thematic territory. *Bruxelles-Transit* is also about displacement and immigration, in this case of Jewish survivors of the Holocaust. There were 40,000 Jews in Belgium in 1947: 5,000 citizens, 20–25,000 legal expatriates, and around 10,000 transients. Despite governmental aid, many of the non-citizens faced serious problems of integration and assimilation, a situation worsened in a difficult period of economic and social reconstruction by a surge of xenophobia tinged by residual Nazi propaganda.[5]

In Le Goff's words, "the Jewish people are the people of memory par excellence" (69). Based on the true story of a single family, *Bruxelles-Transit* is also a work of collective memory, a contribution to the documentation of the Jewish experience in World War Two and the Holocaust. Yet the film breaks with the received history and memory of those events, which Szlingerbaum never directly mentions, though

---

5. See Willy Bok, "Bruxelles-Transit. Les immigrés juifs d'après-guerre," in Samy Szlingerbaum, *Bruxelles-Transit* (Brussels: Editions Complexe, 1989), 89–91.

they are implied in everything we see or hear. Instead, the story begins in Poland in 1947, recounting Szlingerbaum's young parents' and his two-year old brother's ten-day journey by train through Czechoslovakia, Germany, and France to Brussels, where with the help of relatives they abandon their Central American transit visa and make a new home.

For this family, as for the itinerant workers in *La promesse,* a precarious existence after their arrival becomes the norm, defined by short-term renewable visas, rationed food, lack of work permits, shared domestic spaces, and the monotony of a daily routine organized wholly around survival against the odds. As isolated foreigners—and Jews—of extremely limited means, what little contact they have with the native population is restricted to various awkward encounters that heighten their sense of marginality and lack of communication with others. These encounters include a frustrating exchange in a corner bakery, a tense parcelling-out of kitchen space with a haughty neighbor, and a disjointed conversation about their status with a policeman who comes to the door. One of the most vivid scenes is at the bakery. The young woman has prepared *farfeleh* at home, but her kitchen has no oven. With no knowledge of French she tries vainly to persuade the proprietress to bake it for her, later throwing the whole dish into the canal in anger and despair.

We do not see any stage of the family's journey to Belgium, we only hear about it in the voice-over narration (subtitled in French) by Szlingerbaum's mother. This narration in unscripted Yiddish (published later in French translation) is the core of the film's emotional and historical resonance, and the visual images exist in counterpoint to it. Its language gives *Bruxelles-Transit* an extra dimension both as a rare example of Yiddish cinema and as a memory-text that seeks to preserve an endangered culture within Judaism. Though diegetic sound bolsters a mood of documentary realism, the film has no music and little dialogue, further keeping the narration to the fore. Szlingerbaum permits the flow of memory to express itself naturally in the quiet, even tone of his mother's account, one nonetheless not without moments of humor and sadness. At times the account is extremely precise, at other times vague and forgetful. The narrator occasionally succumbs to fatigue or loss of concentration; at one point she exclaims in French, "Samy, that's all for today. Please!" (*Bruxelles-Transit,* 25).

By displaying a preference for long takes, frontal shots, and sound-image disjunctions, Szlingerbaum further distances the film from con-

ventional fictional forms. Reflecting the idiosyncrasies of the narration, some images match it, others do not. These images have a meditative quality, depicting specific incidents but also dwelling on the monotony of daily routine. For instance, as the mother recalls the journey
from Poland to Belgium, the director slowly intercuts shots of the three
refugees arriving at the Gare du Midi in Brussels with obliquely related
shots of passing trains, the station, and its immediate surroundings.
Though these sites are recognizable to those familiar with them,
Szlingerbaum carefully ignores any identifying signs, further allowing
him to abstract his geographical context. By shooting entirely on location in Brussels, using simple dress and plain interior decor and employing no archival footage, Szlingerbaum frees his film from any tendency to represent a historical spectacle. He concentrates instead on
giving expression to subjective memories of a period's impact upon a
close-knit group of individuals—and, by implication, upon all families,
Jewish or otherwise, fleeing from the devastations of war. The film becomes a loose dramatic reconstruction of events recounted by the
mother and interpreted visually by her son. However, this double play
of memory is not personally synchronous, since the boy we see arriving in Brussels in 1947 is Szlingerbaum's brother, the filmmaker having been born two years later. The continuity of Szlingerbaum's own
living memory is thus limited to a period after the events shown in the
first part of the film.

In its formal strategies and exploration of Jewish exodus, the film
resembles Chantal Akerman's *News from Home* (1976), in which random images of New York accompany the voice of Akerman's mother
recounting family news from Brussels to her expatriate daughter.
Szlingerbaum had earlier been an assistant to Akerman (who was executive producer of *Bruxelles-Transit*) and to Boris Lehman, with whom
he forms a trio of filmmakers deeply concerned by their Jewish identity and memories of their Brussels upbringing.

The train stations of European cities and their surrounding districts
continue to reflect a geopolitics of displacement by war, poverty, and
political oppression. For the poor immigrant population of today, as for
Szlingerbaum's own family in the wake of the Holocaust, the station
has a double meaning. As the initial site of a new beginning in a foreign
land, it symbolizes a decisive psychological and cultural step forward.
Yet the network of rails leading to and from the station also represents
an umbilical cord keeping these newcomers in contact, however tangentially, with their places of origin and their past. Lack of confidence

in or acceptance by their host society encourages many to stay close to the points of arrival and departure, as if fearful of venturing further into the unknown and distancing themselves from the point of possible return. This double meaning is particularly ironic in Szlingerbaum's historical context, since Jews and other persecuted minorities soon discovered that the train was for some a means of escape and survival but for others the principal vehicle of deportation to their deaths. Gare du Midi and Treblinka: the peacetime promise of the former and the wartime "promise" of the latter, whose mock façade gaily welcomed new inmates to a camp of no return.

Beyond the particular relevance of the Gare du Midi district to the memories recounted in the film, Szlingerbaum displays a fascination with train images and their associations that has attended both realist and nonrealist cinematic modes from the startling actuality of the Lumières' first films to the staccato, high velocity, time-lapsed images of Wong Kar-Wai's postmodern world. Szlingerbaum's documentary style usurps the traditional monumentality of the station, rendering it instead an ordinary, uninspiring place. With subtle irony he thus dedramatizes the extraordinary arrival of his family in Brussels. At the same time his gentle, cadenced montage of the station interior and of trains at night has a hypnotic, oneiric quality often found in the canvases of fellow Belgian artists Paul Delvaux and René Magritte (and of de Chirico, too). Like these painters, Szlingerbaum defamiliarizes the station and its surrounding area in order to reinvest them with the emotional value of a dreamscape, a locus of enigmatic hopes and fears, of strange journeys, long waitings, and brief encounters in silent, empty, timeless space.

The cityscape of central Brussels changed greatly in Szlingerbaum's short lifetime. Anxieties generated by the transformation of old neighborhoods into wastelands of concrete, glass, and steel—as well as the consequent effects upon their inhabitants' sense of community and identity—have been addressed by a number of other Belgian filmmakers. The approach may be serious, as in André Ernotte's *Rue Haute* (1976), or in *Magnum Begynasium Bruxellense* (1978) where Lehman focuses on the history of the Beguinage, another radically redeveloped district in the heart of the city. Occasionally the approach is lighthearted or satirical, as in Benoît Lamy's *Home Sweet Home* (1973) or in Kaat Beels's *Bruxelles mon amour* (2000). Even *C'est arrivé près de chez vous* (1992), an acerbic parody of violence in the media by Remy Belvaux, André Bonzel, and Benoît Poelvoorde, "is studded with allusions to the demise of the old 'people's Brussels,' as when . . . a friend [of the protagonist, Ben] complains that she has been forced out of the Sablon area . . . by property developers."[6]

One of the most infamous of these redevelopments was the opening in 1952 of the "train station valley," a largely underground rail link between the Gare du Nord and the Gare du Midi. This project involved wholesale demolition of medieval sections of central Brussels and their subsequent replacement by a succession of stark office buildings, parking garages, and roadways. We have seen how the space at the southern end of the "valley" (Gare du Midi) articulates the relationship between place and memory in Szlingerbaum's film. It is a "site of memory" (*lieu de mémoire*) in Pierre Nora's sense of "any significant entity . . . which by dint of human will or the work of time has become a symbolic element of the memorial heritage of any community."[7] The entire "valley" functions as a site of memory as well, having defined the history of various immigrant groups that settled around Nord or Midi, but also having redefined the idea of Brussels in a highly charged and persistent debate over the transformation of a historic, identifiably Belgian city into the capital of European power.

*   *   *   *   *

As we circle out from Brussels into the surrounding region, we realize that Flanders too has faced particular anxieties in the course of its slow and often painful rise from subordinate status to a position of political, linguistic, and cultural equality with French-speaking Belgium. The danger of ideological extremism present in nationalist visions of Flemish empowerment and autonomy has remained one of the most persistent of these anxieties, especially in the historical context of collaboration with the Germans during two World Wars.

Though collaboration had been an issue during World War One and did not occur solely in Flanders, its recurrence in World War Two followed directly on the emergence of militant Flemish politics in the interwar years in the form of right-wing parties such as the Vlaams Nationaal Verbond and the national-socialist De Vlag. After the Liberation, 340,000 Belgians were accused of collaboration, of whom 58,000 were found guilty and 241 executed. The issue lingered in another na-

6. Keith Reader, "Belgian Film Comedy and National Identity," in Joe Andrew, Malcolm Crook, Diana Holmes, Eva Kolinsky, eds., *Why Europe? Problems of Culture and Identity* (New York: St. Martin's Press, 2000), vol. 2, 32.

7. Pierre Nora, *Realms of Memory: Rethinking the French Past*, trans. Arthur Goldhammer (New York: Columbia University Press, 1996), vol. 1, xvii.

tional anxiety, in this case over the ambiguous wartime position of Leopold III that culminated in his abdication in 1953. A collective memory so sensitive that it was rarely discussed for many years, the "Royal Question" recently began to be addressed in Belgian literature and film in the work, for instance, of writer Pierre Mertens and film-maker Christian Mesnil.

The issue of Flemish separatism did not disappear. In the 1960s "language wars" between French- and Flemish-speaking communities became the major anxiety of the Belgian people. Despite his disavowal of political filmmaking, André Delvaux's magic realist *Un soir, un train* (1968) touched on an issue so contentious at the time—following the division of Leuven University along ethnolinguistic lines—that it brought down the national government later that same year. A decade later, when Delvaux made *Een vrouw tussen hond en wolf* (rereleased in a French version as *Femme entre chien et loup*, 1979), Flemish na-tionalist politics was beginning again to harden its stance with the emergence of the Vlaams Blok party. Breaking a longstanding taboo in Belgian cinema on the discussion of wartime collaboration, Delvaux felt a need to warn his fellow Belgians about a potential resurgence of fascism by representing on film a period in which an earlier flirtation with it had taken place. His boldness paved the way for Hugo Claus, Flanders' most renowned living writer, to break a corresponding liter-ary taboo in *Het verdriet van België* (The Sorrow of Belgium, 1983), a highly provocative novel filmed as a serial for Belgian television in 1994 by the Swiss director Claude Goretta.

Delvaux's film focuses on three young natives of Antwerp: Lieve, her husband Adriaan, and her wartime lover François. The film moves from 1939, when Lieve marries Adriaan, to 1952, when she leaves him for an uncertain but independent future. Throughout the war she re-mains in her Antwerp home, torn between Adriaan who, committed to Aryan ideology, is fighting for the Germans on the Eastern Front, and François, the resistance fighter whom she had been hiding from the au-thorities. François helps Adriaan escape severe punishment for collab-oration on his return at the end of the war, but Adriaan soon reverts to his obsessions, reclusively devoting himself to the composition of a lengthy self-defense. Now with a son to care for, Lieve finally rejects both men in her life along with their conflicting beliefs.

Though at first glance an unlikely comparison, *Een vrouw tussen hond en wolf* resembles *Bruxelles-Transit* in several respects. Both films deal with the aftermath of World War Two, both decline the spectacular lure of "History" for a more personal meditation centered on a woman's experience, and both confine the locus of memory to a single place. As for the creative cooperation in this instance, Delvaux and author Ivo Michiels had previously worked together on *Met [With] Dieric Bouts* (1975), Delvaux's television documentary on the Renaissance painter, another original meditation on Flemish identity, memory, and place. Delvaux explains how they approached the making of *Een vrouw tussen hond en wolf*:

> I came to an agreement with Michiels as to how we would do the screenplay and the detail of the film we were to make together. Simply, I had asked him, as a Flemish author, to write this screenplay on the basis of weekly meetings between us. And he wrote down what we discussed. And I accepted that he would publish it under his own name, since it was his writing. But it's a screenplay conceived by the two of us. As a result, we may say that the formula used in the credits is correct: the screenplay is by Michiels and myself, but it has been written by Michiels.[8]

Delvaux's only modification of Michiels's work, carried out in front of the camera with the help of his three main actors, was to give greater balance to their roles by lessening Michiels's emphasis on Adriaan's character. However, Delvaux requested no rewrites and changed nothing in the script, wherein he claimed to find all that he needed to shoot the film. This cooperation yielded two symbiotic texts: Michiels's 1977 prizewinning novel, *Een tuin tussen hond en wolf* (Garden between Dog and Wolf) and Delvaux's film. Michiels's title stresses the wartime symbols of dog (defender) and wolf (aggressor) rather than the other meaning ("twilight garden") conveyed by the title when translated literally into French and incorporated into the English release title, *Woman in a Twilight Garden*. Eventually the film was called "Woman between Dog and Wolf " in both Dutch and French, the title having been changed for French distribution purposes.

As in *Bruxelles-Transit*, a double play of memory structures the film. In this instance a spatial discrepancy exists between the two sets of personal memories since Michiels, unlike Delvaux, spent the wartime period in the Antwerp area and so was able to imbue his script with the authenticity of local experience. Memory in the film is therefore based on parallel recollections that Delvaux transfers to the per-

---

8. My translation from an interview. See my article "From Book to Film: André Delvaux's Alchemy of the Image," *French Review* 67/5 (April 1994): 817–18.

spective of his main characters, especially Lieve, whose viewpoint is the focus of the film. This results in less dependence on what Foucault calls "total" history and more on a "general" principle that "turns to novel ways of making historical evidence intelligible in terms of particular problems."[9] In this way Delvaux's film, like Szlingerbaum's, constructs a "counter-memory" whose main characteristic is a heterodoxical, albeit chronological, historical view.

Unlike in conventional war films, there are no public heroes, famous speeches, or epic scenes of combat. Nor is there any martial music; instead we hear popular tunes performed on radios or in bars and at wedding parties. Colors are not those of flags, uniforms, and panoramic landscapes, but of clothes, interiors, and gardens. By using color and sound thus to express nuances of memory, Delvaux avoids "spectacle elements [that] tend towards a generalized, extrapersonal perspective in portraying historical cause,"[10] offering instead an intimate, painterly chronicle of private lives under circumstances of personal and historical duress. It is as if Lieve, the "woman in a twilight garden" becomes the equivalent, in Delvaux's filmic eye, of a still life by Vermeer.

As Szlingerbaum's film restricts itself to a small area of central Brussels, so Delvaux's film (other than the scene of Lieve's uncomfortable visit to her rural relatives) stays in a single Antwerp neighborhood. Apart from several brief scenes representative of wartime history (air raids, round-ups, partisan actions, Liberation parades) in adjacent streets and squares, most of the film's action unfolds within Lieve's private space. In a further similarity to *Bruxelles-Transit*, Lieve exhibits a strong vein of self-protectiveness. As Szlingerbaum's mother remembers a resigned domestic existence at least to have been safer than an engagement with society at large, so Lieve clings to the sanctuary of her house and garden, whose walls shield her from the madness beyond. And while Lieve might seem to be freer than Szlingerbaum's mother to choose her way of life, she finds herself as trapped by her personal relationships as she is by the war. She cannot prevent that external madness from entering her home when it becomes a refuge, first for a fugitive François and, after the war, for an increasingly uncompanionable Adriaan. A potent symbol of fecundity, rootedness to the land, and religious faith, the pear tree in their garden combines the values of do-

9. Mark Cousins and Athar Hussain, *Michel Foucault* (New York: St. Martin's Press, 1984), 82.
10. Leger Grindon, *Shadows on the Past: Studies in the Historical Fiction Film* (Philadelphia: Temple University Press, 1994), 6.

mesticity with those of the Flemish cause. Driven to the brink of insanity by the collapse of his dreams, Adriaan chops down the tree in a gesture as desperately defiant as that of the raped girl's father in Ingmar Bergman's *The Virgin Spring,* who strips a birch of its boughs in an effort to purify himself before avenging the crime against his child.

Delvaux depicts the consequences of Adriaan's extremism but carefully avoids a simplistic Manichaeism by subjecting the opposing ideology to a measure of critical rememoration. The idealism that drives François in war becomes cynical ambition after the war's end. Delvaux also demystifies, if more gently, the whole memory of the resistance and the process of reconstruction. We witness ruthless partisan recriminations: for instance, women who had associated with Germans get their heads shaven and are openly humiliated. This scene is reminiscent of one in Alain Resnais's *Hiroshima mon amour* (1959), another unconventional film about memories of World War Two, made by a director whose sensibility has much in common with that of Delvaux, and which again involved a creative cooperation between filmmaker and writer (Marguerite Duras). In her preface to the text of the film, Duras describes a sympathetic relationship not unlike that between Delvaux and Michiels: "Readers should not be surprised that Resnais's 'pictorial' contribution is practically never described in this work. My role is limited to describing those elements from which Resnais made his film."[11]

Nor does Delvaux's film spare the Catholic Church, as it portrays the parish priest who acts as mentor to Lieve and Adriaan as a mediocre, unreliable opportunist. Working largely through the low clergy, the Flemish bishops, motivated by a fear of Bolshevism, encouraged susceptible young men like Adriaan to pursue a pseudomystical blend of patriotism and faith by joining the Flemish battalion of the *Wehrmacht,* yet abandoned them once the tide had turned against the Nazis in 1943, swiftly consigning the matter to history. This collective amnesia lasted for a long time, and Delvaux found the Church still reluctant to discuss the history of that period more than thirty years later, when he decided to make his film.

*   *   *   *   *

These films of the Dardennes, Szlingerbaum, and Delvaux reveal complex and unsettling relationships between anxiety, memory, and place

11. Marguerite Duras and Alain Resnais, *Hiroshima mon amour,* trans. Richard Seaver (New York: Grove Press, 1961), 7.

that characterize the history of Belgium and of its constituent peoples. By offering distinctive and personalized representations of a number of these anxieties, I believe these films (and others like them) have helped to open up discussion of issues that Belgians have often found difficult to confront. Two recent films support this view. Julie Vrebos's *Le bal masqué* (1998) is a thinly veiled dramatization of the notorious spate of "supermarket slayings" carried out in the late 1980s by a gang of urban terrorists, a series of events that contributed greatly to a growing feeling of malaise on the part of Belgians regarding the state of their society and the condition of Belgium itself. It needed only the Dutroux murders and their mishandling by the authorities to precipitate a huge crisis of faith in the integrity of the Belgian establishment. Marian Handwerker's *Pure Fiction*, based on the Dutroux affair, was released barely two years afterwards in 1998, suggesting that at least in the medium of cinema the prevalence of collective amnesia in Belgian history seemed to be coming to an end.

FRANÇOISE AUBRY

Victor Horta: Vicissitudes of a Work

In this essay, I shall trace the vicissitudes of some of the works of Victor Horta (1861–1947), for they reveal, as much as political or sociological discourse does, the chaos, blindness, and emotional maelstroms that seem inevitably to accompany architecture in Belgium. An international figure in the heyday of Art Nouveau, Horta saw his glory decline between the two world wars, just as he was realizing his most profound aspirations: the erection of public buildings that would guarantee more enduring general recognition than the private houses commissioned at the start of his career.[1] The Palais des Beaux-Arts, the Gare Centrale and the (aborted) development of the Quartier Royal were to put his stamp on the historic center of the city of Brussels. According to Horta's memoirs, begun in 1939, this was to make up for the feeling he had had in 1922, that he was thought of as a "humble Belgian with only second-rate shops to his credit, as well as houses of dubious taste, and a hospital that had swallowed up millions" (*Mémoires*, 241).[2]

Horta had just been deeply distressed by the mutilations of the Hôtel Roget, a private home he had designed in 1901 and altered personally in 1909 at the request of its new owner, Paul Verstraete (*Mémoires*, 87–90). In 1920, however, Baron Descamps-David had wiped out every trace of Victor Horta's style from the façade, which had then become perfectly dreary. At the time, there were those who saw this action as

1. On the subject of Horta, see especially Franco Borsi and Paolo Portoghesi, *Victor Horta*, trans. Marie-Hélène Agüeros (New York: Rizzoli, 1991); Victor Horta, *Mémoires*, ed. Cécile Dulière (Brussels: Ministère de la Communauté française de Belgique, 1985); *Horta: Naissance et dépassement de l'Art Nouveau*, ed. Françoise Aubry and Jos Vandenbreeden (Belgium: Loudion/Flammarion, [1996]), accompanying the exhibition at the Palais des Beaux-Arts of Brussels, 4 October 1996–January 1997.
2. Horta is alluding *inter alia* to L'Innovation, the Grand Bazar Anspach and the Brugmann hospital.

YFS 102, *Belgian Memories*, ed. Catherine Labio, © 2002 by Yale University.

the vengeance of a conservative senator against the style chosen by the leaders of the Belgian Workers' Party for the Maison du Peuple. On 3 May 1921, a group of artists, "Les figuristes," signed a manifesto addressed to the Minister of Arts and Sciences, in which they argued that the façade showed "a sincere, noble, new Belgian style (that had been its crime!)."[3] Years later, interestingly enough, Franco Borsi concurred, stating that Horta's Maison du Peuple "was without a doubt the most authentically Belgian work in the history of architecture, it expressed both the values of one of the leading industrial countries of Europe as well as those of that linguistic renewal that was about to spread throughout Europe under the name of Art Nouveau."[4]

The question of the creation of an authentic national style had endured through much of the second half of the nineteenth century. What style should the recently formed Belgian state (1830) claim for itself? The Flemish Neo-Renaissance style had seemed appropriate at one point, for it conjured up the Golden Age of the old Netherlands: it was, for instance, chosen for the Belgian pavilion designed by Charles-Emile Janlet (1839–1919) for the Paris World Fair of 1878. Fifteen years later, the construction of the Hôtel Tassel[5] gave a more definitive answer: Horta wanted an architecture that would "create by renouncing [architectural] styles and relying on the generalized application of clearly visible materials" (Mémoires, 30).

If Horta's architecture is the expression of a "Belgian" style, how do we account for the insults it has suffered and the lack of national pride or collective narcissism that should have protected it?

It was because Horta had developed a personal language that had not yet been appropriated by the bourgeoisie, the nobility, or the clergy that he won favor among the leaders of the Belgian Workers' Party. In short: "a new art for a new party." Clearly, however, the views of the progressive young members of the middle-class who had rallied to the party, also played a role in Horta's success. They believed that art had to contribute to the improvement of the quality of life and education of the working class and that artists could only enhance their talent "by

3. "Manifeste des figuristes" (1921), lithograph by Anto Carte, Archives of the Horta Museum (Fondation Jean et Renée Delhaye).

4. Franco Borsi, "Victor Horta et la Maison du Peuple de Bruxelles," in *Architecture pour le peuple: Maisons du Peuple, Belgique, Allemagne, Autriche, France, Grande-Bretagne, Italie, Pays-Bas, Suisse* (Brussels: Archives d'architecture moderne [AAM], 1984), 31.

5. François Loyer and Jean Delhaye, *Victor Horta: Hôtel Tassel, 1893–1895*, trans. Susan Day (Brussels: Archives d'architecture moderne [AAM], 1986).

singing the sadness, the joys, and the hopes" of the People.[6] These ideas came to life in 1891 thanks to the creation of the department of "Art and Instruction" of the Maison du Peuple whose offices were then on the rue de Bavière. Artists invited to teach there, Horta included, did not have to belong to the Party. The creation of the department played a significant role in Horta's career, for his affiliation with the department of Art and Instruction did much to stir interest in his work among many of his future clients, just as his admission into the freemasonry had three years earlier, in 1888.[7]

The construction of the Maison du Peuple[8] (see Figure 1) was intended to strike the imagination and dazzle viewers with a demonstration of the role the Workers' Party wanted to play in political life, even though it had only just obtained parliamentary representation in 1894. Horta intended to "build a palace that would not be a palace, but a house where art and light would be the luxury so long excluded from workers' hovels" (*Mémoires*, 48). He was also aware of the importance of the site, which bordered one of the most working-class neighborhoods in Brussels, the Marolles, which had been crushed some years earlier by the staggering mass of the Palais de Justice. Horta's construction, by contrast, fit into the urban fabric while proudly asserting its presence. From the terraces, visitors experienced the excitement of discovering a vast panorama. The privilege of a beautiful view and the feeling of sovereignty were no longer the exclusive prerogative of the richest classes occupying mansions with noble tiers and balconies. The working-class crowd also took over the public space on days of mass demonstrations, when they were harangued by politicians from the slender balcony hanging above the double door of the monumental hall. The flags of the demonstrators on the square flapped in unison with those hanging on the tapered shafts rising from the balustrade of the coping, flags as red as the bricks and the painted ironwork. In his *Mémoires*, Horta mentions that "in this instance the processions and public demonstrations played as important a role as the inside itself" (50). The Maison du Peu-

6. Auguste Dewinne, in *Le peuple*, 13 October 1898, quoted by Paul Aron, *Les écrivains belges et le socialisme (1880–1913)* (Brussels: Éditions Labor [Archives du Futur], 1985), 86.

7. David Hanser, "Victor Horta, Art Nouveau, and Freemasonry," in *Belgium: The Golden Decades, 1880–1914*, ed. Jane Block (New York: Peter Lang [Belgian Francophone Library 3], 1997) 11–40.

8. Jean Delhaye, *La Maison du Peuple de Victor Horta*, introduced and annotated by Françoise Dierkens-Aubry (Brussels: Atelier Vokaer, 1987).

Figure 1. Façade of the Maison du Peuple, rue Joseph Stevens (just before the inauguration on 1 April 1899). Foundation Jean et Renée Delhaye, Musée Horta, Saint-Gilles, Brussels. © 2002-Horta/SOFAM-Belgium.

ple overshadowed the church of La Chapelle and, as Jules Lekeu emphasized, it was a case of the old faith bowing to the new.[9]

The layout of the Maison du Peuple was quite varied: it included shops offering basic staples (like bread and meat) at the lowest prices to members of cooperative societies, offices and meeting rooms, a clinic, a library, and a large hall. The request for a building permit was submitted on 26 March 1896, and the inauguration took place three years later, on 1 April 1899. Even before World War I, the Maison du Peuple had outgrown its space: in 1911, a request to raise the height of the building was submitted to the city. The following year, a new building opening onto the rue Haute was attached to the rear courtyard, which ruined the natural lighting on the rear façade beyond repair. Over the years, the color palette was dispensed with, while heating, electricity, and plumbing fixtures were coarsely altered. By the time the first rumors of demolition began circulating, the building had already suffered many humiliations. A proposal to give the building landmark status was submitted on 23 December 1963, but was never acted on. An international petition was launched by the Société centrale d'architecture de Belgique (SCAB) and the Société belge des urbanistes et architectes modernistes. The text showed a certain restraint, mentioning "a possibly outmoded ornamentation," but insisted on the quality of the space. The petitioners featured, in no particular order, architects like Alvar Aalto, Mies van der Rohe, I. M. Pei, Walter Gropius, Gio Ponti, and Jean Prouvé, and theoreticians like Bruno Zevi, Siegfried Giedion, Nikolas Pevsner, and René Huyghe. Doubts about the merit of this demolition were nevertheless swept aside by the leaders of the cooperative who wanted "modern and efficient premises."[10] When interviewed, politician Camille Huysmans judged that "Horta [wa]sn't worth bothering about. The Maison du Peuple was a pathetic structure." He even went so far as to assert that Horta had built part of the structure "en l'air," a malicious comment that reveals a complete misunderstanding of the cantilever design of the great hall.[11]

It only took a few months to get the demolition approved, but the outcry had been important enough to make the Minister of Public Works, Georges Bohy, allocate a credit of three million Belgian francs to SCAB for the dismantling of parts of the building under the supervision of architects Jean Delhaye, Pierre Puttemans, and Louis H. De

9. Jules Lekeu, *Vers l'idéal,* special edition of *Le peuple,* 1 April 1899.
10. *Le soir,* 16 October 1964.
11. *Le peuple,* 16 October 1967.

Koninck. White stones, ironwork, and woodwork were numbered and removed for temporary storage at a site in Tervueren controlled by the Musée Royal d'Afrique Centrale. In 1981 the press became concerned about the numerous thefts committed on the site. The thieves may have stepped up their activities because of the Europalia-Belgium exhibit of 1980–81, devoted to Art Nouveau, which had since become widely acclaimed. The components were then moved to an unlocked storage place in the commune of Jette.[12] Two years later, a crook claiming to be the owner of the metal pieces sold them to a scrap dealer for 2.50 francs a kilo.[13] SCAB lamented "a pitiful conclusion fit to be logged as profits and losses under the heading of national cultural indifference." It made the cover of the English-language Brussels weekly, *The Bulletin*, with the headline: "The Second Death of Victor Horta."[14] In time, ambitions for the use of the remaining components were scaled down so much that people actually rejoiced when in 1985 a few guardrails were presented for inclusion in the new "Horta" metro station in the commune of Saint-Gilles. In 1988 the press announced the "last voyage" of the remains,[15] granted to the city of Ghent with a view to enhancing a future museum of industrial archaeology, a project that eventually fell through. Some pieces were then briefly assembled to form a pavilion at the "Flanders Technology" fair, which opened in Ghent on 22 April 1991 (architect W. Slock).[16] One would have to wait until 1995 for another project to take shape, this time in Antwerp. Three years earlier the remains of the Maison du Peuple had been granted by the Stichting voor Monumenten en Landschappen (Foundation for Monuments and Landscapes) to the city of Antwerp, which had been selected as European cultural capital for 1993. The plan was to incorporate the fragments into a commercial complex to be built at 2 Hopland. The Palm Brewery and the Pension Fund of the City of Antwerp agreed to invest 50 million Belgian francs in the project. The construction company was Cosimco, Ltd. and the architects were the Arrow offices in Ghent. The goal was to divorce Horta's architecture from political culture in order to strengthen the image of a company interested in promoting a different kind of culture (Palm's spokesperson

12. *Le soir*, 12–13 July 1981.
13. *Le soir*, 13 July 1983.
14. *The Bulletin*, 15 July 1983.
15. *Le soir*, 23 February 1988.
16. Marcel Celis, "Van Volkshuis tot schroot: Achtergronden van een kwarteeuw falen" (From Maison du peuple to Metal Scraps: Background to Twenty-Five Missing Years), *Monumenten en landschappen* 10/2 (March–April 1991): 23–35.

speaks of a "maison de la culture" devoted to beer).[17] One could speak of a bidding war over the "authentically Belgian": Horta and beer in Antwerp, Horta and comic strips in Brussels (the Magasins Waucquez were converted into the Centre belge de la Bande dessinée, which opened to the public on 6 October 1989). In addition, since almost all the work of Victor Horta, born in Ghent, is actually concentrated in Brussels, it is as though, symbolically speaking, the "Flemish people" were reclaiming one of their native sons many years after they had offered him a faculty position at Antwerp's Institut supérieur des Beaux-Arts, where he taught from 1919 to 1927. The brasserie-restaurant named after Horta, as well as the skeleton of the large Art Nouveau hall, sheltered in a half-cylinder covered with zinc, were inaugurated on 21 September 2000. During the development of the project, all reservations concerning the relevance of the reconstruction were easily brushed aside: the components of the Maison du Peuple had been lying around for thirty years, and had gradually been eroded by rust. As far as public opinion was concerned, only the rescue effort mattered, everything else was merely a quarrel of specialists more interested in their own publications than in preserving Horta's architectural work.[18] In January 2000, the press revealed that the cost to investors had finally amounted to 200 million Belgian francs.[19] The multifunctional Art Nouveau hall can accommodate 600 persons for seminars, wedding receptions, and fashion shows, while the Grand Café Horta can hold 150.

The history of the Maison du Peuple is one of the fables of the modern world: even though the improvident grasshopper starves in the winter, it does not learn from its errors. Torn between the architects who "call upon it"—like a spirit at a séance?—[20] and its cavalier caretakers, the architectural work is being stripped of all materiality. The fragments scattered here and there no longer carry their own weight. Horta's architecture, where structure and ornamentation are one, where light is subtly shaped, and where walking through a house is like strolling in an architectural landscape, has vanished without a trace. It leaves one speechless to realize that elements weighing hundreds of kilos have now been turned into a virtual reality. In September 2000 a journalist of *De standaard* did not hesitate to give his article the cap-

17. *Café-Revue*, June–July 2000.
18. Speech given by W. Verstraete of the Arrow office (*De standaard*, 20 August 1998).
19. *Trends*, 20 January 2000, 62.
20. See—*sic:* "een evocatie van Horta als Hommage aan zijn werk" (An Evocation of Horta as Homage to His Work), *Het nieuwsblad*, 30 October 1998.

Figure 2. Façade of the Maison du Peuple during the demolition in 1965. Fondation Jean et Renée Delhaye, Musée Horta, Saint-Gilles, Brussels. Photo Jean Delhaye. © 2002-Horta/SOFAM-Belgium.

tion: "Victor Horta in handen van Frankenstein," ["Victor Horta in the Hands of Frankenstein"], for "only Frankenstein brings the dead back to life."[21] Sadly, the Maison du Peuple is now much more alive in the hundreds of photographs taken by the architect Jean Delhaye in 1965, right before its demolition, than it is in the Antwerp complex (see Figure 2).[22]

The decision to save fragments of the Maison du Peuple was made

21. *De standaard,* 23 September 2000.
22. Françoise Aubry, "Jean Delhaye, ses croisades pour Victor Horta," *Art et culture* 11 (September 1996): 6–8.

without much concern for the distressing precedent of the destruction of the Hôtel Aubecq, built in 1899, at 540 avenue Louise in Brussels.[23] In 1947, two years after Victor Horta's death, that had been the first important destruction of one of his structures. The custom (!) of the Commission royale des monuments et sites belge did not allow a building whose designer had died only recently to be classified as a landmark.[24] A delay was deemed necessary in order to evaluate the quality of someone's work. Jean Delhaye and Baroness Horta rallied to try to stop the destruction, but were only able to obtain some monies from the Minister of Public Works, Auguste Buisseret, to dismantle the façade visible from the avenue Louise, and the bow window in the corner. The dismantling and demolition took place in 1950. The stones have now been moved five times and are lying in a vacant lot, while the ironwork and frames have been stored in an abandoned building in Brussels.

It would take too long to review the various reconstruction projects. Two of them, published in 1979, had to do with the rue Montagne de la Cour[25] (see Figure 3). In the first instance, the Hôtel Aubecq was to be put on a new base in order to move it from its level site on the avenue Louise to a sloping site across from Saintenoy's Old England, another Art Nouveau building suffering from seemingly endless degradation and neglect.[26] For good measure, the Cousin Hall, a veranda designed by Horta that had been dismantled in 1969 and bought by the Musées Royaux des Beaux-Arts for 48,000 Belgian francs, was then to be added to the façade of the Aubecq house.[27] This second proposal made a mockery of the scale of the original building, its incorporation into a specific urban context, its orientation to the path of the sun, and the complex-

23. Georges Vigne, "Victor Horta et l'Hôtel Aubecq à Bruxelles," *La Revue du Louvre et des Musées de France* 33/1 (1983): 25–34.

24. "Approached about the preservation of that building, we could not consider designation, in view of the relatively recent date of that construction." Letter of 6 May 1949, from the chairman of the Commission, Baron Carton de Wiart, to the director-general of Fine Arts and Letters in the Ministry of Public Education.

25. *Archives d'architecture moderne* (AAM) 16, special edition devoted to La Cambre (1979): 92–99.

26. The restoration of Paul Saintenoy's building and its conversion into a Musée des instruments de musique began in 1989 and was completed in 2000. Eric Hennaut, Liliane Liesens, and Anne-Marie Pirlot, *Old England et la Musée des instruments de musique* (Brussels: Archives d'architecture moderne [AAM], 2000).

27. The "Cousin Hall" was to be incorporated into the future museum of modern art, but this plan was dropped. The elements, parts of which had meanwhile disappeared (particularly the mosaic floor and the bronze mantle trim), were finally transferred to the Musées Royaux d'Art et d'Histoire, where they were to be displayed in the new halls devoted to Art Nouveau.

● VUE AXONOMÉTRIQUE DEPUIS LA
PETITE RUE DU MUSÉE

Figure 3. Proposal for the reconstruction of the Hôtel Aubecq and the Salle Cousin,
rue Montagne de la Cour, Brussels. Axonometric view. Project by the architects
Dominique Delbrouck and Michel Leloup. *Revue des archives d'architecture moderne*
16 (1979): 94 (Special volume on "La Cambre 1928–1978"). © 2002-Horta/SOFAM-
Belgium.

ity of the plan, reflected in the structural alignment of the façades. This project is a good illustration of the Brussels trend, since called "façadism," which rests on the mistaken belief that face-saving is all that matters in architecture. To make matters worse, the furnishings of the Hôtel Aubecq were also scattered: in 1980 the Musée d'Orsay acquired forty-six pieces from the owners of the Hôtel Solvay, M. and Mme. L. Wittamer-de-Camps. As for the Horta Museum, it only owns a few chandeliers and a stool. The armchairs of the drawing room, a table, and an easel are now in the prestigious Gillion Crowet collection.[28]

The fate of another of Victor Horta's works provides an astounding illustration of the vulnerability of a landmark building. In 1889 Victor Horta received a commission for a small structure meant to hold a monumental bas-relief by Jef Lambeaux, "Les Passions humaines." The following year, the newspaper *Le soir* specified that the "very simple and very elegant [building] will be in a Greek style as modernized [*sic*] as possible."[29] Horta's Temple des Passions humaines was barely open to the public.[30] Dedicated on 1 October 1899, it was quickly closed because of a disagreement between Horta and Lambeaux over the lighting of the bas-relief. In 1909 Horta finally altered the pavilion, which was only sporadically open to the public from the time of its official reopening in 1910: the official reason was that there was no guard, but the real problem was the allegedly risqué nature of the sculptures. Designated as a landmark by Royal Decree on 18 November 1976, the building was ceded by Minister Guy Mathot to the authorities of the nearby mosque in order to house an Islamic museum. The possible public re-opening of the Lambeaux pavilion right next to the Islamic and Cultural Center of Belgium constituted something of an embarrassment. Legally, however, the ministerial decree of 12 September 1979, which provided for the removal of the bas-relief by the licensee, at his expense, could not be carried out because it went against the Royal Decree of landmark designation. To get around that obstacle, very serious

28. Michel Draguet, *L'Art nouveau retrouvé à travers les collections Anne-Marie Gillion Crowet* (Antwerp: Fond Mercator, 1999), 37, 52, 53, 237–43.

29. *Le soir*, 26–27 May 1890.

30. Cécile Dulière, "Le Pavillon des Passions humaines au Parc du Cinquantenaire," *Revue belge d'archéologie et d'histoire de l'art* 48 (1979): 85–96; Jo Haerens, "Jef Lambeaux en het reliëf der menselijke passies. Een historisch overzicht" (Jef Lambeaux and the Relief of the Human Passions: A Historical Review), *Bulletin des Musées Royaux d'art et d'histoire* 53/1 (1982): 89–105; Bruno Fornari, "Jef Lambeaux en de menselijke driften" (Jef Lambeaux and the Human Passions), *Monumenten en landschappen* (September–October 1989): 25–39.

consideration was given to putting the entire building, including the bas-relief, on rails and sliding it to another corner of the Parc du Cinquantenaire, where its presence would not embarrass anyone, a move authorized by a Royal Decree of 30 June 1981. This proposal was then developed in 1987 by the promoters of a museum for horse-drawn vehicles, the Bureau ARC, who planned not only to move the pavilion, but also to enlarge it by adding a cafeteria in the back and a long exhibition hall for old vehicles in the basement (see Figure 4). Horta's building had been conceived in the tradition of the temples and fabriques, or follies, that had decorated landscaped parks of the eighteenth century. ARC's plan did ensure the continuing connection of the main elements of the temple to its formal language. Once again, however, the proposed changes would have ruined the very meaning of the architectural work. If the museum were indeed ever constructed, what visitor would still be able to detect a tradition that had been both respected and reinvented by Horta, who created a new kind of profile that inflected the neoclassical quality of the building? Since it is hardly likely that the developers have the financial means necessary to use the type of subtle curves and scientific stone dressing envisioned by Horta, the contemporary building would only magnify the neoclassical elements and make us forget the pavilion itself. Curiously, Horta would then be brought back into the bosom of Alphonse Balat, his teacher, in spite of the fact that the Temple des Passions humaines bears witness to the young architect's resolve to be independent. The cost of demolishing and rebuilding the Lambeaux pavilion was initially estimated at 50 million Belgian francs. Since then, nothing has been resolved and the Lambeaux pavilion, part of the Musées Royaux d'Art et d'Histoire, still stands in the same place—closed!

In 2000, four Horta buildings were chosen by Unesco to appear on the lists of the world heritage. Horta did not think he had created a style, but a work that was "the simple expression of his tastes and his abilities, devoid of all borrowing and which, far from being part of a permanent body of work, tended to be ephemeral. Unless a huge detour caused by a shift in artistic and public tastes were to result in having the work that had resisted demolition take on the characteristics of permanence and definitive preservation" (Mémoires, 60). Horta's prediction has turned out to be partially accurate. His architecture is recognized internationally. The museum established in his own home, on the rue Américaine in Saint-Gilles (Brussels), attracts tens of thousands of visitors every year, the vast majority of whom come from abroad. Today

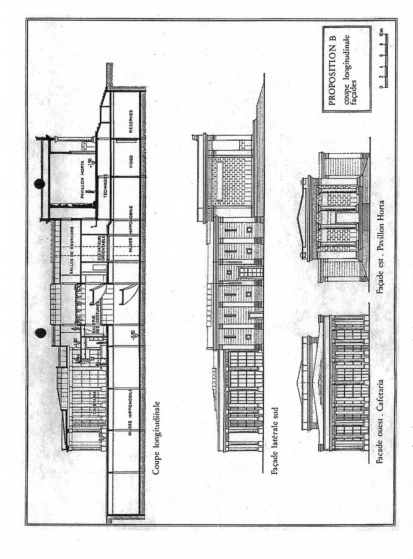

Figure 4. Project for the construction of a hippomobile museum, 1987. Bureau ARC [Philippe de Bloos and Jean-Pierre Hoa]. © 2002-Horta/SOFAM-Belgium.

the building is threatened by its own success. In the last ten years architect Barbara Van der Wee has overseen a major restoration that has succeeded in stabilizing the structural weaknesses. Yet, the building is still overburdened and is literally worn out. Paradoxically, while some of Horta's works have disappeared or been profoundly altered because they met with derision and cultural ignorance, others are now threatened by the enthusiasm they generate. Horta's architecture, which transposed the beauties of the natural world into its structures and decors, has turned out to share the fragility of that world: absent a surge of interest from the political world and public opinion, it will remain on the endangered spaces list. We can dream . . .

—Translated from the French by Barbara Harshav

ALEXANDER B. MURPHY

Landscapes for Whom?
The Twentieth-Century Remaking of
Brussels

Efforts to understand how a nation constructs its past typically focus on the stories told by its most honored historians, the precedents called upon by its political and cultural leaders, the symbolic content of its works of art, and the character of its nationalist icons. Each of these offers insights into how memory is cultivated and kept alive and is a critical component of the construction of national identity.[1] National memory is not only encoded and shaped by individual cultural artifacts, however. It is also embedded in the multifaceted character of landscapes—particularly those of capital cities that serve as symbolic and functional centers of individual nations. These landscapes reflect the outcome of complex contestations over the allocation and use of space that are profoundly influenced by notions of a nation's place in history. As such, the landscapes themselves provide important clues to the national construction of memory.

The most unambiguous symbols of nationalism and memory in the landscape are monuments such as the Arc de Triomphe in Paris or the Brandenberg Gate in Berlin. As such, these are the most common objects of study for those interested in the landscape-identity nexus.[2] Yet monuments are but individual cultural artifacts. What can be said about the larger-scale character of a city's core—its street patterns, complex of buildings, saved historical sites, and sacred spaces? Quite a bit, if the character of many of Europe's capital cities is any guide.

Consider the contrasts between central Rome and central Paris.

1. See generally, John R. Gillis, "Memory and Identity: The History of a Relationship," in John R. Gillis, ed., *Commemorations: The Politics of National Identity* (Princeton: Princeton University Press, 1994), 3–24.
2. Nuala Johnston, "Cast in Stone: Monuments, Geography, and Nationalism," *Environment and Planning. D: Society and Space* 13 (1995): 51–65.

YFS 102, *Belgian Memories,* ed. Catherine Labio, © 2002 by Yale University.

Rome lacks any single monumental center; instead the urban core is a patchwork of areas reflecting the influence of the Roman Catholic Church, efforts to promote the image of an "eternal city" with roots in ancient Rome, the competing influences of different economic interests over the past two centuries, and the city's relatively recent vocation as national capital.[3] Beyond the evocation of a heritage traceable to the greatest European empire of the ancient world, there is little that bespeaks a deeply entrenched sense of national heritage or a generally accepted set of defining national events. And this is hardly surprising given the weak sense of national unity that characterizes modern-day Italy.

Paris, by contrast, presents a very different image. There is a feeling of unity to the urban core with its architectural celebration of high culture and French exceptionalism.[4] Knit together by a complex of national monuments, grand boulevards, and ornately decorated buildings of similar style and appearance, Paris evokes a clearly defined sense of nation that (at least until recently) has been grounded in a nationalist vision of France/Paris as a center of politics and culture unfolding through a grand monarchical tradition, the birth of the nation-state ideal, and a centuries-old role at the political and cultural center of Europe. Consciously or unconsciously, that vision has found its way into the millions of decisions, small and large, that have shaped the evolution of the Parisian landscape core over the course of the last century and a half. The vision never operates independently of the political-economic forces that shape landscape change, but it interacts with those forces to produce a landscape that says much about how the French see themselves and their history.

THE PLACE OF BRUSSELS

What does the landscape of central Brussels tell us about the nature of identity and memory in Belgium? That is the main question of this essay. Founded in the tenth century, Brussels grew and developed as a modest-sized central place shaped by both its economic and administrative roles. At the time of Belgian independence in 1830, Brussels was still largely confined to its central "Pentagon," although urban expansion along the major roads leading out of town had produced tentacles of development that connected the city to several of the surrounding

3. John Agnew, *Rome* (New York: John Wiley & Sons, 1995), 74–80.
4. Daniel Noin and Paul White, *Paris* (New York: John Wiley & Sons, 1997), 207–30.

towns.[5] In keeping with the settlement patterns established in prior eras, the wealthier citizens of Brussels lived in the relative comfort of the upper town to the east, which also played host to many of the institutions that sprang up to serve the business needs of the rapidly industrializing Belgian state. Here also were most of the important historical monuments that had been bequeathed to nineteenth-century Brussels from the past. The working people and the poor, by contrast, were found in the lower town to the west and south, where industrial, artisanal, and trading activities were concentrated.[6]

During the decades immediately following independence, urban development was driven by the city's rapidly changing economic role and the desire of the Belgian elite to build a national capital. The former led to a rapid expansion of the city, facilitated by the arrival of the railroad and the development of an urban transportation system based on horse-drawn omnibuses. The result was the emergence, or in some cases the expansion, of distinct manufacturing zones near the Pentagon. The latter led to the first efforts to cast Brussels as a fitting capital for a would-be nation-state—complete with the types of public buildings necessary to house the new Belgian government and express its significance. To facilitate this endeavor, a high-profile commission was established in 1835 to oversee the construction and maintenance of buildings and monuments in Brussels, followed by the founding of a society in 1837 for "l'agrandissement et l'embellissement de la Capitale de la Belgique" [the growth and beautification of the Capital of Belgium].[7]

By the middle of the nineteenth century, the stage seemed to be set for Brussels to emerge as a grand national capital. The economic advantage afforded by Belgium's early industrialization provided a potential source of revenue to realize that vision, and the country's political and economic elite was bent on building a modern nation-state. As

5. See generally Lisette Danckaert, *Bruxelles. Cinq siècles de cartographie* (Tielt: Lannoo; Knokke: Mappamundi, 1989), 103–09 (also published in Dutch). In 1830 some 100,000 people were concentrated in the Pentagon and another 40,000 in the towns that would eventually become part of the metropolitan area. See Thierry Eggerickx and Michel Poulain, "1,000,000 de Bruxellois. Esquisse démographique des communes de la région Bruxelloise," *Les dossiers Bruxellois/De dossiers Brussel* 12/13 (Brussels: DIRE, 1990): 139.

6. Marie-Rose Thielemans, "La localisation des industries aux alentours de 1830," in Arlette Smolar-Meynart and Jean Stengers, eds., *La région de Bruxelles. Des villages d'autrefois à la ville d'aujourd'hui* (Brussels: Crédit Communal, 1989), 246–61 (also published in Dutch).

7. See generally *Espace Bruxelles-Europe* (Brussels: Ministère de la Région Bruxelloise, Administration de l'urbanisme et de l'aménagement du territoire, 1987).

such, there were arguably both the means and the proclivity to create a city that could stand for—and encourage—an integrated social and cultural tradition. A stroll around central Brussels today, however, reveals a relatively disaggregated urban landscape in which function often seems to have taken precedence over form, and in which the landscape can change dramatically within a few hundred meters. Spaces of enormous historical significance and beauty are juxtaposed with monotonous buildings and transportation arteries in a manner that seemingly defies any sense of overall vision.

How and why did this happen? The conventional explanation lies in the economic arena. Josef Konvitz has argued that, over the last two centuries, cultural considerations have been overshadowed by economic forces in most Western cities—and this seems to have been particularly true of Brussels.[8] The commitment of many in the ruling Belgian elite to the ideals of classical economic liberalism is well established, and this group did much to facilitate Brussels's economic development through projects designed to tie the city to the surrounding countryside and to expand opportunities for large-scale commercial ventures. In the social arena, it prevented any significant intervention on behalf of the destitute or of a working-class population that was poorly compensated in comparison to its counterparts in Paris and Amsterdam; it was assumed that menial laborers and the poor would simply have to cope with whatever urban development schemes seemed to be in the overall best interests of the city.[9]

Even though the economic orientation of the new Belgian state played an undeniably significant role in the transformation of Brussels, economics does not exist in a cultural vacuum—particularly in a city that is consciously being made into a national capital. Thus, even as the Belgian elite was embracing a form of relatively unrestrained capitalism, it was also wrestling with the construction of a state in the age of nationalism. Yet the struggle was also being carried out against the backdrop of a rapidly changing internal sociocultural order that greatly complicated the nation-building process. The landscape of Brussels bears witness to the complexities of the struggle, and, in the process, provides important clues to the social construction of memory in Belgium.

---

8. Josef W. Konvitz, *The Urban Millenium: The City-Building Process from the Early Middle Ages to the Present* (Carbondale, IL: Southern Illinois University Press, 1985).

9. See generally Carl Strikwerda, *Urban Structure, Religion, and Language: Belgian Workers, 1880–1914* (Unpublished Ph.D. dissertation, The University of Michigan, 1988).

SETTING THE STAGE

The overall character of the central Brussels landscape owes much to processes that unfolded during the early decades of the reign of Leopold II (the Belgian king from 1865 to 1909). The city emerged as the dominant urban area in Belgium, encompassing more than 10 per cent of the country's population and sprawling out over the surrounding countryside.[10] Moreover, the city acquired many of the trappings of a significant turn-of-the-century European capital: broad avenues, great monuments, splendid parks, and pretentious public buildings. One of the driving forces behind these changes was the desire of the (largely Francophone) aristocracy and upper middle class to promote urban growth and to build a capital city in the image of Paris.[11]

The early decades of the Leopold II era have sometimes been called the Golden Age of Brussels because of the general economic prosperity of the time. The country's wealth came from the continued economic advantages of early industrialization and, toward the latter part of Leopold II's reign, from the exploitation of people and resources in the Congo. The massive urban development projects of Leopold's reign were built on the prosperity of the time. They were funded by a combination of public money and contributions from the king himself, who saw urban development as a way of expanding the Belgian economy.[12] The less well-off segment of the Brussels population often suffered in the wake of urban development schemes, but there was little they could do to change the situation. Laws had been enacted in 1858 and 1867 allowing for the public expropriation of private land, and these could be invoked when necessary to allow projects to proceed.[13] The immediate impetus for these laws was the fear of disease, but they provided a juridical basis for large-scale expropriations even where disease was not the primary issue.

Leopold II's interest in remaking Brussels into a model European capital surfaced even before he acceded to the throne. In a speech before the Belgian Senate in 1860, Leopold tied urban renewal to national stature and prestige.

10. Bernard Jouret, *L'agglomération bruxelloise II. Définition spatiale du phénomène urbain bruxellois* (Brussels: Éditions de l'Université de Bruxelles, 1972).

11. Inter-Environnement and Archives d'Architecture Moderne, *Les espaces publics bruxellois. Analyse et projets* (Brussels: Fondation Roi Baudouin, 1981), 38.

12. Liane Ranieri, *Leopold II, urbaniste* (Brussels: Hayez, 1973), 12–15.

13. Marcel Smets, *L'avènement de la cité-jardin en Belgique* (Brussels: P. Mardaga, 1977), 42.

All around us capital cities and other urban areas are making astounding progress. Our country, with its economic and cultural riches, cannot be left behind by its neighbors. Belgium, situated at the heart of Europe and safeguarded by its power, should live up to its role and its potential. I myself would like some evidence of our free existence and prosperity stamped into each of our edifices.[14]

Joined by a ruling elite that shared similar ambitions, Leopold II set about remaking Brussels. In 1863 he presented a list of twenty-five urban development projects to the Belgian government, most of which were to be implemented during his years as king. In drawing up his plans, Leopold II's model was avowedly Paris. He sought to follow in the footsteps of the prefect Baron Haussmann, who oversaw the remaking of the Parisian landscape and, in the process, lent his name to an approach to urban renewal based on the creation of grand public spaces, the rigid separation of public and private spaces within the city, and the blending of different architectural styles.[15]

Leopold II did not confine himself to the formal commune of Brussels; rather he thought in terms of the Brussels region as a whole. His plans thus set the stage for greater integration of the metropolitan area. Three kinds of projects were characteristic of the era: the construction of splendid public buildings and monuments; the creation of large, straight streets cutting through the urban fabric; and the establishment of urban parks at key locations. Figure 1 shows the most important of these projects in and around the Pentagon. As the figure reveals, the urban development plans of the Leopold II era affected most parts of the central city. In some cases, older neighborhoods were torn up to make way for new projects (e.g., the central boulevards through the Pentagon), whereas in other cases new arteries were constructed in places that had been little developed (e.g., the Military Boulevard to the northeast).

The projects of Leopold II, when viewed as a whole, clearly signal the impetus to make Brussels a capital appropriate to a nation of growing importance. There is little to suggest that the character of that nation, or the memories that defined it, were seen as particularly problematic. Instead, Leopold and his contemporaries seemed to be looking

14. Quoted in Louis Verniers, "Les transformations de Bruxelles et l'urbanisation de sa banlieue depuis 1795," *Annales de la Société Royale d'Archéologique de Belgique* 37 (1934), 135, my translation.
15. See generally Leonardo Benevolo, *The European City,* trans. Carl Ipsen (Oxford: Blackwell, 1993), 171–86.

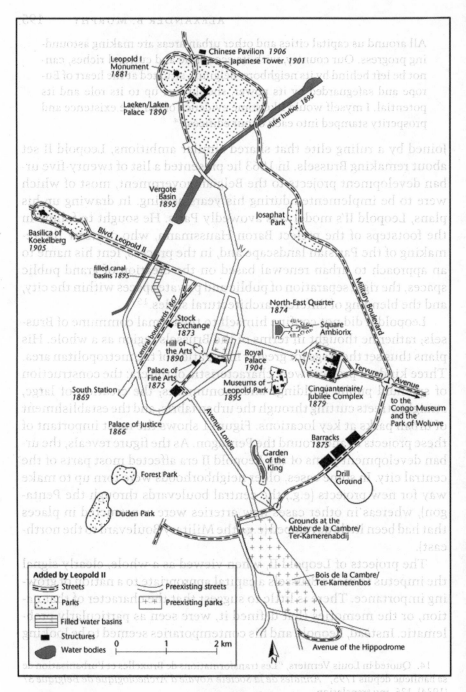

Figure 1. Major changes in the Brussels Region during the Reign of Leopold II. Dates indicate when construction began.

to the needs of a new state within the context of a century that had elevated the doctrine of nationalism to a position of commanding promi-
nence. Economics was part of that vision, for Belgium had long presented itself as an economic crossroads of Europe. Hence, included in
the mix of urban development projects was the construction or widening of roads and canals to facilitate commerce, as well as the building
of a significant urban port (the Vergote basin). Economic imperatives
were not separable from political and cultural ones, however; instead,
they reinforced each other.

In sum, the emerging Brussels landscape of 1890 reflected a sense of
a nation in the making—complete with the governmental, economic,
and cultural infrastructure appropriate to a country of substantial ambition. There was little evidence of a narrow or particular set of historical memories on which the dominant sense of nationhood was based,
however. Instead, it was rooted in a vision of centuries of external dom-
ination and in the new possibilities offered by freedom from that dom-
ination.

The particular character of the landscape vision that dominated
Brussels can be seen in the Palace of Justice, constructed near the western edge of the Pentagon. The site selected for the building was a raised
plateau directly overlooking a working-class district called the Marolles; fittingly, it was here in the Middle Ages that the gallows were
located. The architect Joseph Poelaert was commissioned to draw up
plans for a palace that would symbolize the strength and power of Belgium and its constitution. The Greco-Roman style building he designed was of enormous proportions, larger than any other single edi-
fice in the Brussels region. Its dome was over 100 meters in height and
the total floor area was larger than that of St. Peter's in Rome. To construct the building, a considerable portion of the eastern section of the
Marolles had to be destroyed, bringing further misery to the city's lower
classes. And once completed, the building loomed over one of the poor-
est sections of the city, providing a constant reminder of the strength
and aspirations of the Belgian state.

THE UNRAVELING OF A UNIFIED VISION

Beginning in the last decade of the nineteenth century, and extending
through much of the twentieth century, the apparent coherence of the
city envisaged by Leopold II at the start of his reign came under fundamental challenge and ultimately gave way to the present reality.

Two large-scale turn-of-the-century urban renewal projects in the Pentagon both reflected and shaped what was happening: Leopold's Hill of the Arts (Mont des Arts/Kunstberg) project and the initiative to link the train stations on either side of the Pentagon. In the first of these, Leopold II sought to reconvert the slopes leading down from the Place Royale/Koningsplaats to the lower city into a grand public cultural space. Charles Buls, the mayor of Brussels at the time, objected to the plan because of his concern for preserving the buildings that were already in place. Buls was unsuccessful in stopping the project, and it unfolded in a way that ultimately frustrated the objectives of both mayor and king. After expropriating land and demolishing a number of buildings, the project was halted in the late 1890s because of uncertainties about where it fit with other plans for the central city. Aside from some landscaping that was done to clean up the site in 1910, work did not resume for several decades. By that time the old buildings were long gone, but Leopold's original vision could no longer be realized either.

The second signal project was born out of a plan to construct a rail link between the North and South stations on either side of the Pentagon—and to build a central railroad station in the middle. Much of the rail link was to be built underground at the lower end of the break-of-slope between the lower and the upper city. Construction required cutting a wide swath through the Pentagon, however, as well as clearing significant areas of land to make way for the central station. Nonetheless, the project was approved in 1903 and demolition began immediately thereafter. The project had profound implications for the character of the central city.[16] And although significant areas were cleared, fiscal problems, war, depression, and political in-fighting intervened to prevent comprehensive reconstruction for more than a half a century. Hence, long after the rail link was completed, a great scar shattered the functional and aesthetic integrity of the Pentagon. That scar, in turn, made it easy for later generations to approach the development of the urban core without any coherent vision for the Pentagon as a whole.

How do we explain the fate of these two projects? The course followed by each can certainly be attributed in part to particular fiscal and political circumstances. Yet something larger seems to have been at work as well: a challenge to the monist vision of memory and nationalism embodied in the early Leopoldian city. That challenge opened up

16. See generally ARAU (Atelier de Recherche et d'Action Urbaines), *Brussel/Bruxelles/Brussels*, special issue of *Wonen-TA/BK*, 15/16 (1975): 1–76.

the question, "For whom is the urban landscape being made?"—and the obvious difficulty in answering that question helped to pave the way for a functionalist vision of the city with minimal reference to a defined sense of cultural-historical memory. In short, those with the power to shape what happened developed a distinctive approach to urban design in which attachments to traditional, backward-looking symbolic forms frequently gave way to the construction of a city that transcended the political and cultural geography in which it was embedded. It was almost as if the marginalization of nationalism and memory provided the only way forward. In the process, however, the market became the most obviously important force in the making of the city, and the nation-building project itself took on a more functionalist cast.

Several economic and demographic developments of the late nineteenth and early twentieth centuries are at the heart of the shifting sociocultural milieu. Most obviously, the population of the Brussels region swelled as the demands of Belgium's industrial economy spawned an increasingly complex financial, commercial, and administrative support system. Immigration accounted for a significant proportion of the growth: between 1880 and 1910 there was greater immigration to Brabant—the province over which Brussels presided—than to any other Belgian province.[17] Yet the new inhabitants of the Brussels region did not settle in the central city. Instead, more and more people were being pushed out of the urban core to make way for transportation arteries and for structures devoted to finance, commerce, and administration. By the turn of the century, emigration exceeded immigration in the Pentagon—the beginning of a trend that was to accelerate during the course of the twentieth century.[18] With workers concentrating in the industrial regions to the west and the middle class moving to the east and southeast, an increasingly dichotomized social geography was emerging that reflected and exacerbated class divisions.

Importantly, the contrasts between different parts of the city were growing. During the waning years of the nineteenth century the

17. Paul Deprez and Christian Vandenbroeke, "Population Growth and Distribution, and Urbanization in Belgium during the Demographic Transition," in Richard Lawton and W. Robert Lee, eds., *Urban Population Development in Western Europe from the Late-Eighteenth to the Early-Twentieth Century* (Liverpool: Liverpool University Press, 1989), 229.

18. H. Van der Haegen, C. Pattyn, and C. Cardyn, "The Belgium Settlement System," in H. Van der Haegen, ed., *West European Settlement Systems*, special issue of *Acta Geographica Lovaniensia* 22 (1982): 251–363.

wealthier sections of Brussels saw the opening of many new theaters, concert halls, restaurants, and covered markets. In the poorer neighborhoods, amenities were few and retail activities were conducted primarily in the open air. These contrasts were set against the backdrop of an increasingly tension-laden relationship between capital and labor. The small size of the urban proletariat meant that Brussels had been spared some of the labor upheavals of the 1870s and 1880s in Belgium's industrial centers, but by the 1890s the Belgian Workers Party (founded in Brussels in the 1880s) had gained considerable influence, and Brussels found itself at the center of the Party's efforts to expand the franchise and to push for labor reforms. Strikes broke out in Brussels (and beyond) throughout the 1890s and early 1900s, including two general strikes in 1902 and 1913,[19] and any illusion of social homogeneity was destroyed. The challenges that emerged to Leopold II's vision for the Hill of the Arts were clearly a product of that environment, and the inability to resolve those challenges reflected how entrenched and polarized things had become.

Sociocultural fragmentation in turn-of-the-century Brussels was not solely a product of class relations, however. Disagreements raged over the role of the Catholic Church in public affairs—particularly in education—and the different communal administrations in the metropolitan area often worked at cross-purposes. Of particular interest for the subsequent development of the city, however, was the growing controversy surrounding the issue of language. The closing decades of the nineteenth century saw a rapid Frenchification in the Belgian capital.[20] Although precise data are lacking, the number of monolingual speakers of variants of Dutch declined precipitously in Brussels between 1880 and 1900, and by 1910 there were more monolingual Francophones in the Belgian capital than there were monolingual speakers of Dutch and related dialects. More than half of the population still knew Dutch or one of its variants, but the city "presented a predominantly French image. The street names, the showrooms, the press, the administration were in French only."[21]

The increasing concentration of commercial, financial, and admin-

19. Janet Polasky, "A Revolution for Socialist Reforms: The Belgian General Strike for Universal Suffrage," *Journal of Contemporary History* 27 (1992): 449–66.

20. See generally Hendrik Aelvoet, *Honderd vijfentwintig jaar verfransing in de agglomeratie en het arrondissement Brussel, 1830–1955* (Brussels: Simon Stevin, 1957).

21. Jeanine Treffers-Daller, *French-Dutch Language Mixture in Brussels* (Amsterdam: Ph.D. thesis, University of Amsterdam, 1991), 15.

istrative functions in Brussels furthered the Frenchification process by fostering growth in the city's middle class. As the size of the middle class expanded, an ever-larger number of the capital's citizens entered into a world dominated by French. Language shift was particularly strong among this group, often occurring over the course of two or more generations. Though not large in number, immigrant Walloons also contributed to the Frenchification of the city. As a result, Brussels came to symbolize the challenges faced by speakers of Dutch and related dialects in the Belgian state.

Exacerbating the situation was the strong geographic and class dimension to language change in Brussels. Dutch dominated in the working class communes to the west and southwest of the central city, whereas French was strongest to the east and southeast. By 1890 the linguistic contrasts from place to place in the metropolitan area were stark. Almost 50 per cent of those living in the commune of Ixelles/ Elsene to the southeast spoke French only, and another 34 per cent were bilingual.[22] Yet only 12 per cent of the residents of the western commune of Anderlecht spoke French only, and 39 per cent were bilingual. The commune of Brussels itself (at the center of the city) was a microcosm of the larger metropolitan area. Variants of Dutch remained relatively important in the western sections where the working class population dominated, but farther east French was the principal language.

The Frenchification of Brussels came at a time when the so-called "communities problem" in Belgium was becoming increasingly visible.[23] Brussels was not one of the principal centers of Flemish activism—Ghent and Antwerp played that role—but as the fight for linguistic equality intensified, the Belgian capital was inevitably drawn into the fray. Boards of inquiry operated out of the Belgian capital and the Parliament seated in Brussels was the focus of the most important political struggles. The city was also instrumental in the birth of a reactive Walloon movement. The first Walloon political organization was founded in the commune of Saint Gilles/Sint-Gillis in 1886 by Walloon civil servants, and many Walloons subsequently looked to Brussels as a critical venue for the protection and promotion of Walloon interests.

22. Eliane Gubin, "La situation des langues à Bruxelles au XIXe siècle à la lumière d'un examen critique des statistiques," *Taal en Sociale Integratie* 1 (1978): 72.

23. See generally Alexander B. Murphy, *The Regional Dynamics of Language Differentiation in Belgium: A Study in Cultural-Political Geography* (Chicago: University of Chicago Geography Research Series 227, 1988).

By the end of Leopold II's reign, then, the process of language shift had proceeded apace, and the Belgian capital was neither a typical Flemish city, nor was it a Walloon city. Rather, it was a city whose inhabitants were predominantly of Flemish background, but where French was overtaking Dutch and related dialects as the principal language. Linguistic intermixing could be found throughout the city, but a number of different parts of Brussels had distinctive linguistic identities. Under these circumstances, the whole notion of a single Belgian nation was under significant attack—undermining any notion that the capital city could embody a landscape that represented one people. The middle class "Bruxellois" who had come to use French were among the most enthusiastic participants in Leopold II's vision of Brussels as a great national capital. Their cultural identities were no longer rooted in local particularisms, but were instead forged in a capital city caught up in an age of unselfconscious nationalism. Yet many other residents of Brussels, together with their sympathizers in other parts of Belgium, had a very different vision—and those differences fostered an environment in which the inscription of memory in the cultural landscape could easily engender conflict. As a result, a certain social and cultural gridlock developed that helps explain the subsequent evolution of the Brussels landscape.

THE WAY FORWARD

The most obvious consequence of the disintegrating social and cultural consensus was the stagnation of projects such as the north–south railroad connection. More broadly, however, the absence of consensus precipitated a reorientation of the focus of large-scale urban planning, away from culturally based nation-building. What form would that reorientation take? In the absence of a unified cultural-historical vision, the alternative was necessarily more economistic and functionalist. If there was any sense of a socially cohesive memory, it lay in the centuries-old notion of Belgium as a crossroads—a center of commerce and trade. Fueled by growing possibilities for Belgium to play a wider regional and international role as the twentieth century wore on, this vision came to play a significant role in the development of Brussels.

The trajectory of Brussels's development became increasingly clear after the city and country began to recover from the hardships brought by World War I. By the mid-1920s Brussels's political, financial, and industrial leaders once again found themselves in a period of economic expansion. Car ownership was on the rise and the city's public transportation system was taxed to the maximum. Under these circumstance, and given the larger urban planning reorientations described above, it is not surprising that priority was given to projects that would facilitate interactions between Brussels and its hinterland—road, railroads and the like.[24] Moreover, the dissected urban landscape left in the aftermath of the Hill of the Arts and Central Station projects made it easy to think of the grand boulevards of the late nineteenth century as transportation corridors and to entertain plans for the construction of new corridors through quarters that were already disrupted by prior urban development initiatives. Work resumed for a time on the rail link through the Pentagon; a great curved thoroughfare, consisting of the rue Montagne de la Cour/Coudenberg and the rue Ravenstein, was constructed around the Hill of the Arts; and, in the vicinity of both projects, roads were widened and lengthened, streets were reconfigured to eliminate dead ends, and new long and straight arteries were built radiating out from the center to accommodate the growth in automobile traffic.

Belgium was hit hard by the Great Depression, and many of the more ambitious urban projects of the 1920s had to be suspended. Work stopped again on the rail link through the central city, and new housing projects came to a virtual halt. As Brussels fought its way out of the depression, however, the focus of attention was ever more on functional, rather than aesthetic considerations. During the 1930s the first tall buildings appeared in central Brussels. Built adjacent to the zone of destruction created by the attempt to construct a rail link through the Pentagon, these monumental, cubist-influenced structures had little in common with older architectural elements in the urban core. They thus further undermined whatever aesthetic cohesion the central city might have inherited from the past.

Following the German occupation of Belgium in 1940, most major metropolitan building projects were suspended, including the long-standing effort to complete the rail link through the central city. The liberation of Brussels in September 1944 was accomplished without major physical damage to the city. Bombing was minimal and a German attempt to burn down the Palace of Justice was thwarted before

24. J-F Herbecq, "L'évolution du territoire de la ville. Projets d'agrandissement et annexions après la Première Guerre Mondiale," in Arlette Smolar-Meynart and Jean Stengers, eds., *La région de Bruxelles: Des villages d'autrefois à la ville d'aujourd'hui* (Brussels: Crédit Communal, 1989), 330–35 [also published in Dutch].

the fire had spread too far. Even though the buildings and streets survived the occupation more or less intact, post-war Brussels faced substantial economic and social problems. The Belgian economy had to be rebuilt, and Brussels had to cope with a new round of social tensions resulting from the wartime experience. The country responded to these tensions by embarking on a new course. Shortly after the end of the war, the Belgian Parliament passed legislation guaranteeing a minimum standard of living regardless of age or physical well-being, thus paving the way for the country's emergence as a "welfare state." Against this backdrop, emphasis was necessarily placed on the construction of new, minimally acceptable housing, which furthered the pre-war functionalist orientation of urban planning.

As Belgium entered the 1950s, international issues began to demand more and more attention. The country found itself caught up in a widening debate over the need to reconfigure the West European political economy so as to head off another major conflict, to combat growing Soviet influence to the East, and to recapture a position of leadership in world affairs. Belgium was at the heart of the push for a more integrated Europe, and the emergence of Brussels as the chief administrative center in the realization of that vision brought new opportunities and challenges for the city in the second half of the twentieth century. Inevitably, the direction the city took in the face of these developments was influenced by that which had come before—including a variegated landscape that bore the marks of the lack of a strong cultural consensus about the nature and meaning of national memory.

It would take another essay to sketch even the broad outlines of the changes that swept through Brussels in the wake of the rise of the European Economic Community (now European Union), the establishment of NATO headquarters in the city, the arrival of a multitude of multinational corporations, and associated developments that produced an increasingly internationalized city in the second half of the twentieth century. Yet a few themes dominate. The Brussels elite, inspired by the city's potential as the focal point of a strategically located and economically prosperous region, facilitated the spread of the city into the surrounding countryside while promoting commuting to and from Brussels on a grand scale. They also built up important political and economic institutions in Brussels and created places of grandeur within the city. At the same time, significant parts of the urban core were destroyed in the name of progress—even as poorer sections of the city continued to languish. Contemporary Brussels, then, presents a series of contrasts between rich and poor, harmonious and discordant, compact and spread out, beautiful and ugly, grandiose and intimate.

The city's contrasts are not simply the result of a particular economic orientation run wild. Of course, free market capitalism is inscribed in the Brussels landscape. Yet its influence bears witness not just to the power of the market, but to a particular set of contestations over the nature and meaning of nationalism and memory. Faced with social and cultural changes as the nineteenth century gave way to the twentieth, the Belgian elite could not turn to any particularly cohesive set of cultural memories to carry forward the nation-building project embodied in Leopold's design for Brussels. The way out was through a culturally neutral concept of nationalism and memory that found expression in a plan that treated the city more as a political or economic node than as a human habitat. There were historically important parts of the city that did not interfere with that vision (e.g., the Grand Place/Grote Markt), and these were preserved and maintained. Yet in many places, the older urban fabric gave way, often in a rather haphazard way.

The loss of an internally integrated urban core allowed Belgium to avoid a direct confrontation with its past—with certain positive implications for the Belgian polity. Most obviously, it helped to distance the capital city from some of the controversies surrounding the nature of Belgian nationalism. As such it represented the kind of pragmatic compromise that so often seems to occur in Belgium in the face of cultural and social conflict. Yet the reluctance to confront the inscription of memory in the Brussels landscape carries with it costs as well. The aesthetic and environmental ones are the easiest to see, but there are social and psychological costs as well. In the absence of significant markers of the ethnolinguistic, class, or political conflicts that shaped the country's historical emergence, the landscape of Brussels's urban core fails to provide a solid cultural foundation on which new projects and initiatives can be built. As a consequence, the default foundation tends to be pragmatic and economic, with the inevitable narrowness in perspective that this implies.

In recent years, a growing number of questions are being asked about what has been lost in the twentieth-century transformation of Brussels, and steps are being taken to introduce at least an array of new environmental and aesthetic concerns into urban planning.[25] There is

25. Discussed in Jean Annaert, "L'environnement bruxellois. Perception et comportement," *Revue Belge de Géographie* 188/1–2 (1994): 9–21.

great promise in some of these initiatives, and they may mark the beginning of a new phase in the development of the city. Yet they must necessarily contend with a present-day city that reflects particular notions of memory developed against the backdrop of an ambiguous Belgian nationalism. How they confront, and seek to rework, those notions will fundamentally influence both the direction these new initiatives take and their chances for success in the future.

Contributors

FRANÇOISE AUBRY was born in Charleroi, Belgium. She has been the Curator of the Horta Museum in Brussels since 1981. She has written extensively on Art Nouveau, including *The Horta Museum, Saint-Gilles, Brussels* (1990) and *Art Nouveau in Belgium: Architecture and Interior Design* (with Jos Vandenbreeden), both of which also came out in French, Dutch, and German. She is also the author of *The Nineteenth Century in Belgium: Architecture and Interior Design* (with Jos Vandenbreeden, 1994) and *Victor Horta à Bruxelles* (1996), as well as the editor, with Jos Vandenbreeden, of *Horta: Art Nouveau to Modernism* (1996). She has recently curated the exhibits "Europalia-Horta" (Palais des Beaux-Arts, Brussels, 1996) and "Prague Art Nouveau. Métamorphoses d'un style" (Palais des Beaux-Arts, Brussels, 1998).

LUC DE HEUSCH is an ethnologist, writer, and filmmaker. An emeritus professor at the Université Libre de Bruxelles, he is the author of numerous works, including *Mythes et rites bantous* (Gallimard, 1972–2000), *Why marry her? Society and Symbolic Structure* (Cambridge University Press, 1981), *The Drunken King, or, the Origin of the State* (Indiana University Press, 1982), *Le sacrifice dans les religions africaines* (Gallimard, 1986), *Ceci n'est pas la Belgique* (Complexe, 1992), *Postures et imposture. Nations, nationalisme, etc.* (Labor, 1997), and *Mémoire, mon beau navire. Les vacances d'un ethnologue* (Actes Sud, 1998). He has directed film portraits of Michel de Ghelderode, Magritte, Alechinsky, Ensor, as well as other films dealing with Belgian society.

SOPHIE DE SCHAEPDRIJVER is Associate Professor of Modern European History at the Pennsylvania State University. She has published works on nineteenth-century urban history (with a focus on topics

YFS 102, *Belgian Memories*, ed. Catherine Labio, © 2002 by Yale University.

such as prostitution, newcomers to the city, and social topography, with particular reference to Brussels), as well as on linguistic nationalism, especially with respect to Belgium. Her second book, *De groote oorlog. Het koninkrijk België in de Eerste Wereldoorlog* [*The Great War: The Kingdom of Belgium in the First World War*], was published in Dutch in 1997 (Amsterdam: Atlas), and is now in its fifth printing. A French translation is scheduled to appear in 2002 (Brussels: Labor, "Archives du futur" series); a revised English version is currently being prepared. The book was awarded the 1999 Belgian/Flemish "Free Speech Award" (*Arkprijs van het Vrije Woord*).

JACQUES DUBOIS is emeritus professor at the Université de Liège. He specialized in nineteenth- and twentieth-century French literature and the sociology of culture. His most recent publications include: *Le roman célibataire. D' À rebours à Paludes* (Paris: Corti, 1996, with Jean-Pierre Bertrand, Michel Biron, and Jeannine Paque), *Le roman policier ou la modernité* (Paris: Nathan, 1996), *Pour Albertine. Proust et le sens du social* (Paris: Seuil, "Liber", 1997), and *Les romanciers du réel. De Balzac à Simenon* (Paris: Seuil, Points-lettres, 2000). He is President of the Centre d'études Georges Simenon at the Université de Liège and is in charge of the "collection Points-lettres" for the Éditions du Seuil.

CATHERINE LABIO is assistant professor of Comparative Literature and French at Yale University. She has published articles on the history of the novel and the history of ideas in seventeenth- and eighteenth-century Europe. She is the author of *The Aesthetics of Knowledge: Origins and the Enlightenment* (forthcoming) and is working on a book-length project on literature and economics.

PIERRE MERTENS was born at the dawn of the Second World War. Having had a "hidden childhood," a Jewish mother and a father in the resistance has fueled his entire professional life, both in the literary and the legal fields. His novels include: *Les bons offices* (1974) on the Israel-Arab tragedy; *Terre d'asile* (1978) on the end of Allende's Chile; *Perdre* (1984); and *Les éblouissements* (1987; Prix Médicis) on the betrayal of German intellectuals in the Nazi era. *Une paix royale* (1995) earned him the Prix Jean Monnet de littérature as well as a lawsuit—which he won—by the Belgian royal family. His latest novel is *Perasma* (2001). Pierre Mertens is also an observer for numerous humanitarian organizations.

PHILIP MOSLEY is Professor of English, Communications, and Comparative Literature at Pennsylvania State University—Worthington Scranton. He is the author of *Split Screen: Belgian Cinema and Cultural Identity* (2001).

ALEXANDER B. MURPHY is Professor of Geography at the University of Oregon, where he also holds the James F. and Shirley K. Rippey Chair in Liberal Arts and Sciences. He specializes in cultural and political geography, with a regional emphasis on Europe. In 1991, he was the recipient of a National Science Foundation Presidential Young Investigator Award. Professor Murphy is a Vice-President of the American Geographical Society and North American editor of *Progress in Human Geography*. He is the author of numerous articles and several books, including *The Regional Dynamics of Language Differentiation in Belgium* (University of Chicago Press, 1988).

MARC QUAGHEBEUR is Commissaire au Livre and Directeur des Archives et Musée de la Littérature and teaches the course on Belgian Francophone literature at the Université Catholique de Louvain. In the last twenty years or so, his research has generally focused on the corpus of Belgian letters written in French, always with a view to bringing together historicity, language, and aesthetics. He works on other Francophone areas as well, especially Central Africa, and attempts to bring out the dynamics peculiar to today's *francophonies*. He is also a poet. His latest volume, *La Nuit de Yuste* (1999) was published by the Éditions Le Cormier in Brussels.

SERGE TISSERON is a practicing psychiatrist and psychoanalyst and *directeur de recherche* at the University of Paris X. He became known with *Tintin chez le psychanalyste* (Aubier, 1985) and has written some eighteen books on the varied nature of our relationships to images, including *Psychanalyse de la bande dessinée* (PUF, 1987), *Psychanalyse de l'image. Des premiers traits au virtuel* (Dunod, 1995), *Y a-t-il un pilote dans l'image?* (Aubier, 1998), and *Nos secrets de famille. Histoires et mode d'emploi* (Ramsay, 1999). In 1997 he was put in charge by the Ministry of Culture and the *direction de l'Action sanitaire et sociale* of a three-year research program on children's and teenagers' appropriation of images (see *Enfants sous influence. Les écrans rendent-ils les jeunes violents?* [Armand Colin, 2000]). Serge Tisseron also writes and draws comic strips, the latest of which is *Bulles de divan* (Calmann-Levy/Ramsay, 2001).

ANTOINE TSHITUNGU KONGOLO is a published poet, novelist, and essayist. He is the editor of *Aux pays du fleuve et des grands lacs.*

Chocs et rencontres des cultures (Brussels: Archives et Musée de la Littérature, "Documents pour l'histoire des francophonies," 2001), a thematic anthology aimed at introducing the Congo, Rwanda, and Burundi and their histories (from 1885 to the present) through the corpus of African and Belgian Francophone literature. His earlier research on the cultural interactions of the Congo, Rwanda, and Burundi resulted in the publication of an anthology of tales entitled *Les dits de la nuit* (Labor, "Espace nord," 1994) and in a long series of scholarly articles published over a ten-year period. Other works include a novel, *Fleurs dans la boue* (Kinshasa: Mediaspaul, 1995) and a collection of poems, *Tanganyika blues* (Paris: L'Harmattan, "Poètes de cinq continents," 1997). He is currently writing a doctoral thesis in comparative literature at the Université Libre de Bruxelles.

PIET VAN DE CRAEN is Professor of Linguistics at the Vrije Universiteit Brussel. His research interests lie in the field of psychosociolinguistics and multilingual education. He has published extensively on these subjects in English, French, and Dutch. He is cofounder of the European Language Council and is currently secretary of this organization.

ANTOON VAN DEN BRAEMBUSSCHE has been teaching the philosophy of history and the philosophy of art at the Erasmus University of Rotterdam since 1980, first as a lecturer and subsequently as an associate professor. He has also been teaching art criticism at the Free University of Brussels for the past four years. Among his publications are: *Theorie van de maatschappijgeschiedenis* [Theory of the History of Society] (Baarn: Ambo, 1985); *Rose und Kartoffel. Ein Heinrich-Heine-Symposium* [Roses and Potatoes: A Heinrich Heine Conference] (Amsterdam: Rodopi, 1988); *Different Elements for a General Science of Culture,* with C. Blok et al. (London: Avebury, 1990); *Denken over kunst* [Thinking about Art] (Bussum: Couthinho, 1994; 3rd ed., 2000); and *Voorbij het postmodernisme* [Beyond Postmodernism] (Best: Daimon, 1996). He is currently working on a publication entitled *The Silenced Past,* a systematic inquiry into the nature of historical taboos and traumas.

The following issues are available through **Yale University Press,** Customer Service Department, P.O. Box 209040, New Haven, CT 06520-9040.

69 The Lesson of Paul de Man (1985) $17.00
73 Everyday Life (1987) $17.00
75 The Politics of Tradition: Placing Women in French Literature (1988) $17.00
Special Issue: After the Age of Suspicion: The French Novel Today (1989) $17.00
76 Autour de Racine: Studies in Intertextuality (1989) $17.00
77 Reading the Archive: On Texts and Institutions (1990) $17.00
78 On Bataille (1990) $17.00
79 Literature and the Ethical Question (1991) $17.00
Special Issue: Contexts: Style and Value in Medieval Art and Literature (1991) $17.00
80 Baroque Topographies: Literature/History/

Philosophy (1992) $17.00
81 On Leiris (1992) $17.00
82 Post/Colonial Conditions Vol. 1 (1993) $17.00
83 Post/Colonial Conditions Vol. 2 (1993) $17.00
84 Boundaries: Writing and Drawing (1993) $17.00
85 Discourses of Jewish Identity in 20th-Century France (1994) $17.00
86 Corps Mystique, Corps Sacré (1994) $17.00
87 Another Look, Another Woman (1995) $17.00
88 Depositions: Althusser, Balibar, Macherey (1995) $17.00
89 Drafts (1996) $17.00
90 Same Sex / Different Text? Gay and Lesbian Writing in French (1996) $17.00
91 Genet: In the Language of the Enemy (1997) $17.00

92 Exploring the Conversible World (1997) $17.00
93 The Place of Maurice Blanchot (1998) $17.00
94 Libertinage and Modernity (1999) $17.00
95 Rereading Allegory: Essays in Memory of Daniel Poirion (1999) $17.00
96 50 Years of *Yale French Studies,* Part I: 1948-1979 (1999) $17.00
97 50 Years of *Yale French Studies,* Part 2: 1980-1998 (2000) $17.00
98 The French Fifties (2000) $17.00
99 Jean-François Lyotard: Time and Judgment (2001) $17.00
100 The Cultural Wars (2001) $17.00
101 Fragments of Revolution $17.00

Special subscription rates are available on a calendar-year basis (2 issues per year):
Individual subscriptions $26.00
Institutional subscriptions $30.00

ORDER FORM   **Yale University Press,** P.O. Box 209040, New Haven, CT 06520-9040
I would like to purchase the following individual issues:

_____

_____

For individual issues, please add postage and handling:
Single issue, United States $2.75   Each additional issue $.50
Single issue, foreign countries $5.00   Each additional issue $1.00
Connecticut residents please add sales tax of 6%.

Payment of $_____ is enclosed (including sales tax if applicable).

MasterCard no. _____   Expiration date _____

VISA no. _____   Expiration date _____

Signature _____

SHIP TO _____

_____

See the next page for ordering other back issues. Yale French Studies is also available through Xerox University Microfilms, 300 North Zeeb Road, Ann Arbor, MI 48106.

The following issues are still available through the **Yale French Studies Office**, P.O. Box 208251, New Haven, CT 06520-8251.

19/20 Contemporary Art $3.50	42 Zola $5.00	54 Mallarmé $5.00
33 Shakespeare $3.50	43 The Child's Part $5.00	61 Toward a Theory of Description $6.00
35 Sade $3.50	45 Language as Action $5.00	
39 Literature and Revolution $3.50	46 From Stage to Street $3.50	
	52 Graphesis $5.00	

Add for postage & handling

Single issue, United States $3.00 (Priority Mail)   Each additional issue $1.25
Single issue, United States $1.80 (Third Class)   Each additional issue $ .50
Single issue, foreign countries $2.50 (Book Rate)   Each additional issue $1.50

YALE FRENCH STUDIES, P.O. Box 208251, New Haven, Connecticut 06520-8251
A check made payable to YFS is enclosed. Please send me the following issue(s):

Issue no.	Title	Price

Postage & handling _____

Total _____

Name _____

Number/Street _____

City _____ State _____ Zip _____

The following issues are now available through Periodicals Service Company, 11 Main Street, Germantown, N.Y. 12526, Phone: (518) 537-4700. Fax: (518) 537-5899.

1 Critical Bibliography of Existentialism	19/20 Contempoary Art
2 Modern Poets	21 Poetry Since the Liberation
3 Criticism & Creation	22 French Education
4 Literature & Ideas	23 Humor
5 The Modern Theatre	24 Midnight Novelists
6 France and World Literature	25 Albert Camus
7 André Gide	26 The Myth of Napoleon
8 What's Novel in the Novel	27 Women Writers
9 Symbolism	28 Rousseau
10 French-American Literature Relationships	29 The New Dramatists
11 Eros, Variations...	30 Sartre
12 God & the Writer	31 Surrealism
13 Romanticism Revisited	32 Paris in Literature
14 Motley: Today's French Theater	33 Shakespeare in France
15 Social & Political France	34 Proust
16 Foray through Existentialism	48 French Freud
17 The Art of the Cinema	51 Approaches to Medieval Romance
18 Passion & the Intellect, or Malraux	

36/37 Structuralism has been reprinted by Doubleday as an Anchor Book.
55/56 Literature and Psychoanalysis has been reprinted by Johns Hopkins University Press, and can be ordered through Customer Service, Johns Hopkins University Press, Baltimore, MD 21218.